Fish and Chips and the British Working Class, 1870–1940

महद्

Fish and Chips and the British Working Class, 1870–1940

John K. Walton

Leicester University Press
Leicester, London and New York

First published in Great Britain in 1992 by Leicester University Press (a division of Pinter Publishers)

Editorial offices
Fielding Johnson Building, University of Leicester, University Road, Leicester, LE1 7RH, England

Trade and other enquiries
25 Floral Street, London, WC2E 9DS, England

British Library Cataloguing in Publication Data
A CIP catalogue record for this book is available from the British Library.
ISBN 0–7185–1327–4

For enquiries in North America please contact PO Box 197, Irvington, NY 10533

Library of Congress Cataloging in Publication Data
A CIP catalog record for this book is available from the Library of Congress

Typeset by Florencetype Ltd, Kewstoke, Avon
Printed and bound in Great Britain

Contents

For my students, past and present

Acknowledgements

This book has benefited enormously not only from the help of friends and colleagues, but also from numerous kindnesses vouchsafed by total strangers. At one time the list of acknowledgements threatened to occupy more space than the text itself. In response to this problem, most people will find their contributions gratefully recognised in individual footnotes. Inevitably, however, there are exceptions.

Jenny Smith has been a mine of references, suggestions and bright ideas throughout; and without her encouragement the project would never have got under way in the first place. I acknowledge her contribution with love and gratitude. Mr Parrington and the headquarters staff of the National Federation of Fish Friers at 289 Dewsbury Road, Leeds, gave me unstinted access to essential source material and provided friendly and congenial working conditions. Gill Parsons offered moral support and practical help at a time when both were particularly important; and my Lancaster students in general have taken a sustained interest in the project and helped to impel it on its way. Bev Smith put me in touch with her grandmother Mrs Vincent, whose delightful reminiscences were invaluable in several respects. The fish and chip shops in Ullswater Road, Lancaster and Broadgate, Preston kept me in touch with the current state of the trade. Many people in various institutions have heard my thoughts on fish and chips, and commented on them: I remember with particular pleasure the sessions at the Institute of Historical Research in London (starring Geoff Crossick and Judith Rowbotham), the Victoria and Albert Museum (starring Ray Batcheler), the Norman McCord retirement symposium at Newcastle University (starring Norman McCord), and the Lancaster University History Society. This brings me back to my students: and it is to this long-suffering, lively and stimulating group of people that this book is dedicated.

Lancaster
24 July 1991

List of abbreviations

ER	Elizabeth Roberts oral history collection, University of Lancaster.
FFR	*Fish Friers' Review*
FN	*Fishing News*
FTG	*Fish Trades Gazette*
MO	Mass–Observation Archive, University of Sussex.
NCF	Northern Counties Federation of Fish Friers
NFFF	National Federation of Fish Friers
PP	Parliamentary Papers
UKF	United Kingdom Federation of Fish Friers' Associations

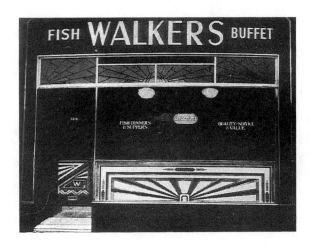

A shop front from 1933 for aspiring friers to emulate

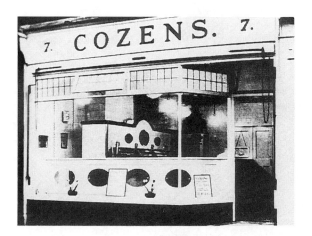

Another shop front - as self consciously up-to-date as a
new trolley bus

The model interior of Walkers Central London shop
(see top)

The interior of Harry Ramsden's Guiseley restaurant in all its
early glory (1933)

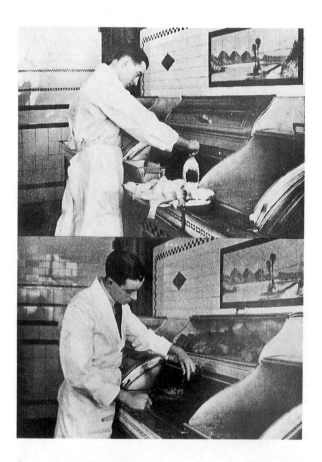

Preparing processes: battering the fish (above)

Separating the portions. A rare view of the hidden life
of the fish frier (below)

se's 'Terrace De-Luxe' range as advertised in 1931

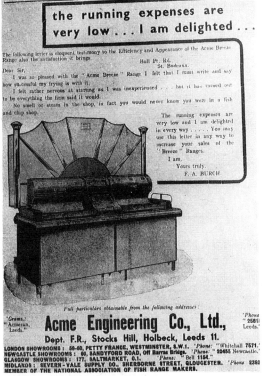

The Acme Breeze range (1937): up-to-date styling and
a new approach to the trade's oldest form of fuel

A novel advertising pitch, in 1937, for an essential
ingredient

A haughty fish frier rejects the Food Council's advice to
fry herrings (1928)

Going up, Sir?
Why walk up the stairs,
when you can take the lift?

A classic portrayal of the
value of combination and
mutual assistance (1928)

The original sign of the
National Federation. It could
be displayed in the shop to
reassure customers or worn on
a lapel badge as a mark of pride

1 The Importance of the Fish and Chip Trade

Fish and chips is generally recognized as a great and quintessentially British institution; but it is difficult to persuade people to take it seriously as a subject of historical enquiry. This is partly because it is presumed to be, for practical purposes, timeless: it has 'always' been there, but it has no 'history' in the sense of transforming itself, affecting people's lives for good or ill in significant ways, or interacting with the self-evidently important concerns of statesmen and diplomats. Fish and chips is often recognized as a constituent of a broad and emotionally resonant national cultural identity, but always in vaguely allusive or nostalgic vein. Thus the up-market right-wing quarterly *This England*, evoking in 1968 the homesick longings of affluent exiles:

> after just so long in the air-conditioned splendour of the new world they yearn for the sight of whitewashed walls and thatched roofs, of old familiar places, and dear faces; of fog, football and even fish and chips.[1]

'Even' is a telling word, of course: there remains something shamefaced about the acceptance of fish and chips as a component of 'Englishness' among the 'better classes'. It can be celebrated as 'The Great British Dish', as in a recent advertising campaign that made lavish and prominent use of the Union Jack, playing on a set of associations that was nicely pulled together by the trade journalist John Stephen as early as 1933:

> Have we another food-catering trade so national in character as the fried-fish trade? I doubt it. Fish landed by British ships, manned by British fishermen, searching the seas from close inshore to the Arctic regions, in fair weather and foul; potatoes grown on our home farms, dripping from home cattle, ranges made by British labour in British factories, and the fuel, coal or gas, from British mines.[2]

This set of perceptions attaches fish and chips to potent patriotic images of land and countryside, industrial might (the whole agenda of the widely disseminated popular song, 'There'll always be an England'), and, above all, the notion of Britain as a gallant seafaring nation whose little ships do battle with the elements and the foreign enemy to feed and protect the people. The convivial, open, public nature of the purchase and often the eating of fish and chips also enables it to be appropriated in support of cosy visions of democratic solidarity of a kind that transcends divisions of class or status. Bill Naughton's autobiography captures this well in evoking his Bolton childhood:

> there was about fish-and-chips a sound democratic touch that no other food possessed; the poorest person could shop alongside the poshest . . . You were all one in the kingdom of fish-and-chips.[3]

Viewed in other moods and seen from other angles, of course, the image and associations of fish and chips could be very different. They expressed ethnic diversity as well as simplistic national solidarity, from the strong East End Jewish element in the early days of fish frying in London, through the strong Italian presence in the trade from the turn of the century, in urban Scotland and Ireland especially, to the growing importance of the Chinese and Greek Cypriots in the post-Second World War decades. And because the fish and chip shop was an open, democratic institution, it was also 'common', as well as having enduring associations with decidedly ungenteel smells and behaviour, with dubious hygiene and an associated threat of poisoning and illness. To the chagrin of socially aspiring members of the trade, such ideas kept many middle-class people, especially women, at arm's length; some patrons of fish and chip shops were unwilling to admit to this demeaning activity in the presence of their betters. The detective novelist Margery Allingham captured this social unease in a story first published in 1936. Mrs Tripper, a caretaker, is explaining her movements to the coroner, to establish where she was at a critical moment:

> It was a shop in Red Lion Street – a fried-fish shop, if you must know. It was very foggy and I hadn't been able to get about to do my ordinary shopping, and I knew my husband would like something hot for his supper and so I thought I might as well try some of their more expensive pieces. Some of these places are very high class, and the Red Lion shop is very nice indeed.[4]

The queasy ambivalence of attitudes and expectations revealed by this morass of self-justification loses none of its impact when we adjust for the nature of the source: this is popular fiction at its most observant and it helps us to understand the socially divisive aspects of the widening awareness of the fish and chip shop and its social connotations.

Fish and chips thus came to carry powerful images and social messages. This was sometimes recognized, but it could also be dismissed almost in the same breath, by the same commentator. Thus A. H. Halsey, in a textbook on *Change in British Society*, offers a list of carry-overs from Victorian society into the late-twentieth century:

> Yet it is, in a similar range of trivial and serious senses, the same country. Fish and chips and Sheffield Wednesday and Cambridge and the monarchy are still parts of the social continuity which is Britain.[5]

Fish and chips is important enough to figure at the head of this list; but it is probably fair to assume that the first two items on it are 'trivial' in Halsey's eyes, while Cambridge (presumably the University) and the monarchy are 'serious'. This reflects a broad set of academic assumptions about the serious and the trivial and about the 'proper' subjects of academic enquiry. It helps to explain why most historians still focus pre-eminently on politics, diplomacy, 'high' culture and the exercise of power, while relegating the examination of the daily lives, attitudes and values of 'ordinary' individuals, families and communities to the status of a 'fringe' pursuit, of little relevance to the issues that really matter. The rise of social history and oral history, to say nothing of feminist history, has done a great deal to redress the balance; but it has had more impact within academe than beyond it. Dismissive contempt for the study of the 'popular' and the 'everyday' is still pervasive within the historical profession itself. Fish and chips is a particularly appropriate candidate for this condescension, for the more basic and essential an activity is, the more likely it is to be loftily dismissed by the advocates of a narrow and exclusive political history. This is why a book on fish and chips needs to be justified, perhaps rather assertively. The project has generated a great deal of interest, much, though not all, of it at a rather trivial and sensational level; but it has also provoked less-supportive responses. They may be summed up in two episodes. A colleague's wife, after enquiring about the current progress of my research, expostulated: 'But surely even you can't pad out fish and chips into a whole book!' Of wider interest, perhaps, was the fate of my first article on the subject. An excerpt from it appeared, immediately, in the *Pseuds' Corner* column in *Private Eye*. The offending paragraph was the part of the introduction describing the agenda for the rest of the article.[6] I conclude that in the eyes of *Private Eye* and in its perceptions of its readers' likely responses, the very act of treating fish and chips as a serious historical subject is in itself 'pseud', presumably because it is held to be investing something essentially trivial and risible with a ludicrously inflated importance. This is an interesting reaction. It is almost certainly influenced by the status of the trade, over many years, as a butt of comedians and sketch-writers in a variety of media, beginning with the music-hall and the comic postcard. This trend was already well-established in 1907, when newspaper reporters refused to take seriously the idea of a federation of fish friers. It was picked up again by the *Fishing News* in 1932; a contributor to the *Saturday Review* the following year defended fish and chips against 'funny men with red noses (who) mock my fried fish, as they mock mothers-in-law, or the half-legendary Wigan Pier.'[7] Fish and chips as the object of sustained derision, on the part of decidedly down-market comedians, lost any credentials it may have had as a potentially serious subject in the eyes of orthodox opinion. And the opinions generally purveyed in *Private Eye* are impeccably orthodox, reflecting as they do the public-school, middle-class, masculine values that hold the status of 'common sense' in the ruling circles the magazine purports to satirize.

Clearly, then, the relevance and significance of the fish and chip trade for the understanding of ourselves through our past will have to be justified at the outset. But I shall have to avoid the pitfalls set out by the fish and chip trade's own satirist, 'Gossipyum', in the *Fish Friers' Review*, using a characteristic contemporary approach to the deflation of academic windbaggery and pomposity:

Professor Schweinessen proved to his own satisfaction that Fish and Chips, like Salmon and Gluckstein, Robinson and Cleaver, Preston and Thomas, Ham and Eggs, were natural partnerships. And as such, admitted of no argument. His lecture on the subject, which will ever be regarded as the classic example of saying nothing, interlarded with scientific analogies, remains in the annals of the University of Boon, Been and Bane to this day.[8]

The actual historiography of fish and chips is very limited. Even Derek Oddy's chapter on 'Food, drink and nutrition' in the *Cambridge Social History of Britain*, the most recent contribution to the literature, has nothing to say about it, although it provides a lot of invaluable contextual material.[9] The only book-length history devoted to the trade is a lively journalistic piece by the late Gerald Priestland, better known as the BBC's religious affairs correspondent, which uses the trade press as well as interviews and personal observation.[10] Academic historians have neglected this book; the few who mention fish and chips in work on diet, consumption patterns and popular culture depend heavily on a brief pioneering piece by W. H. Chaloner which dealt mainly with the origins of the trade.[11] Beyond this, Hamish Fraser has some interesting additional things to say in his survey of the origins of the 'mass market' between 1850 and 1914, and Elizabeth Roberts discusses some possible implications of the rise of the fish and chip trade in urban Lancashire, using interview evidence from her oral history project, in her *A Woman's Place*.[12] But in general social historians of diet, living standards and popular culture in Britain have followed the example of R.N. Salaman, whose monumental and seemingly exhaustive *History and social influence of the potato* does not even mention fish and chips, although it does include a brief discussion of the rise of the potato crisp.[13]

This neglect of a national institution reflects historians' priorities, expectations and agenda-setting rather than any shortage of source material. It is perhaps significant that fish and chips cannot be pursued through neatly ordered, calendered and indexed runs of documents, directly concerned with the subject in hand, in county record offices or major libraries. There is material in the Public Record Office, especially in the files of the Ministry of Agriculture and Fisheries for the inter-war years when the trade's economic importance was recognized to the extent that the leaders of its organizations were regularly consulted about policy-making, and a small group of civil servants devoted considerable energy and ingenuity to finding out about the practices and problems of fish friers. But this evidence has to be teased out from files that deal mainly with other topics.

The staple source for the historian of fish and chips is the voluminous and remarkably informative trade press, the *Fish Trades Gazette*, *Fishing News* and, from 1925, the National Federation of Fish Friers' own monthly, the *Fish Friers' Review*.[14] Beyond this, at local level there are trade directories and medical officers' reports and those oral history archives that incorporate questions on diet, health, leisure and employment. The Mass-Observation archive also includes interesting detail on the place of fish and chips in working-class life in Bolton and Blackpool on the eve of the Second World War. Ultimately, however, fish and chips became so culturally pervasive that useful and telling references to it occur incidentally in an enormous range of published sources, especially autobiographies and popular novels. Popular journalism, especially of the sort that combines atmospheric description with nostalgic reminiscence,can also be used in a variety of ways. A recent piece by Keith Waterhouse in the *Daily Mail* is particularly effective in evoking the mystique of fish and chips and its intimate association with essential regular and recurring aspects of working-class life, from supper by the fire to cinema-going and courtship.[15] There is clearly no danger of fish and chips being undervalued or condescended to in this particular quarter.

More generally, however, a case for the relevance and importance of studying fish and chips in its social, economic and political setting still needs to be made. I intend to argue that fish and chips has had sufficient economic, social and (I am unrepentant about this) political significance to deserve extended analysis, involving explanation and assessment as well as narrative and description. In the rest of this introduction I shall outline this argument, before going on to develop key themes in greater depth in the main body of the book. We begin with the economic dimensions and implications of the rise of the fish and chip trade.

By the beginning of the twentieth century the trade was rapidly emerging and spreading from its down-market, back-street origins. Shops multiplied, locations became more respectable, capital requirements and technological sophistication increased and standards of hygiene improved, while the characteristic smell of frying became more effectively restrained and controlled. In 1907 a *Fish Trades Gazette* editorial asserted that: 'the estimated number of friers in the United Kingdom is no fewer than 10,321', but the basis for this remarkably precise figure is unknown. The usually well-informed Manchester frier, William Loftas, who became the pioneer fish and chip trade journalist and all-purposes expert under the pseudonym 'Chatchip', claimed many years later that there were already between 10,000 and 12,000 fried fish shops in Britain as early as 1888.[16] No hard evidence is provided in support of this claim either, but it accords better with the same authority's contemporary estimate that there were as many as 25,000 friers in the United Kingdom in 1910.[17] This became the generally accepted figure on the eve of the First World War, although there is no surviving source enabling us to test its accuracy. Even the trade directories, then at their peak of coverage, turn out systematically to understate the number of fish and chip shops when they can be compared with Medical Officers' returns – which in turn are only available for that minority of boroughs in which the trade was regulated and inspected under the offensive trades legislation of 1907.[18]

The First World War brought a temporary halt to the rapid expansion of the trade, under the pressure of inflation, conscription and successive crises in raw material supplies, but growth picked up again in the inter-war years. By 1927 the National Federation of Fish Friers could tell the Food Council that there were 35,000 fish friers in Great Britain.[19] This was the highest estimate ever made, however, and in 1935 the NFFF delegation, which gave evidence to the Sea-Fish Commission, would only commit itself to a figure of 'at least' 30,000.[20] In 1939 official estimates ranged from 25,000 to 30,000, with an admission that the true figure could be 35,000 or more; but counting was becoming more difficult because growing numbers of shops and restaurants combined the sale of fish and chips with a variety of other items.[21]

Whatever the exact figures might add up to, the orders of magnitude are clear enough. Fish and chips had become a major industry by the eve of the First World War, and consolidated that position during the 1920s and 1930s. In

January 1931 a columnist in the *Fish Friers' Review* calculated that the trade employed at least 70,000 people directly (including friers' wives and assistants) and 200,000 indirectly (in transport, on the docks, as coopers, and so on).[22] This may well be a conservative estimate: it certainly does not allow much for assistance (especially from children and part-time staff) in the many shops that did a really substantial trade. Even so, in employment terms it put fish and chips on a par with a lot of other industries that have attracted extensive and sustained research and debate on the part of economic historians. Comparatively speaking, the growth of the fish and chip trade during the first three decades of the twentieth century was remarkable. In a sample of 12 towns studied by P. Ford in 1935, fish and chip shops showed by far the fastest growth rate among the retail trades during 1901–31 in terms of the sheer numbers of outlets. The number of such shops per thousand population went up by 177 per cent, while the next most dynamic trades, opticians and confectioners, respectively doubled their representation and increased it by 72 per cent. Most trades actually declined in importance relative to the population as a whole.[23]

The industry's importance as an employer and as the most dynamic sector of retailing (in number of outlets if not in scale of operations or organizational development) is only the beginning of the story. Fish and chips became vitally important to several other major sectors of the British economy and its influence also extended much further afield. Most obviously, it was central to the growth and transformation of the British fishing industry from the later nineteenth century onwards and its impact on agriculture should not be underestimated. It generated its own specialist engineering and hardware industries and it stimulated demand for oils and fats, paper, fuel, salt, vinegar, mineral waters and a range of other products. More needs to be said about all this.

The fried fish trade grew in step with the great transformation of the fishing industry in the later nineteenth and early twentieth century. The trade helped materially in opening out the demand for cheaper fish, packed in ice rather than being kept alive for the fishmonger's slab, for a more proletarian and less fastidious market. This in turn made the steam-trawling revolution possible, as the trawl delivered the fish dead on the deck and necessitated new ways of disposing of them. The fried fish trade also provided markets for fish species that had long been ignored or wasted, such as plaice and haddock. Fish and chips was thus essential to the economics of the new long-distance trawlers which sought their quarry in Icelandic waters and then beyond. It was an essential ingredient in the growth and prosperity of the new industrial fishing ports, especially Hull, Grimsby and Aberdeen and later Fleetwood, North Shields and Milford Haven.[24] The fish trade journalist John Stephen expressed all this pithily and convincingly in 1934:

> We can reasonably say that had it not been for the frying trade, steam trawling as we know it to-day would not be. Suppose we imagine . . . that there were no fried fish shops at all. If that were so, then there would be no need for at least half the biggest trawlers and the supplies of fish from the North Sea would be nearly sufficient for the wet fish trade.[25]

The concentration of the industry into a few large ports and the decline of the old fishing villages were part of the same process. Obviously none of these things could have happened without the improved inland distribution facilities provided by the railways; but without the demand which was generated in new quarters and for new products by the fried fish trade, the changes in the fishing industry would have been slower and less dramatic.

Various estimates were made, at different times, of the proportion of the white-fish catch that went to the frying trade. Fish friers' consumption on the eve of the First World War was calculated at between 100,000 and 150,000 tons per year. At the lowest estimate, deducting herring, mackerel and 'prime fish, like soles, turbot, brills, halibut and lemon soles', the friers would be using about $17\frac{1}{2}$ per cent of the annual catch. A figure of 20 per cent or more is likelier and the 25 per cent suggested by one commentator is perfectly possible.[26] And this consumption was, of course, socially skewed towards the working classes: as the official annual report on sea fisheries remarked in 1914: 'Outside the fried fish shops . . . comparatively little fresh fish is consumed by persons of small means.'[27]

Inter-war figures are even more impressive, as the trade took more than its fair share of steadily growing fish consumption. By January 1935 the NFFF was claiming that the friers were 'responsible for between 60 and 70 per cent of the edible fish sold'. This was queried by one of the civil servants at the Sea-Fish Commission to which this statistic was submitted; he provided a list of alternative estimates. The report of the Imperial Economic Committee in 1927 offered 40 per cent; that of the Food Council in the same year 'not far short of 50 per cent'; the Economic Affairs Committee in 1931 estimated the proportion at 50 per cent; and the Fishmongers' Federation, who might have been expected to play down the importance of fish and chips, offered 'something over 70 per cent' in evidence to the Sea-Fish Commission.[28] These successive calculations are compatible with a steady increase in the proportion of fish going to the friers between 1927 and 1935, continuing what must already have been a strong trend. But the highest point seems to have been reached in the mid-1930s, when the trade's own statistician, T. Harrison of Portsmouth, calculated that the friers took 65 per cent of the white fish landed; the other figures must also refer to white fish, leaving out (most importantly) herring and mackerel. By 1939 a plateau had apparently been reached: the chairman of the White Fish Commission put the friers' share at nearly 60 per cent, adding the important qualification that this calculation was 'merely by weight' and that the friers used 'the cheapest kinds of fish'. The trade's own estimate at this time was two-thirds.[29] But this was a plateau at a remarkably high level, clearly indicating the overwhelming importance of the inter-war fried fish trade to the fishing industry.

The friers also had a capacious appetite for potatoes. On the eve of the First World War they consumed half a million tons per annum: about 10 per cent of the crop in a poorish year and a rather lower proportion in a good one.[30] Again, the friers' share of consumption increased in the inter-war years; but in the case of potatoes the trade's statistician was widely at variance with the official figures. The Ministry of Agriculture's report on the marketing of potatoes in England and Wales commented in 1926 that: 'In some districts, the extent of this business (fish and chips) and its effect on the potato trade are enormous; taking the country as a whole, it is estimated that about 15 per cent of the potatoes consumed pass through the hands of the "chip" trade.' There were marked regional variations: in the factory towns of south Lancashire, 60 per cent of the potato consumption was in the form of chips; in Nottingham the figure was more like 25 per cent; in South Wales between 20 and 25 per cent, but in London only between 5 and 10 per cent.[31] It was claimed in 1924 that Lancashire friers consumed three-quarters of the potatoes grown in the county.[32] But the national figure of 15 per cent is confirmed by official figures from the beginning of the Second World War and it may have been relatively constant through the inter-war years.[33] How, under these circumstances, Mr Harrison of the NFFF could tell an audience of Sheffield friers in 1935 that the friers took between 40 and 45 per cent of the farmers' potatoes must remain a mystery, although the phrasing must mask a difference of definition from the basis of the official figures.[34] The friers were clearly less important to the potato growers than they were to the trawlermen; but theirs was a far from negligible contribution to overall demand.[35]

William Loftas reckoned in 1910 that fish and chip frying consumed nearly a thousand tons a week of frying oil and dripping. He subsequently modified this assessment downwards, but not by much; the accuracy of his estimate (on his own showing) came as a terrible shock to officials of the Ministry of Food in the supply crisis of 1917.[36] By 1935 consumption had apparently risen more than threefold to 165,000 tons, although this is an uncorroborated estimate by the Mr Harrison whose assessment of the friers' proportion of the potato crop was so much higher than the other calculations.[37] We cannot readily assess the contribution of the fish and chip trade as a proportion of the output of the oil and fat industries because different frying media were used in different districts. Within the northern textile area, for example, cotton-seed and later other vegetable oils were used in most of Lancashire, lard was favoured in the north Lancashire weaving towns around Burnley and dripping was, and remains, at the heart of the claim that the West Riding of Yorkshire made the best and most popular fish and chips anywhere. But a lot of friers mixed their frying media, combining lard with dripping, dripping with cotton-seed oil, or cotton-seed oil with ground-nut or soya oil.[38]

What is clear is that from the early twentieth century the seed crushers and oil and fat refiners recognized an important market. They sought to stimulate it by improving the quality of the product to reduce the 'nauseating and objectionable features' of the frying trade as then conducted.[39] Thus in 1910 the Southern Cotton Oil Company (GB) opened a factory in Bootle to produce 'Snowdrift' hogless lard for frying: the liquid oil was being double and treble refined to improve its taste and reduce odour.[40] The frying trade's links with the wider world economy embraced Egyptian cotton-seed oil (with which the trade had practically begun) as well as the American variety. At about the same time, importers were bringing in Australian beef dripping and advertising it to friers in the *Fish Trades Gazette*. In 1921, by which time Argentina was also exporting beef dripping to Britain, Loftas decried these products as 'far too heavy for fish frying, and should never be used alone'; but this was a matter of taste and Loftas was no enthusiast for dripping in general as a frying medium.[41] Fish and chips might be seen as essentially a British institution but it was far from being insular in its quest for raw materials. In this respect we should not forget the German, Belgian and Dutch potatoes that augmented the friers' home-grown supply when local crops were short, or the Canadian frozen fish that helped to keep the trade going in the depths of the war years and continued to be used by some friers thereafter.[42]

The peas and beans that were often sold along with fish and chips over much of northern and midland England also brought the friers into contact with distant producers. In 1910 the 'Dutch Imperial' was said to be the fish frier's ideal pea; but by 1920 the varieties in use included 'Jap Marrowfats' and 'Australian Blues'. Some at least of the former were definitely being imported: it was more than just a matter of nomenclature. In 1920 also Loftas listed the beans used by friers: 'English haricots, French haricots, English butters, Dutch butters and Rangoons, all white varieties, besides one or two brown varieties.'[43]

This relatively localized and limited aspect of the trade was much more important to the friers concerned than to the growers or merchants; much the same can probably be said of the lesser food ingredients of the frying trade. But it made its mark on a variety of other industries. Just as the friers provided a market for the lower grades and smaller sizes of fish (especially 'chat' hake and haddock), so they offered an outlet for the lower grades of flour and eggs for use in batter-making. The trade was certainly important enough to attract specialist firms; by 1933 a trade journalist could advise that 'a number of mills specialise in producing Friers' flours'. By that time there were also several patent batter mixes devised for the fried fish trade, such as 'Egbata'. Beyond this, the Midland Vinegar Co. of Birmingham was directing its advertising at friers in 1908; the Agricultural Chemical Co. was pushing its 'Amberine' as a colouring agent to make friers' batter look more appetising, as an alternative to the annatto that was already being widely used for this purpose; and Hancock, Collis and Co. of Billingsgate were developing special lines in 'chip-potato bags' that enabled uniform portions to be given, as well as greaseproof wrapping paper (to go inside the still-ubiquitous newspaper) and other requisites.[44] There were specialist wholesalers emerging by this time, too, like G. Crawford of Billingsgate, who offered 'all supplies' for 'the fish friers' trades'. A Manchester firm of this sort was described at length in 1911. G. Radcliffe, Ltd. specialized almost completely in oil, dripping, Crispit (their patent frying medium), flour and peas and beans for the fish and chip trade. They employed three travellers, 10 carters and 'numerous warehouse staff'. They used five horses and lorries in Manchester, three in Bolton and two in Wigan to distribute their goods and they employed 22 women and girls in their pea-and-bean picking department. There were at least three similar firms operating in Manchester at this time.[45]

On the fuel side, too, friers were important enough as customers to attract special attention. They were heavy consumers of coal, coke and gas and their organizations took a keen interest in wartime coal rationing and other threats to fuel supplies. During the great coal dispute of 1921, it was claimed, fish friers in many areas were put in a 'privileged category', along with bakers, and were able 'to procure preferential supplies of fuel' while stocks lasted. Similar measures were taken five years later in the General Strike and the longer-running dispute in the mining industry.[46] Some coal merchants also went out of their way to court the friers' custom: Baldwin's of Bristol advertised in 1925 'Special

Nuts for Fish Friers: Cheaper than Gas and more Reliable.'[47] As the tone of this advertisement suggests, gas really began to make headway as a friers' fuel in the inter-war years, but it was already being employed at the turn of the century in some areas. At Leicester, coke was actually displacing gas during 1904–6 as it became significantly cheaper.[48] In 1909 the *Fish Trades Gazette* presented the classic trade-off: gas cost nearly double the rate for coal or coke but gas furnaces were much cleaner.[49]

Furnaces were not the whole story: a Manchester firm introduced a 'midget gas engine' early in the new century specially for fish friers' potato-peeling machines: Loftas remembered that 4,700 were installed for this purpose within a few years.[50] But it was not until the late 1920s that gas companies really began to recognize the importance of the friers as consumers. By 1927 municipalized gas managements were generally willing to offer industrial concessionary rates to friers but private firms were still 'very chary'. Five years later the South Metropolitan Gas Company was making sustained efforts to attract the custom of the friers in its area, designing ranges to reduce gas wastage and trying to use friers' gas consumption to 'balance the load' in the evenings when the big industrial users had shut down and domestic consumers had switched to electric light. Loftas set this growing interest in context later in 1932 by making an heroic calculation, based on an extrapolation from fish friers' gas consumption in Great Yarmouth, that the trade as a whole might get through 8,000 million cubic feet of gas per year: an important contribution to the industry's revenues. Electricity, meanwhile, was largely a thing of the future for the frying trade, although the first commercial range appeared as early as 1928.[51]

Fish friers' hardware and engineering equipment had long been a major industry in itself. In 1909 Hancock, Collis & Co. offered the following 'fish friers' requisites': fish trays, potato scuttles, potato scoops, wires, back trays, potato baskets, potato shovels, fine skimming shovels, salt and pepper boxes, rubber pan cleaners, egg whisks, batter bowls, fish slicers, vinegar bottles and cork sprinklers. They were not alone: it was clearly well worth while to assess and cater for the needs of over 20,000 potential customers.

But the really big money was made where fish and chips intersected more directly with the engineering industry. This began in the earliest days of the trade, as manufacturers of frying ranges and potato washing and peeling equipment proliferated in the later nineteenth century. The early friers used iron cauldrons and crude brick furnaces made by local tradesmen on demand; but specialist firms soon emerged in the Manchester and London areas before spreading to the West Riding of Yorkshire and elsewhere. Faulkners of Hollinwood, between Manchester and Oldham, claimed in 1909 to have begun operations in 1862, although the son of the founder remembered the year as 1872 in his old age.[52] Nuttalls of Rochdale and Teuten of London have also claimed foundation dates in the 1860s.[53] Washing, peeling and chipping machines for potatoes began to be designed by engineers and put into commercial production in the 1870s and 1880s. By the early twentieth century there were perhaps two dozen specialist firms making frying ranges and other machinery for the trade. One of the biggest by 1914 was Acme Engineering of Leeds, which originated in 1879 as Acme Wheeleries, a safety-bicycle firm owned by the Whiteley brothers. In 1899 A. E. Wilkinson joined the firm and at the same time it moved into making potato peelers. In Edwardian times it took up range manufacture and abandoned bicycles, at the height of the great cycling boom: impressive testimony to the attractions of the frying trade for discerning entrepreneurs.[54] Another name to conjure with, Mabbott of Manchester, began in 1880 with the founder and a single employee; by 1910 it employed 150 people on fish and chip machine manufacture and repair at Manchester and Chapel-en-le-Frith.[55] At a cautious estimate, this direct spin-off from the rise of fish and chips must have been employing several thousand people nationally when the war broke out.

Development continued apace in the 1920s and 1930s as ranges became technically sophisticated and more elaborately decorated. The cost of new equipment increased strikingly. The range-makers became organized into the National Association of Fish Restaurant Engineers, submitting their own proof of evidence on the importance of the fish and chip trade to the Sea Fish Commission in 1935. As early as 1928 Nelson & Co. of Preston, who were not regarded as giants in the industry, had made 6,000 ranges of one particular type, which cost £72 each new at that time.[56]

Fish-friers also became important customers for refrigerating equipment. Again, this was mainly a product of the inter-war years. In 1910 a *Fish Trades Gazette* contributor expressed surprise that so few friers seemed to realize that: 'there is money to be made . . . by the judicious use of the cold store', at a time when 'mechanical refrigeration' was beginning to supplement older patterns of ice-box. By 1933 a standard friers' manual urged that: 'It is also necessary to instal either an ice-box or a refrigerator', although the author was prepared to advise 'the small frier' who was short of capital on how to make a do-it-yourself ice-chest, at least as a stopgap. But the ideal was a modern electric automatic refrigerator; the needs of the fish trades must have provided important stimuli to innovation in this field.[57]

Fish friers also took their share of the expanding market for shop fittings, with a distinctive appetite for tiles and waterproof surfaces and coatings stimulated by the increasingly demanding requirements of the public health inspectorate. These pressures grew from the early twentieth century, especially after the Public Health Act of 1907 allowed local authorities to schedule and regulate fish frying as an offensive trade. Regulations became more stringent in many places during the inter-war years and these developments combined with friers' rising aspirations and pursuit of a better class of customer to create a bonanza for manufacturers. Tiles were replacing wallpaper, especially in most owner-occupied shops; new patent vitreous wall-coverings had made headway by the 1930s, such as Opalite and Marmorene. The needs of the fried fish trade thus boosted demand for new Pilkingtons' products and also for several Czech manufacturers. Leaded lights and decorative mirrors were also being installed as friers sought to improve their image. Firms like Northern Terrazzo Ltd. of Leeds began to find it worth their while to direct their advertising at the trade press.[58]

More friers also began to attach restaurants to their premises and standards rose in this respect as well. H. T. Reeves in 1933 contrasted the older era of 'plain deal-top tables, now and again . . . covered with some cheap American cloth, and a few Windsor kitchen-chairs', with the more elaborate arrangements that were now becoming popular. He recommended coloured wall-papers, electric lighting with carefully chosen light-fittings, parquet floors, purpose-built restaurant tables with hygienic tops (cellulose was preferred), stainless steel cutlery and a wireless speaker to supply unobtrusive music.[59] This was a matter of ideal rather than widespread reality, but it illustrates the ways in which friers' requirements provided multiple stimuli for other trades and industries as the more enterprising members of the trade sought to propel themselves up-market.

Some of these links between fish and chips and the wider economy are obviously more powerful than others, but the case for studying the trade on the criteria of basic economic importance is very clear indeed. An even stronger case can be made for the social significance of the rise of the first fast-food industry. In the first place, it came to be almost ubiquitous in industrial Britain by the early twentieth century, after a period of accelerating growth in shop numbers and colonization of new territories from the late 1870s and early 1880s. By 1905 there were, on one calculation, fewer than 400 people per fish and chip shop in Oldham and Leeds and only about 600 in Bolton and St Helens. Not all of the northern manufacturing towns showed such high densities: in Bury, Bradford and Stockport, for example, the figure was between 800 and 1,000. Parts of London's East End and the working-class South Bank must have been on a par with these ratios, although provincial capitals, ports, county towns and market towns, from Newcastle and South Shields to Gloucester and Bristol, were much less obviously in thrall to the fish and chip habit.[60] In Glasgow (especially), Edinburgh, the Clyde coastal towns and, indeed, much of urban Scotland the fish restaurant, usually run by Italian immigrants, was becoming a popular institution; the trade was also gaining a foothold in Belfast and Dublin, in urban North Wales and the Rhondda Valley. Even at this early stage, the fish and chip shop was a familiar sight – and generated a familiar smell – over most of urban England; many rural areas were being visited by horse-drawn fish and chip vans. In the early heartlands of Pennine Lancashire and Yorkshire, and in some working-class areas of London, there was a fish and chip shop on almost every second corner. The trade continued to consolidate and to spread into new districts through the inter-war years; by the 1930s sustained efforts to attract white-collar and middle-class custom were beginning to bear fruit. The universality of fish and chips as a cultural reference point, whether as the butt of jokes or a focus for nostalgia, was firmly grounded in an ubiquitous physical presence.

It is not surprising to discover that fish and chips became an important element in the regular diet of a large proportion of working-class families. As early as 1904 a survey conducted by Southwark's Medical Officer of Health purported to show that 42 per cent of the population within a quarter of a mile of one fish and chip shop had 'recently' eaten fried fish from it, while a further 16 per cent had consumed some from elsewhere. Some sceptical comments were made in the trade press; but even if the claims were exaggerated, the popularity of fish and chips was undeniable.[61] In 1917 Bradford's fish friers calculated that the city's 303 shops supplied between 800,000 and 900,000 meals per week, or 2.5 for each man, woman and child in the population. This calculation was part of a propaganda drive to secure special treatment for the trade during the worst months of the First World War; but it coexists quite happily with other evidence suggesting that many – perhaps most – working-class families in industrial areas used the fish and chip shop three or four times a week.[62]

Contemporaries certainly attached importance to the level of fish and chip consumption and it became a major focus of controversy among commentators on public health and working-class living standards. In its early days, especially, the trade was widely perceived as a health hazard. A combination of appalling smells from unrefined frying media and primitive technology, with visibly defective hygiene and occasional well-publicised prosecutions for the sale of fish which was nasty as well as cheap, made such a perception understandable. It was well-developed by the early twentieth century and it helped to secure fish and chips the status of an offensive trade, alongside such salubrious crafts as gut-scraping and tallow-melting, in 1907: a designation that persisted officially until 1940.[63] Medical Officers of Health persistently tried to demonstrate links between fried fish consumption and enteric fever; even when such attacks became less frequent and less threatening in the inter-war years, voices within the trade continued to warn of the bad publicity and potential for disaster presented by the older and dingier back-street shops:

> I have seen fish displayed on a window slab open to all the dust and filth of the street, which have already been fried, and taken from there and put back into a pan to heat up . . . Scores of shops to-day do not use a potato peeler, but just scrub the potatoes and leave all the diseased parts of them to go into the pan with the rest. The customer picks them out.[64]

This was in 1932, after many years of steadily improving standards in the upper levels of the trade. It underlines the point that the public health issue was a serious matter of sustained importance, to which we shall have to return.

There was also a contemporary debate over fish and chips and working-class living standards. Critics alleged that fish and chips was indigestible, expensive and unwholesome. It was seen as a route to, or an aspect of, the 'secondary poverty' which arose from the incompetent or immoral misapplication of resources that would otherwise have been sufficient to sustain an adequate standard of living. It was presented as part of a pathology of culinary ignorance and the failure to use cheap ingredients to their best advantage. Above all, perhaps, it was seen as an easy way of avoiding the full burden of household responsibilities. The trade's apologists took a very different view, of course, emphasizing fish and chips' food value, cheapness, convenience for hard-pressed housewives (and especially women who combined housework with industrial employment) and palatability. They could call on eminent medical testimony like that of the brain surgeon Dr Crichton Browne, whose presidential address to the Sanitary Inspectors' Conference of 1910 provided the friers with propaganda for a generation, as he emphasized that fish and chips was warming, sustaining, nourishing, an escape from monotony and perhaps even 'a useful auxiliary in the fight against tuberculosis'. Above all, though, the friers argued that fish and chips was the most effective way of boosting fish consumption at working-class level, offering as it did a way of making fish attractive to consumers without requiring them to invest in expensive domestic technology or to use up too much of that important but underrated working-class commodity, time. This was a sustained debate, which arouses echoes in today's historiography. It reveals as much about contemporary values and expectations as it does about diet and consumption patterns. It deserves and will receive extended discussion in a later chapter.[65]

These controversial aspects of the fish and chip trade helped to call its respectability into question among some who might otherwise have been potential customers. The public nature of the purchase and (often) the consumption of the dish, with its all-too-visible newspaper wrapping, was embarrasing to those people in the working class who prized privacy, aloofness and independence above neighbourliness and communal give-and-take, espousing cleanliness as a cardinal virtue alongside privacy. At higher social levels these barriers were much more in evidence. Dorothy L. Sayers might plausibly send Lord Peter Wimsey out for a fish and chip supper with a sculptress in a novel set in 1921, but this is clearly a daringly Bohemian act following a visit to a rather plebeian music-hall; there are strong overtones of recreational 'slumming' about the episode.[66] In any case, aristocrats (especially imaginary 'younger sons') had a lot more freedom to be unconventional without loss of caste than did their middle-class – and especially lower middle-class – contemporaries. The tyranny of 'what will the neighbours think' was only too well understood in the trade. It generated a large crop of perhaps apocryphal but genuinely illustrative stories, like this one from 1932:

> I heard of a doctor's wife who would have paid the grocer's boy a few coppers to fetch the fish from the shop as she waited at the end of the street, as she did not think it would do her husband any good if the public knew he ate fish and chips.[67]

Evidence of such fears and taboos constantly surfaces in conversations with people who grew up in the 1920s and 1930s. There is, for example, the well-brought-up young lady in a small West Riding industrial town whose friends conspired to send one daring young man to the fried fish shop at the end of a summer evening at the Lawn Tennis Club, so that they could consume the forbidden treat on the verandah of the club-house away from prying and censorious eyes; or the woman from a highly respectable family in a small Lancashire town whose main confession of sin at the end of her first term, at a Manchester University whose English department also contained the young Anthony Burgess, was that she had compromised herself by entering a fish and chip shop. Such attitudes were in steady decline during the 1930s, as we shall see, as the trade began to attract middle-class custom and to be more favourably treated by officialdom of all kinds; but it was a long haul and the stigma of the early years was never to disappear completely.[68]

At the level of the working-class neighbourhood, however, the steamy atmosphere of the fish and chip shop drew its customers together for the exchange of gossip and sociability. It opened its doors freely to women and children as well as men and became particularly important as a focus for gatherings of adolescent boys. It was also, later in the evening, an inevitable accompaniment to courting. As the trade's publications pointed out from time to time, the successful frier needed to nurture a sense of cheerfulness and community by providing a steady flow of backchat and badinage, carefully adjusted to the preferences and marital status (if female) of individuals. Evidence on these attributes of the fish and chip shop is remarkably ubiquitous in working-class novels and reminiscences, from Jack Common's evocations of the Tyneside railwaymen's quarter of Heaton in the first decades of the twentieth century to the autobiographies of the Gorbals' Ralph Glasser and Hunslet's Richard Hoggart.[69] All shops were social gathering points and sociable queuing was a way of life; but the fish and chip shop, with its associations of warmth, pleasure and comfort, was especially important, particularly as its opening hours were restricted, well defined and responded to a neighbourhood consensus about mealtimes. Indeed, it may well be significant that the rise of the fish and chip shop coincided with the beginnings of the long decline of the pub.[70]

But the study of fish and chips is not just a matter of the trade's customers, working class or otherwise. It also provides a window on the lives of the small shopkeepers who have been so numerous in urban Britain, but so systematically neglected by historians whose main concerns have involved the landed interest, the wage-earning working class, and (most recently) the more substantial layers of the commercial and professional middle class. Serious studies of the petty bourgeoisie in Britain before the Second World War can almost be counted on the fingers of one hand. In recent years we have had books by Mike Winstanley and John Benson (although the latter's 'penny capitalists' were really poor working-class people trying to make ends meet by whatever means come to hand); edited collections of essays on the lower middle class in general, presided over by Geoff Crossick, but paying more heed to white-collar workers than to small traders; several essays from historical geographers on the changing spatial patterns of urban retailing; and precious little else.[71] By contrast, the literature on department stores and multiple retailers is relatively abundant; so is material on the rise of the Co-operative movement.[72] The publican and the drink trade have also attracted plenty of attention, though more from a social reform perspective and in terms of the rise of the music-hall than from an urge to examine the vicissitudes and problems of the trade on its own terms.[73]

The small shopkeeper has provided less obvious grist to the historian's mill. There is no clear-cut agenda to match the place of the department store or the rise of multiples like Liptons in heroic business history, or the role of the Co-operative movement in the making of the working class and its institutions, or the fierce moral and governmental controversies generated by the drink trade and its opponents. There was, after all, no national moral crusade against the fish and chip shop, except perhaps in Scotland on the eve of the First World War.[74] British shopkeepers encountered and dealt with their problems on a local rather than a national stage, although their attempts to federate in defence of their interests deserve more attention than they have so far received; their campaigns against local taxation and expenditure affected municipal policy in a wide range of Victorian and Edwardian urban settings. Above all, what is needed to redress the balance is a series of studies of particular shopkeeping and trading occupations. Grocers, greengrocers, drapers, confectioners and a host of other traders were important in terms of the numbers for whom they found a living and in terms of their impact on suppliers and customers. But they are more difficult to study because they have never been concentrated into particular towns or areas; they are spread too thinly to generate sources for the local case-studies that have been one obvious route to a deeper understanding of economic and social change in the nineteenth and twentieth centuries.

This study of the fish and chip trade will begin to fill this gap in the literature and in our understanding of the social structure of industrial Britain. Fish friers were located on the difficult, shifting margin between the lower middle and upper working classes. They recruited extensively from the ranks of skilled and supervisory labour and in many cases a fish and chip shop was a supplementary source of income for a family whose bread and butter came from one or more wage-earners working outside the home. Often, the shop was a short-lived expedient to tide a family through a difficult period, especially when the children were too young to earn. Even when a fish and chip shop was envisaged as the first step on the road to independence and a comfortable retirement, many – probably most – aspiring friers soon found themselves back in the ranks of wage labour again. And even while the business was being conducted, the overwhelming majority of friers continued to live among their customers, remaining culturally part of the working class in important respects even while their income came from trading rather than from waged manual labour. The pursuit of social advancement, if desired, was further hampered in many cases by the distinctive smell of the business, which all too often penetrated Sunday clothes as well as everyday wear, helping to perpetuate the trade's bad image.[75]

The fish and chip trade was overwhelmingly composed of single-family businesses. Chains were unusual and rarely pulled together more than a handful of shops. Managers were sometimes employed, perhaps especially in London, and many of the larger shops had paid help. But a study of the inner workings of the trade sheds light on the conduct of small businesses in general (though some problems were specific to fish and chips) and especially on the role of the family. The division of labour between husband and wife forms a major theme here: male friers liked to see fish frying as a craft and were eager to embrace and promote its skills and mysteries, while relegating the women to counter service; but it is clear that women often ran the shops and even more frequently did their share of the frying. But the fish and chip trade, like many others, maintained a heavy dependence on child labour well into the twentieth century. The trade required a lot of basic labour of a light and repetitive kind (as well as a good deal of hard manual work) in the preparation processes. The frier's children were a resource which could not be ignored, especially but not exclusively in the strenuous years before the First World War. The frier himself might have achieved the desired goal of independence from an employer, but he had to exploit his children and to work long hours for small hourly rewards in order to sustain this position. Child labour in these conditions was less visible than in factories or sweat-shops, but we should not ignore the issues it raises.[73]

In most towns of any size and even in some villages, the fish and chip trade was highly competitive: friers had to cultivate the virtues of rugged individua-lism in order to survive. But these values coexisted uneasily with the traditions of craft solidarity and trade-union consciousness from which many friers were recruited; they also cut across expectations of solidarity and mutual aid in working-class neighbourhoods. The need to organize the trade, which was felt most strongly in respect of problems of raw material supply and the restraint of competition, was regularly canvassed from 1907 onwards. In 1913 a lasting national organization was formed. Its active members formed an élite within the trade and some of the leaders justified their policies in terms of protecting a wider public interest as well as the sectional concerns of the friers. There was even a proposal that the National Federation of Fish Friers should affiliate to the TUC.[77] There was certainly a distinctive socialist presence among the friers during the inter-war years. But by the 1930s much of the Federation's campaigning, from whatever political standpoint within the membership, was directed against the regulatory bodies for the fishing and potato industries in the new corporate state. They seemed to be advancing the interests of the big producers at the friers' expense, imposing red tape and rising prices on hard-pressed small businesses with tight margins. The Keighley friers reported an interesting, though far from representative, set of opinions in 1935: 'Some members expressed the opinion that a Capitalist system was at work behind these Control Schemes, and that the Banks had a big word to say in the matter.'[78] More generally, friers experienced the state, both locally and nationally, as an interfering, threatening entity, taxing, inspecting, imposing standards, prosecuting and failing to protect. In the long run – and for most members of the trade – this was more likely to promote individualism or the sectional defence of friers' perceived corporate interests; membership of the National Federation languished except when a particular, identifiable threat needed to be faced.

But the politics of fish frying were far from being a negligible or laughable entity; here, as elsewhere, the friers' experiences provide a window that will cast light on the attitudes and values of the petty bourgeoisie in general.[79] This is no insignificant matter: the petty bourgeoisie became a major and distinctive political force in many European countries, most famously in Germany, during the period covered by this book. Explanations for its much weaker presence as a distinctive entity in British politics will only begin to carry conviction when more work has been done on the culture and concerns of small shopkeepers and petty tradesmen.[80]

The friers themselves liked to think they had a direct and telling influence on British politics in a more general sense. This belief was expressed particularly pungently in an editorial in *The Frier*, the mouthpiece of the short-lived Northern Counties Federation of Fish Friers, a Yorkshire-based secession from the National Federation, in 1919:

> Now the war is over, Government interest is dead. We have served their purpose, keeping off hunger, stemming revolution.

This reflected a central theme of the presidential address to the NCFFF, reported in the same issue:

> [During the war] all our energies were directed to . . . compelling the Government to recognise that we stood between the Government and grave discontent in congested districts, and that we stood, more than any other trade in the country, between the very poorest of our population and famine and revolt.[81]

This was not just a retrospective perception. Fish friers' spokesmen, especially in Yorkshire, had been articulating such sentiments through the spring and summer of 1917, reaching a crescendo at the end of the year in the face of a mounting crisis in oil and fat supplies that threatened the industry's ability to continue. By September efforts were being made to get fish frying listed as an 'essential trade' for conscription purposes. Mr Lackie of Bradford argued that 'many fish friers were doing far better national service by keeping open their shops to supply food . . . than by being in the Army.'[82] By early December the Bradford friers, in particular, were becoming almost apocalyptic in their language. Thus John Pullan, the NFFFF president:

> . . . the poor and working class had to have something to eat, and women generally were too busy munition-making to cook for their families if they could afford to get anything to cook or cook it with. If, therefore, the Government would not help the trade to find them a reasonably priced alternative, then it could look out for trouble.[83]

A week or so later another trade spokesman, William Pott, was talking in terms of a potential famine, which the control and conservation of fish supplies for the friers might help to alleviate. It was in this context that the organized friers put out a series of pamphlets, one of which was called 'Famine, or Fried Fish.'[84]

These claims were taken sufficiently seriously by the wartime coalition government for it to modify its policies to protect the friers' interests and ensure that the trade could continue to operate. There were clearly real and sustained fears in government circles in 1917–18 about the current levels of unrest and agitation over high food prices and intolerable queues for basic essentials, and ministers were aware of the impact on food supplies of the U-boat campaign and of world food shortages.[85] The evidence on whether the nutritional content of working-class diets really declined in these years is inconclusive but J. M. Winter, who has adopted a guardedly optimistic posture after a careful review of the evidence the government used, accepts that in so far as living standards were maintained, it was probably achieved by changing the balance of the diet towards blander and less palatable fare.[86] Winter takes no account of fish and chips in his assessment, nor does it feature in the memoirs of wartime politicians or in the official war histories. But this does not mean that it was not important or that policy-makers at the time took no account of it. Perceptions of living standards were as important as actual nutritional levels: the warmth, tastiness and time-saving qualities of fish and chips should not be underestimated.

Nor were they. In January 1918 a special Advisory Committee to the Fish Friers' Trade was convened under the auspices of the Ministry of Food, bringing together fish friers, oil and fat manufacturers and distributors and consumer representatives to work out policy on the supply of oils and fats to friers.[87] It does not seem to have met until July 1918 and the friers' representatives did not get all their own way in its actual deliberations; but its establishment expressed a sea-change in government policy that was soon noted and praised in the trade press. In January a *Fish Trades Gazette* editorial praised the Ministry of Food's recognition of the fried fish trade, especially the decision to provide 'everyone in the frying trade' with an adequate supply of cotton-seed oil.[88] This proved to be an over-simplification, but oil and fat supplies were indeed guaranteed and efforts were also made to resolve the enduring problem of fish supplies arising from the conscription of trawlers into war service.[89] Fish and chips was seen to be particularly important with the advent of rationing and as a private enterprise alternative to the 'National Kitchens' which were being canvassed as feeding stations: for both fish and potatoes remained unrationed and the ubiquity of the trade's outlets meant it could be encouraged to meet basic nutritional needs with the minimum of government interference.[90] The change of attitude was also expressed in a growing willingness to grant exemption from conscription to fish friers on the grounds that their work was of vital importance to the war effort.[91]

The events of 1917–18 provided an enormous boost to the trade's collective self-esteem. They gave rise to a widespread and enduring notion among friers that fish and chips had not only prevented revolution by feeding the disaffected poor, but also played a crucial part in winning the war by keeping the munitions workers fed and sustaining their morale. How much truth there was in this dual contention can never be established but it would be a mistake to laugh it out of court altogether. The stirring events in Russia and Germany in 1917 and afterwards were set against a background of severe and chronic food shortages, and Winter's conclusions about the importance of food supplies in general to the outcome of the war are carefully weighed and worthy of consideration:

> In this context it is possible only to suggest that if German workers in 1917–18 had commanded the real incomes of their British counterparts, and if their families had been able to maintain the nutritional levels we have described above, the outcome of the war may well have been reversed . . . it was precisely on the level of defending civilian living standards that the German war economy failed. The consequences were clear: better health among British civilians; much greater deprivation, stress and despair as well as deteriorating standards of health among a German population which paid the price British civilians never had to pay for their country's war effort.[92]

This is a verdict that leaves fish and chips out of the account. At the least it seems clear that if the work of the friers were added into Winter's equation, fish and chips might be held to have tilted the balance in the war of food supplies, health and morale that was so important to the outcome of the entire conflict.

The friers themselves were perfectly clear about all this, and events surrounding the outbreak of the Second World War show that the relevant government departments took their claims seriously in determining policy. When the NFFF presented its memorandum asking the Sea-Fish Commission for better treatment for the frying trade in 1935, it contained the argument that: 'It was demonstrated during the last war that the fried fish shop was a necessity . . .'[93] And in 1941 the trade was quick to latch on to a comment in the *Northern Daily Telegraph* that: 'Your fish and chips will help to win the war . . . Britain's sixpenny suppers . . . helped to win the World War of 1914–18 . . .'[94] In keeping with these expectations, the fish friers were well treated by government during the Second World War, after an uncertain start. They were consulted about the preparation of emergency plans for food supplies in wartime, and the correspondence between the NFFF and the Ministry of Agriculture and Fisheries on this subject between 1938 and November 1940 was deemed so sensitive that it has been kept hidden from researchers under the Public Record Office's 50-year rule, although this probably says as much about the absurdities of state secrecy as about the intrinsic importance of the file in question.[95]

The friers were also represented at the meetings in 1939 which set up an emergency fish distribution plan for war conditions, although they opposed the draconian scheme that was adopted root and branch and claimed part of the credit for its abandonment after a mere 19 days.[96] They suffered from shortages and soaring raw-material prices, but they were recognized as an important interest-group throughout, without having to make the special case that had been necessary in the previous war. Thus the prices paid by friers for their distinctive potato grades were subjected to government subsidy during a difficult period in 1940–1. Price controls on white fish were introduced in June 1941, while oil and fat allocations were safeguarded throughout. The friers' representatives were never completely satisfied by their treatment and throughout 1940 they argued for strict maximum white-fish prices; but no attempt was made to regulate their own selling prices in turn, under circumstances in which the usual consensus governing price levels had broken down. The in-house historian of the Ministry of Food's Fish Division in the war years was clear that he, at least, thought the friers had had a good deal:

> There were frequent and justified complaints from the public about the prices charged by many friers, who themselves benefited considerably from the controlled prices of all their raw materials, and Fish Division would have liked to put an end to the abuse.[97]

They were unable to take action because of the insoluble problems of definition and regulation that bedevilled the trade, rather than through any lack of conviction or will. But whether we see the fish friers through the civil-service lens, as hard-faced profiteers who did well out of the war, or from their own perspective as much-abused but resilient providers of a vital public service, there is no denying their wartime importance and its recognition by central government.

Arguments about the political importance of fish friers could be extended to peacetime and especially to the depressed years and distressed areas of the inter-war years. George Orwell, in *The Road to Wigan Pier*, included fish and chips in his famous list of little luxuries that helped to make life bearable and pushed revolution to the margins in the depressed areas of the 1930s.[98] The notion that it was fish and chips, above all, that warmed and filled the hungry bellies of the poor, gained wide currency. It re-surfaced, for example, in an *Observer Colour Supplement* feature in 1966:

> Between the wars, fish-and-chip shops burgeoned across the depressed areas, new ones opening all the time. For sixpence they provided a meal tasty and filling for a whole family.[99]

We shall see that this over-simplifies a complex set of issues. But it is significant that the man quoted in support of the contention came from Sunderland. It was above all in north-eastern England that the fish and chip trade came to be seen in this light, as both a humanitarian and a stabilizing influence. In 1935 it came to the attention of a government inquiry into the white fish industry. The Sea-Fish Commission took evidence at North Shields from a deputation of friers. It found them to be struggling to make ends meet due to a combination of rising prices and impoverished customers. Mr Cole of Middlesbrough claimed that some friers were having to sell at the pre-war price of a halfpenny fish and a halfpennyworth of chips. The commissioners asked in amazement: 'Can anybody expect to get a presentable meal for a penny?' Mr Muirhead of Sunderland spoke for most of his colleagues in his reply:

> We look at it in another light, that we have people who are living on the dole; we have people who are living on the P[ublic] A[ssistance] C[ommittee] and we are the only salvation of those people, at our cost.[100]

This was not a matter of quixotic humanitarianism on the fish friers' part: it was a question of basic economic survival. They would have liked to sell larger portions of better quality fish at higher prices and wider profit margins, but their customers could not afford to pay. For their part, the commissioners were worried about the future of the fishing industry. How could profit margins for trawler-owners and fishermen be sustained if large numbers of consumers could not afford the lowest possible prices for the poorest grades of fish? The sustained interest shown by government in the fish friers during the 1930s was a reflection more of this concern for the health of the industry than for the eating habits of the poor in the distressed areas; but evidence like this showed that the two issues were ultimately inseparable. The fish friers of north-eastern England, and (for example) in Glasgow,[101] helped to keep starvation and despair at bay among the unemployed in the depressed years, with consequences that should not be ignored or underestimated merely because they are incalculable.

The obvious importance of the friers to the fishing industry ensured that their spokesmen were taken increasingly seriously by civil servants and MPs. This was particularly apparent in the deliberation of the Sea-Fish Commission in 1935, as we have seen, and also when the White Fish Commission of 1938–9 sought to impose a marketing scheme and a system of compulsory registration on the fish trades. This was partly a response to the growing strength and representativeness of the NFFF in these years, and the urbanity of its president, Mr Youngman of Leeds, and other senior officials. The trade's views were meticulously recorded and proposals were adjusted to take account of the expert advice as well as the fears and concerns of its spokesmen.

Not that all was plain sailing. The friers found it much more difficult to make an impact on the agricultural vested interests that dominated the Potato Marketing Board from its establishment in 1934 and there was much complaint about its policies.[102] Commissioners and civil servants were often sceptical about the friers' case on aspects of fisheries policy, too. In 1939 the chairman of the White Fish Commission expressed himself as 'disappointed' at the friers' attitude to restrictions on landings from distant waters. He confided to his colleagues that: 'Probably the real difficulty is that these folk are not sufficiently educated or not sufficiently broadminded to take the trouble to understand the real effect of the regulation scheme they criticise.'[103] A similar condescending attitude surfaced when the secretary of the Sea-Fish Commission described

William Loftas, who was being a nuisance, as 'the literary fish frier, who wrote such blether about the Honorary Accountants'; and in 1940 a civil servant discussing potato-subsidy arrangements commented: 'It is generally known that, in many cases, the smaller type of shop is conducted by persons who are not exactly well-educated . . .'[104]

But the fish friers were not alone in sometimes falling foul of the overweening self-esteem of the governing class. The bottom line – the key point that made the friers worthy of attention and even a measure of respect from central government – was expressed in the Sea-Fish Commissioners' parting shot to the north-eastern friers in 1935: 'It is quite clear that any section of the consuming trade that takes as much as 50 per cent of the production is an important section . . . and must be so conducted as to expand, not contract, the sale of fish . . .'[105] The commissioners may have underestimated the friers' proportion of the white-fish landings, but this comment, and others, made government appreciation of the trade's importance only too apparent.

The case for the importance of the fish and chip trade can thus be made from a variety of perspectives, not least from that of central government and policy-making. We can now move on from justification to execution. We begin with a fuller examination of the origins, growth and spread of the trade from its Victorian origins to its years of maximum ubiquity and importance in the 1920s and 1930s.

2 Origins, Growth and Spread

The fish and chip trade grew out of existing petty trades in fried fish and cooked potatoes, which were carried on separately in the streets and alleys of London and some of the industrial towns in the middle decades of the nineteenth century. They were brought together under uncertain circumstances during the 1860s, in the Pennine textile-manufacturing towns around Oldham in Lancashire and in London. It is not clear which area, and still less which individual, deserves the credit for bringing about the momentous marriage of fish and chips: this is a matter of murky and probably insoluble dispute. It was obviously an idea whose time had come and the industry may well have had more than one fountainhead. At any rate, the spread of the industry from these two starting points was first steady, then spectacular, but it is difficult to chart in any detail, especially in the early years. The sources are scanty, anecdotal and resistant to quantification. But we must begin by saying what can be said about roots and origins.

The fried fish side of the trade can be traced back further than the chipped-potato branch. Its origins are clearly metropolitan. The friers themselves chose to celebrate the centenary of the 'fish frying industry as a separate branch of the food distributing industry' in 1949, on the basis of a reference to a fried fish warehouse in Chapter 26 of Dickens' *Oliver Twist*.[1] As Gerald Priestland points out, however, the book in question was first published in serial form between 1837 and 1839, which takes the origins of the trade back at least to the beginnings of Queen Victoria's reign.[2] The biographers of the famous chef, Alexis Soyer, writing in 1859, took it for granted that fried fish was readily obtainable in the Soho of the early 1840s:

> who could believe that the elegant, white-kid gloved Soyer, chatting with and amusing a dozen different parties . . . would afterwards quietly and slyly often dive into some obscure place and purchase two-pennyworth of fried fish! eating it with the greatest relish as he walked along.[3]

Sir Shirley Murphy, the Medical Officer to the London County Council, claimed in 1906 that surviving 'veterans in the trade' could still identify the locations of the 'few fried fish shops' that were operating in 1851; and he also found (and quoted at length) the passage in Mayhew's *London labour and the London poor* which dealt with the business methods and way of life of the 300 vendors of fried fish who figured among the city's street traders in 1861.[4]

Mayhew locates these friers, who fried fishmongers' leftovers that were distributed by costermongers, in obscure alleys in three parts of London: the streets around the Inns of Court, the fringes of the East End in the Bishopsgate area, and the Borough district just south of the Thames near London Bridge. This is clearly only part of the story: Chatchip's identification of Soho as the birthplace of the fried fish trade and London's Jewish community as its originators deserves to be taken seriously.[5] Substantial and lasting fried fish shops were being set up in the 1850s and 1860s in various parts of London. Malin's of Old Ford Road survived for more than a century to be fêted in 1968 as 'the world's oldest fish and chip business'.[6] But we do not know at what point they, or anyone else, began to sell chips with their fried fish; and rival contenders for the status of the first fish and chip shop can be found in the very different setting of the industrial Pennines.

Before we look at this alternative tradition in more detail, it should be said that there were no real impediments to the combining of fish and chips in mid-Victorian London. The baked-potato trade seems to have emerged in London at about the same time as the fried fish trade, although it seems to have remained separate and distinct;[7] but recipes for fried potatoes were readily available in cheap cookery books long before the advent of *pommes de terre à la mode* from France in the early 1870s, which was widely supposed to have brought chips into the range of acceptable English foods. Thus the *Modern Housewife*, published in 1848–9, offered 'fried potatoes' to be cooked in boiling fat, 'throwing a little salt over'; and Soyer's *Shilling Cookery*, issued in about 1854, contained a recipe for fried potatoes that required them to be cut very thin, fried in about two inches of fat and manipulated with a skimmer to prevent them from sticking together.[8] We do not know whether, or when, these ideas were adopted by London fish friers, or whether the impetus to the marriage of fish and chips came, as has been generally believed, from other sources at a later date.

Chatchip, whose active involvement in fish and chip frying and interest in its history dated from the early years of the twentieth century, had a clear perception of an enduring contrast between London and Lancashire. This was based on long talks with veteran friers from both areas; his assertive style and shortage of verifiable references should not lead us to set his work aside. In seeking to explain the consistently higher ratio of fish to chips in friers' portions in London, he announced that:

> Lancashire was the birthplace of the chipped-potato trade in England as London was the birthplace of fried fish, and just as in London the fried-fish trade was carried on for years without potatoes, so in Lancashire was the potato trade . . . without fish. Londoners are learning to like chipped potatoes, especially in those shops where a Lancashire potato peeler has been installed, and Lancastrians are learning to like fried fish, especially from those shops where the losses on 'spuds' are not transferred to the selling price of fish.[9]

The use of the present tense is a little startling in a piece written as late as 1920 and the tone of the second sentence is deeply misleading. The comments on the economics of fish and chip selling in Lancashire are also highly debatable. But the basic historical argument is at issue now; and in 1911 Chatchip had elaborated it in interesting ways:

> Until, perhaps, twenty years ago, what fish was sold in the Northern districts used to be fried by wholesale fish friers, from whom it was obtained by the local potato frier – as a matter of fact, this custom still obtains in some parts, particularly in the Welsh border districts.[10]

According to him, the growth of the fish and chip trade in Lancashire and later in northern England generally came when the existing potato friers went over to frying their own fish as well. So in contrast with Malin's and other London claimants to the title of 'oldest fish and chip shop', any Lancashire contender would have to establish at what point it began to fry, or at least to offer, fish as well as chips.

Gerald Priestland encountered this problem when he went to Mossley in pursuit of Lees' fish and chip shop, Lancashire's answer to Malin's. He performed prodigies of investigative journalism and found several interesting people to interview; but he was unable to discover when fish joined chips in a business that was apparently founded in 1863 as a pea-soup and pig's trotter hut, going over to 'chipped potatoes in the French style' a few years later and advertising itself as 'The Oldest Chip Potato Restaurant in the World' in 1902.[11] Various other claimants to primacy emerged from Priestland's efforts, but all that could be shown conclusively was a considerable increase in activity in the chipped-potato trade in the industrial Pennines during the 1860s, with the emergence of specialist range-making firms. When the fish joined the chips remained an open question, although some point in the 1860s seems the best guess from the available evidence.

Chatchip was certainly right about the primacy of the potato in the early years of the frying trade in Lancashire and its environs. There was a strong tradition of eating baked potatoes at the local wakes and fairs and in the 1850s and 1860s specially built 'locomotives for roasting potatoes' were much in evidence at fairgrounds in the Oldham area.[12] Chips made their appearance alongside these delicacies during the 1860s. Fried fish came in during the next decade, but in the 1890s trade directories still listed 'chipped potato dealers' alongside the 'fried fish dealers'. At Church and Oswaldtwistle, for example, the Barrett directory for 1894 listed only three fish friers, all of whom were also present among the 19 chip dealers. In the mill and market town of Clitheroe, eight chip dealers were listed, but not a single fish frier. But in the larger towns of Blackburn, Accrington and Darwen they were all 'fried fish, &c., dealers'.[13] This suggests a transition in perceptions and priorities – as well as providing another cautionary tale about the problems and inconsistencies of trade directories, even at this point of maximum coverage and apparent reliability. But in parts of Lancashire, chips without fish were a long-lived institution. In 1938, when the White Fish Commission was considering ways of regulating the fish and chip trade, its civil servants were told that:

> The friers were rather concerned about certain shops, particularly in the Oldham neighbourhood, which they described as potato shops. These dealt mainly in fried potatoes but only to a very small extent in fish.[14]

All this suggests that the introduction of *pommes de terre à la mode* from France in 1870, which was put forward by Sir Shirley Murphy as the basis of the marriage of fish and chips, was a red herring as far as Lancashire was concerned; it seems likely that chips came in during the 1860s and that their provenance was uncertain. Nor is there any hard evidence in support of Priestland's romantic hunch that the Pennine industrial towns saw the first successful consummation of the long marriage of fish and chips. There is circumstantial evidence in his favour, especially the long-established local attachment to the potato as a recreational as well as a workaday food; but ultimately all remains shrouded in speculation.[15]

Outside Lancashire, fried fish seems to have held sway before chips came on the scene, even in areas like Staffordshire where chips were more widely and enthusiastically eaten than fish in the early twentieth century. This is at least suggested by the evidence that in 1906 not all friers sold chips as well as fish in Stafford, Walsall and Nottingham; even in Leeds, which was to become one of the proudest centres of the fish and chip trade, some friers did not offer potatoes in 1909. In Macclesfield, too, only a short distance from the trade's Lancashire heartland, the earliest friers in the 1880s seem to have specialized in fish: chips were a later introduction by an Irish immigrant.[16]

By the early twentieth century, however, fish and chips had already become an established institution over most of industrial England and there were few parts of the country where its influence had not penetrated. Outside London and the Pennines, fried fish shops were already operating in the 1860s in places as different and as widely separated as Portsmouth and Coventry; the trade spread and consolidated its hold in the later nineteenth century.[17] The exact pace and pattern of growth cannot be recovered, for friers appeared belatedly and erratically in trade directories and other more or less official sources. But the *Fish Trades Gazette* commissioned a wide-ranging occasional series, 'The Trade in the Provinces', which provides a lot of information about the nature and distribution of the trade during 1905–9. Stray additional pieces of information enable quite a convincing basic picture to be put together. Sir Shirley Murphy, in his London County Council report, counted 250 fried fish shops in the Post Office Directory for London in 1888 and 600 in 1906. That these figures were (characteristically) incomplete was shown by the efforts of the LCC's inspectors, who uncovered 1057 shops; Murphy thought the real total was probably about 1200.[18] Meanwhile, fish friers (and chip dealers) were beginning to appear in significant numbers in the trade directories of the Oldham area in the early 1880s. Listings spread westwards through Lancashire over a decade or so, reaching Preston in 1885 and Blackpool by the end of the decade. This, along with the West Riding of Yorkshire, was the area which the 'Trade in the Provinces' feature found to be the most prolific in fish and chip shops in Edwardian times.

The *Fish Trades Gazette*'s roving reporter certainly did the rounds, as his despatches came in from places as far apart as Darlington and Bristol, Weymouth and Morecambe. He had a sharp eye for local peculiarities in everything from preferences in fish and frying media to social customs, as we shall see in later chapters. Sometimes he offered precise-looking renderings of the number of friers in a town, but often he contented himself with vague generalities. Where numbers are on offer, too, it is seldom clear whether his definitions of town boundaries coincide with the administrative divisions used by compilers of official statistics. So a formal statistical table would be misleading. But some idea of orders of magnitude can be given. The heaviest concentrations of fish and chip shops he records were in Oldham and Leeds, where there were probably fewer than 400 people per shop: perhaps one shop to every substantial working-class street, if the friers were evenly distributed through the town. But they were not. Thus in Leeds: 'Very few are to be found in the heart of the city and none in the principal thoroughfares, but they abound in the outside wards and townships.'[19] There was no need to add that they were also absent from middle-class residential areas. But the Leeds pattern was not universal. Most of Worcester's shops seem to have clustered in the town centre, while Bristol's were 'all over' the city, although Birmingham was closer to the Leeds model: 'The shops are spread all over the city, and in some of the poorer districts there are one or two in nearly every street. There are comparatively few near the centre of the city.'[20]

After Leeds and Oldham in overall density came Bolton and St Helens, with about 600 people per shop. Bolton was said to have 'a shop in nearly every street, and in some thoroughfares there are half a dozen'. St Helens must have shown a similar pattern, offering a reminder that fish and chips could be every bit as ubiquitous in centres of mining and heavy industry with little waged work for women as it was in the cotton towns.[21] After this came Bury, Bradford, Stockport and Halifax, with ratios of between 800 and 1000 or so to each shop. A mixed batch of towns occupied the band of ratios between 1,100 and 1,500 people per shop: the resorts of Morecambe and Weymouth, the Yorkshire textile centre of Cleckheaton, the administrative, transport and mixed-industrial economies of Stafford, Stockton and Lancaster, and the railway town of Darlington. Even at this level of density the fish and chip trade was far from negligible, although its presence became less pervasive in the county towns and regional capitals of Bristol, York, Derby, Newcastle, Worcester and Gloucester, with ratios of between 2,000 and 3,500.[22] Comments from the *Fish Trades Gazette* correspondent suggest that fish and chips was more strongly established in Nottingham and Birmingham than in other midland county towns and regional capitals, and that Liverpool, with its enduring partiality for oysters, was less of a fish and chip centre than St Helens, Warrington, the cotton towns, or even Manchester and Salford.[23] The Manchester area itself, indeed, was given a celebratory write-up by Chatchip in 1911:

> If London may claim to be the birthplace and the Jews the fathers of the fried fish trade, Manchester can claim to be its home, and Lancashire people to be its foster-mother, for nowhere in the British Isles are there so many fried fish shops in so little area as can be found in Manchester and the neighbouring cotton manufacturing towns.[24]

He claimed that there were 2,000 fried fish shops within a five-mile radius of Manchester Town Hall, with over 500 more in Oldham and district. This reiteration of Lancashire primacy is given further support from a comparative angle by this comment on Hanley in 1906, which was later applied to the Staffordshire pottery towns in general:

> Fried fish, however, does not seem to be such an important 'institution' here as it is in most Lancashire towns. The majority of the shops are rather small, and in every respect they compare unfavourably with those in the sister county. Chipped potatoes rather than fried fish seem to be favoured by the poorer class of people in the Potteries, and they are frequently seen leaving the shops with large quantities of the vegetable and comparatively very small portions of fish.[25]

This comment not only points up contrasts in living standards and eating habits which will be discussed later: it is also a reminder that simply counting shops and comparing them with population figures tells only part of the story – and perhaps a misleading version at that.[26]

Stray reports on matters of concern to the trade in the *Fish Trades Gazette* during the early years of the twentieth century reveal a wide distribution across England and Wales, although it is difficult to guess from this evidence how thick on the ground fish friers were in any particular locality. In Edwardian times fish and chips had gained a firm footing in south-coast resorts from Thanet to Bournemouth, with an outpost even at up-market Bexhill; it was in evidence in the Bristol Channel resorts like Clevedon and Weston-super-Mare, at Southend and Great Yarmouth, at the proletarian northern seaside resorts, especially Blackpool, and even at sedate little Saltburn-by-Sea. There were about 25 shops in Gillingham, Kent, in 1907, and at about the same time naval ports like Portsmouth and Southampton were developing thriving fish and chip trades, as were fishing ports like Hull, Grimsby and Fleetwood, which took a pride in consuming their own catch. Oxford and Cambridge were not left out, nor were the manufacturing towns of the south midlands, from Reading to Northampton and Peterborough. The trade was spreading into London's more salubrious outer suburbs, although it did not go unresisted: as Barnes and Mortlake's populist Councillor Kitley pointed out when restrictions were envisaged there, 'Councils all over the suburbs were stopping the fried fish trade.'[27] From Carlisle to Bodmin, from Bedlington to Bognor, the trade expanded to cover the whole of England, including villages and small market towns like Bedale, Hailsham, Dursley, Sherborne, Faringdon and Saxmundham. It was also colonizing Cardiff, Tonypandy and the South Wales valleys and becoming established in Swansea. A fish and chip map of England and Wales would have matched Bradshaw's Railway Guide in its colourful, comprehensive coverage.

It would be interesting to put together a more detailed perspective on the rise of the fish and chip trade, comparing different areas more systematically than the *Fish Trades Gazette* surveys and looking at change over time through a long period. The most plausible way of doing this would involve the use of trade directories, which are at their fullest and most convincing in the crucial years of the late nineteenth and early twentieth century.[28] But in the case of fish and chips the directories are far from foolproof. Not only do they tell us nothing about shop size and turnover: they also systematically understate the number of shops in business at a given time, in unpredictable ways.[29] In the first place, the trade was well-established, in its disreputable early back-street form, by the time the directories began to take notice of it in the 1880s and 1890s. In Blackpool and no doubt elsewhere, the Medical Officer of Health noted and counted the shops before the directories did. This is not surprising: in its earliest days, with makeshift premises and no control over smell and steam emission, the trade was more a matter for nuisance prosecutions than for commercial listings. But even as the lists lengthened in the directories at the turn of the century and beyond, it is clear that large numbers of friers continued to be omitted. Sir Shirley Murphy's LCC survey made this clear for London; but there is also disquieting evidence from the provinces. In July 1913 'Rambler', an experienced trade journalist, recollected that when he took his first shop in Burnley in 1896 there were 'from 200 to 250 chip shops' in the town; but Barrett's *Directory* for 1899 lists only 133 'fried fish, *etc.*, dealers', with no separate heading for chipped-potato dealers.[30] And for Carlisle between 1913 and 1931 it is possible to compare the entries for two firms of directory compilers with the number of friers recorded in the annual reports of the Corporation's Sanitary Inspector. When the Carlisle City directory could be compared with Kelly's, the latter had more entries than the former; but each omitted some friers who were listed in the other. Thus in 1914 Kelly listed 21 fried fish shops to the City directory's 20 but when the two lists were combined the consolidated total was 33. Meanwhile, the Sanitary Inspector listed 28, but in later years his total was significantly higher than that of the City directory, with 25 shops against 16 in 1920, 34 against 23 in 1927 and 38 against 28 in 1931.[31]

This kind of evidence does not inspire confidence in large-scale number-crunching exercises using trade directories; and any attempt to cross-refer to other sources, even if they were available, would generate a disproportionate amount of labour to little purpose. As a tentative indication of basic trends in a northern industrial town, Table 2.1 may not be completely misleading, however; but it will have to be treated with considerable caution. It gives a directory's eye view of the rise of the fish and chip trade in Preston. This was a cotton town but not a representative one: it had a larger administrative and commercial middle class than its peers and a more diverse manufacturing economy.[32] Fish and chips also spread here rather belatedly, as compared with its apparent northern cradle in the spinning towns north of Manchester. But the overall trend may not be wildly untypical and the same firm's trade directories, those of Barrett and Co., are used throughout.

Table 2.1   Fish and chip shops listed in Preston directories, 1885–1936

Year	Number	Year	Number	Year	Number	Year	Number
1885	22	1898	129	1913	133	1932	172
1889	32	1904	134	1917	120	1936	155
1892	70	1907	148	1922	140		
1895	93	1910	142	1926	166		

The pattern that emerges fits in quite well with contemporary assessments of what was going on, whatever reservations we might harbour about the representativeness of the directory coverage: this was, after all, the same firm whose count of fish friers in Burnley in the late 1890s was so much less than that of a well-informed local frier turned trade journalist. So we see very rapid late Victorian growth, followed by Edwardian consolidation; and the *Fish Trades Gazette*'s roving reporter captured the town's trade at the height of this early prosperity. Preston's friers were said to be 'numerous' and remarkable for their cleanliness and good order. Fish and chips was popular in the town: 'While many have it regularly for supper others frequently make their mid-day meal of it, and seem to thrive upon it.'[33] But a setback seems to have followed after 1907, at a time when friers generally were complaining about rising raw-material prices and increasing local government regulation and restriction and the first trade protection organizations were emerging and federating.[34]

The impact of the First World War can be seen in the reduced listing for 1917; but the fall in numbers is much less than contemporary comment would lead us to expect. Successive crises in the supply and price of fish, potatoes and oils and fats first provoked complaint and then despair from spokesmen for the trade. Early in 1917 a Tyneside commentator claimed:

> The trials and troubles of the fish and chip dealers are now come to a climax. The majority of them on Tyneside are contemplating the closing of their businesses, and going in for munitions or other work.

At the same time Bradford friers were talking of 'a notable struggle for existence' and phrases like 'total extinction' were being bandied about.[35] A little earlier Sir E.H. Busk and Sir J. Wrench Towse, writing on behalf of the Fish Food Scheme Committee of the National Sea Fisheries Protection Association, had announced that:

> The great majority of the fish friers and of the fish hawkers and small fishmongers have gone out of the business. These were really the backbone of the industry . . . It is estimated that only about one-fifth of these remain.[36]

This was outrageously apocalyptic as far as the fish friers were concerned, although it was taken seriously in a *Fish Trades Gazette* editorial a fortnight after it was first published.[37] But numbers did fall much more sharply in some places than the modest dip in the Preston directory entries would suggest. By early 1918 Hull's friers had apparently halved in numbers to 300 since the start of the war, while Leeds' had declined from 800 in 1909 to 500 in February 1918.[38] In Carlisle, however, the Sanitary Inspector found 22 fish and chip shops in 1918, as against 28 in 1914: a noticeable but less spectacular decline.[39] We are left wondering whether Preston's directories, and perhaps those of other towns, may have systematically excluded friers in a limited way of business or in low-status areas, who were not part of a trade élite; these would have been the most likely people to suspend operations, or to go to the wall, during the most difficult months of wartime. So a study based on directories alone would only show casualties among the more substantial members of the trade, without taking account of the carnage among the weaker brethren. This seems the most convincing way of reconciling the contradictions in the quantitative evidence.

Similar problems of selective under-recording in directories probably persisted in the inter-war years. The Carlisle evidence supports this notion and Preston's Medical Officer of Health reported 174 fish friers in the town in 1930, with five more recently sanctioned. This was only a few more than the highest directory figure, but enough to give pause for thought.[40] The modest post-war recovery in Preston's fish and chip shop numbers does not match the expectations aroused by the fish frying organizations' complaints of new friers flooding into the trade at this time; nor does it correspond with the experience of Leeds and Bradford, where the number of fish friers never again reached the pre-war high-water mark.

Complaints about unfair and proliferating competition were legion within the trade during the 1920s. The most vehement statement of the fears in the trade in the immediate post-war period came from the Northern Counties Federation, whose leaders fulminated against the prospect of a return to the 'former mad competition state' and threatened to bar new friers who competed with existing members from the NCF and the trade benefits which went with membership.[41] A lot of the newcomers at this stage were discharged soldiers with grants from the Ministry of Pensions, administered through local pensions committees; the Halifax branch of the NCF persuaded its local committee to send applicants to them to enquire about vacant shops, rather than allowing them to set up at random in competition with existing friers, many of whom were themselves returning from the war.[42] The ex-service recruits attracted sympathy as well as animosity and 'Macte Animo' of the *Fish Friers' Review* was at pains to emphasize the help given from within the trade to those newcomers who had forfeited their apprenticeships in order to join up in the war and thus had been denied the skilled craftsman status to which they would have been entitled.[43] In any case, the influx of ex-servicemen was a temporary phenomenon; fears on this score were soon displaced by worries about the unemployed, as the first of the postwar depressions began to bite. William Pott of Hadfield was certain, in 1925, that: 'We truly have had a flood of new frier shops in our country since the war': he ascribed this more to the trade's attractions for unemployed workers than to any other cause.[44] More generally, 'Macte Animo' identified a boom period immediately after the war, when large numbers of new entrants came into the trade and overstocked it, although he blamed lax administration by local authorities rather than the spur of unemployment as such.[45]

The quantitative evidence, for all its limitations, does not support these perceptions from within the trade. There is interesting countervailing material on the barriers to the proliferation of shops and the changing character of a lot of the businesses. Chatchip, perhaps predictably, went against the prevailing orthodoxy in 1920:

> Scores and hundreds of fried-fish shops [had stopped trading in wartime] . . . the proprietors of which either went fighting or munition-making . . . Those friers who went on munitions will never come back, they learned how to make a living better and easier . . . Those who went into the fighting forces and *have* returned, cannot get shops. Landlords will not let them; they want to sell at three times their economic value. There are no would-be fish friers who can afford to buy property. People who

can afford to pay fancy prices for shop property are not attracted by the fried-fish trade.[46]

This was an exaggerated and short-term view but it did draw attention to genuine constraints on the expansion of the trade. The 1920s saw sustained complaints about the difficulty of setting up new shops on the new suburban housing estates, whether provided by private developers or the local authority. The 'offensive trade' label made life difficult for the aspiring frier who wanted to follow his customers to the suburbs and the Town Planning Act of 1925 erected further obstacles, effectively banning fish friers from large areas of designated and controlled development. Some headway was being made on council estates in cities like Leeds by the late 1920s, but these constraints on expansion helped to stem the flow of new recruits to the trade, channelling what growth there was disproportionately into the older town centres and working-class districts, where competition from newcomers in what was often a dwindling market was particularly keenly felt. This pattern of development may help to explain the apparent paradox of persisting complaints about the overcrowding of the trade that do not seem to be borne out by the head-counts in directories and other quantifiable sources.

In this context the experience of the fish frying trade in Bradford is revealing, though certainly not representative. The city's Inspector of Fried Fish Shops, Mr G. Driver – himself a unique and pioneering appointment – reported in 1929 on the current state of the trade, reflecting on more than 20 years' experience. Bradford's frying trade had reached its high-water mark in terms of sheer numbers on the eve of the First World War, when there were 317 shops. There were now 286 (and an earlier report showed that there had been 280 in 1925). The decline in numbers was said to be due to strictly enforced local by-laws: in 1925 it was claimed that without such restrictions, 'had all the people been allowed to open who applied there would have been over 800'. Under this regime the loss of shops due to street improvements and the demolition of 'insanitary areas' was not being made good; Driver pointed to some shops that had closed down 'voluntarily rather than bring the business up to the sanitary standard required'. But there was another side to this story, which points up the limited value of calculations based simply on raw shop numbers without taking account of the size of individual businesses. Driver went on to assert that:

> There has never been more fried fish consumed in Bradford than now. There are twelve wholesale firms who cater for fish friers most exclusively; in 1917 there were a large number of friers with single-pan ranges, today there are not half-a-dozen.

So there were fewer, bigger and better shops and a substantially increased trade. Driver made it clear that he and his paymasters recognized the value of well-conducted fish and chip shops:

> There is a greater demand than ever for cooked foods, and fried fish seems to have priority over any other, and in cities where women are engaged in the textile and other trades, the fried fish shop is a blessing, as the children get some good, wholesome food, where otherwise they would only receive a ration of margarine and bread, probably not so sumptuous even as that.

In this spirit of appreciation, Bradford's Health Committee was allowing one fish and chip shop to be established on each of its new housing estates.[48]

Bradford was famous for its uniquely careful – and sympathetic – regulation of the fried fish trade and Driver was justifying, on his retirement, the policies with which he had long been identified. But the trends towards tighter regulation and increasing size of business were much in evidence elsewhere: the apparently limited growth of the trade in the post-war decade in some of its heartlands needs to be seen in this perspective.

In terms of the sheer number of outlets, the fish and chip trade in Preston reached an all-time peak in the early 1930s, to judge from the directory evidence in Table 2.1. This experience was much more common in the northern and midland industrial districts than the eve-of-First World War high-water mark in Bradford. But R. A. Taylor, counting fish and chip shops in Kelly's street directories, found that the number of shops continued to grow, both absolutely and in relation to the total population, throughout the 1930s in several large southern towns, although Manchester and Hull showed a downward trend. In Southampton the ratio of fried fish shops per thousand population increased from 0.24 to 0.36 during the decade; Portsmouth increased from 0.39 to 0.51. Reading, Norwich and even Bournemouth showed less marked increases. This growth came from much lower starting figures: the corresponding ratios for Manchester and Hull in 1930 were 0.80 and 1.05. Taylor's conclusion that, 'By 1930 the trade was past or at least passing its peak in the North, whereas in the South it was still growing fairly rapidly', perhaps overdraws the contrast, owing to the limitations of the directory evidence and the undoubtedly growing size and turnover of the 'average' northern business; but there are real differences in trend here nevertheless.[49]

In some depressed areas of northern England, however, the 1930s saw a considerable expansion of fish and chip shop numbers at the bottom end of the market, involving the sort of traders who were least likely to find their way into the trade directories. In 1932, while other contributors to the *Fishing News* speculated that depressed working-class purchasing power in industrial areas, coupled with high prices, might mean that fish and chips had already reached its 'utmost degree of popularity in this country', Chatchip offered a different but complementary emphasis. He agreed with a correspondent that the means test was pushing unemployed men with savings into trying to retrieve their fortunes by starting fish and chip businesses, using ranges which the makers were supplying all too readily on easy hire-purchase terms. This was leading to a proliferation of incompetently run shops operating on a shoestring in already-congested districts.[50] This perception is confirmed for the north-eastern coalfield by the evidence given to the Sea-Fish Commission by the local friers in 1935. Friers complained that wherever the trade was unregulated by local government, as in Bishop Auckland, people were coming off the dole with minimum capital expenditure and overheads to compete with the established businesses and drive prices down. Similar trends were evident in Jarrow, Sunderland and even in Newcastle itself.[51]

All this suggests there were different trends in different places, with persisting expansion in the number of outlets being a product of relative prosperity in southern towns and of survival strategies among the unemployed in the distressed areas. In some industrial settings, however, a fall in the number of shops might mask a continuing increase in the popularity of fish and chips, as smaller, older and more insanitary shops gave way to larger, more up-market premises with a higher turnover and a wider social range among their customers.

Part of this trend was the spread of the high-class fish restaurant, usually on a town-centre site, during the inter-war years. This was not a completely new development. Chatchip remembered that by 1896 Sam Isaacs was running a chain of fried-fish restaurants in London, which offered fish, chips, tea, bread and butter for ninepence and were 'palaces' by the standards of the time.[52] By the turn of the century similar things were happening in the provinces. G. Pye of Portsmouth spent over £1,000 on a purpose-built fish and chip shop in 1900; in 1906, in the small Lancashire port and resort of Fleetwood, Theodore Clegg provided sitting accommodation for 70 people: 'and he divides his customers into three classes – first, second and third, according to their personal appearance and social status'.[53]

But the most widespread and impressive developments began in the early 1920s, using prime city-centre sites. Chatchip, looking back from the early 1950s, chose to highlight Holmes' Fish Café in Margate and Nathan Duce's Picton's Fish Café in Reading, with its floodlit 'old-world' exteriors.[54] He might equally have mentioned Foster's Fish Restaurant and Café in Leicester, which was operating in 1923 in a completely rebuilt building, with oak tables, seating for more than 100 people and fancy cakes to go with the staple fare. Or there was A. Buckley's Imperial Fish Restaurant at Shepherd's Bush, which was said to have a: 'distinctive appearance . . . in that clean white tablecloths and good class silver plate adorn the tables'.[55]

The next decade or so saw a further string of initiatives. Leeds became particularly well-endowed, as Henry Youngman's city-centre restaurant was joined by Harry Ramsden's famous venture on the outskirts at Guiseley. Chatchip remembered that it was 'considered, by myself and by the hundreds of friers who subsequently visited it, the best set of premises for a fried fish restaurant that had, to that date, ever been devised'. Ramsden's opened in 1931, with seats for 200 people. It soon acquired wall-to-wall carpeting, leaded windows, chandeliers (though not yet crystal ones) over the tables and music. But the lunch-time custom of the local millworkers, with their bulk orders for takeaway meals, was of basic importance to Ramsden's trade: he did not depend solely on the up-market restaurant traffic he had generated and this dual clientele probably explains the unique extent of his success.[56] Chatchip's own venture, a 'Fish and Chip Palace' in Oxford Road, Manchester, in the city's central entertainment district, was opened by an MP with a great fanfare of publicity in 1934. Much was made of its spotless cleanliness, its use of new materials such as 'staybright', opalite and chromium, and its comfortable furnishings; but it seems to have been a disastrous failure and this may have been partly due to a failure to make concessions to an older and less affluent type of clientele. This is a reminder that the big, new, heavily capitalized restaurants on prime sites were still unusual, high-risk enterprises and we should not overstate their importance to the trade as a whole.[57]

Fish and chips was moving up-market in other ways in the inter-war years. It was featuring, increasingly as a matter of course, on general restaurant menus.

This was a source of some disquiet within the trade but it seemed that nothing could be done about it. Chatchip reckoned that the Alexandra Coffee Palace in south London became, in 1911, the first popular general café to offer fish and chips.[58] By 1932 it was a different story:

> Every café, restaurant, cookhouse, hotel, hostelry and city stores' 'snack rooms' now figure them prominently on their menus . . . In some of the cafés it is a well-established fact that as much, and more than [sic] 60 per cent of their total turnovers are taken for fried fish and chip meals.[59]

This is a characteristic piece of hyperbole but, as usual with Chatchip, it contains a significant element of truth. In the same year *The Caterer and Hotel-Keepers' Gazette*, an up-market publication aimed at the more opulent levels of the hotel trade, featured alongside its characteristic advertisements for warm-air hand-driers and fake-oak beams and panelling a fish frying unit 'specially designed for small-space kitchens' by Bartlett's of London, W2.[60] During the decade, department-store restaurants were also giving fish and chips a high profile, although in the case of Brown's of Chester this was part of a campaign to make the store attractive to the skilled working class, who were accused by the manageress (who was not happy about the policy) of 'eating with their knives and eating huge meals of fish and chips in the afternoon'.[61] By 1939 the *Fish Friers' Review* was taking the line that all the large stores were extending their catering business in this direction and turning it into a major money-spinner at the expense of fish friers whose customers would not want their wares in the evening after an afternoon blow-out as part of a shopping trip.[62] Mass-Observation's portrayal of working-class eating habits in Bolton and Blackpool in the late 1930s certainly bears out the impression that fish and chips was a ubiquitous – and universally popular – feature on menus of all kinds.[63]

Fish and chips was thus spreading beyond the specialist shops that had completely dominated the market before the First World War, as it invaded restaurants, hotels and department stores. It also had an important place in the works canteens that some major employers introduced in the inter-war years. The Montague Burton factory at Leeds opened its new canteen in 1934, deploying a 10-pan Acme frying range that could supply fish and chips to 2,000 workers at lunch-time, a quarter of the building's total capacity.[64] Conversely, however, many fish friers were diversifying in their own businesses, offering alternatives or supplements to the traditional bill of fare. All this complicates attempts to assess the extent and changing importance of the fish and chip trade, as such, in the inter-war years.

Even before the First World War, not all fish friers were exclusive specialists in the trade. Most obviously, from the earliest days of the industry many shops in London and the southern counties sold fried fish alongside wet, dried and sometimes shellfish; under these conditions fish frying itself might account for only a small proportion of the turnover of the business.[65] In Manchester and other parts of Lancashire, on the other hand, many Edwardian friers also sold tripe and cowheels. Chatchip, in his opinionated way, insisted that this was the only other business that could be suitably combined with fish frying. It apparently offered opportunities for better window-displays and allowed sensitive people to pretend to their friends that they were buying tripe rather than fish and chips. More to the point, no doubt, was that Chatchip had combined the trades himself.[66] The Mason's Arms at Headington Quarry, near Oxford, was a converted cottage with, in 1905, a drinking parlour at the front, a fish and chip shop in the middle and a sweet shop at the back.[77] Elsewhere we find a Merthyr Tydfil steeplejack selling fish and chips and tobacco on the same premises, prompting the *Fish Trades Gazette* to speculate on the possible uniqueness of this combination of occupations, and a Preston blacksmith who was also a fish-frier.[68]

By the early 1920s, however, matters had gone much further in parts of northern England. The summer of 1921 found Chatchip in denunciatory vein:

> In some Yorkshire and Lancashire towns one can see greengrocery, grocery, fire-wood and firelighters, ice-cream and sweets being retailed from fried-fish shops, and in one Derbyshire town I saw tobacco, sweets and grocery all mixed up in one shop with the frying trade.[69]

This detracted from the frier's concentration on his proper vocation and got in the way of the essential cleaning of the frying equipment. Four years later, however, a Durham frier offered a different point of view. He reckoned that: 'There are very few fish shops in the country that can live entirely by the sale of fried fish and chips' and his response was to branch out into fresh and dried fish, rabbits, eggs and groceries to such an extent that fish and chips now accounted for only one-fifth of his trade.[70] The relatively high fish prices of the 1930s, when rival foodstuffs were becoming cheaper, accentuated this trend. Loftas told the Sea-Fish Commission in 1935 that: 'The tendency in Manchester since fish has got so dear is that they have dropped off fish and gone on to pies . . . they have created a demand for other things instead of fish.'[71] When the White Fish Commission began an abortive scheme to register and regulate all the fish frying businesses in Britain in 1938, it had to reckon with problems of definition that not only encompassed the fish frying activities of Woolworths, Marks and Spencer and the Lyons Corner House, but also the much humbler activities of many

> persons in the North who sell fried fish and chips . . . together with such foods as peas, beans, tripe, meat pies and other cooked meats, or sweets, biscuits and ices. They claim that they carry on a general catering business.[72]

These café proprietors claimed that fish and chips was incidental to their business; but the specialist friers were indignantly adamant that they should not escape regulation. For present purposes, however, what matters is that fish frying was not always a specialist trade. In the inter-war years it became increasingly entangled with other kinds of activity in ways that make it even more difficult to establish precise statistical trends and that prefigure the growing complexity and diversity of the trade in the years after the Second World War.

Despite the cross-currents and complexities, however, an overall pattern of development for the fish and chip trade in England and Wales emerges quite clearly. It begins in London and the Pennine manufacturing towns in the 1870s.

By the early twentieth century it has gained a strong foothold in most of the manufacturing districts and has almost reached saturation point in some of the textile and heavy industrial towns of northern and midland England. It is beginning to go up-market in the Edwardian years and by the First World War hardly any market town or substantial village is without at least one fish and chip shop. Its early development shows an affinity for industrial economies that generate a lot of waged work outside the home for wives and mothers, but it also flourishes in mining and metalworking districts that offer little industrial employment for women. This raises issues to which we shall return. It suffers a setback during the First World War, but recovers thereafter, although the recovery takes different forms in different places. It may reach its peak, at least in terms of specialized shop numbers, in the early 1930s in most of northern and midland England, while continuing to expand in the south; but this part of the picture is complicated by the spread of fish and chips beyond its original specialist outlets, while at the same time some fish friers are diversifying into other lines. An overall view of the trade's distribution in 1939 can be found in the listing of branches of the National Federation of Fish Friers in the *Fish Trades Annual* for that year. The NFFF was well-established as the sole trade organization for fish friers by this time, but some branches had far more members than others and the Federation's writ ran more effectively in some areas than others. The picture is also distorted by the whole of London and the Home Counties being subsumed under a single branch. But of the 137 branches listed in England, 32 were in Lancashire and 29 in Yorkshire, with 15 in Durham and Northumberland. The rest were widely scattered, with surprisingly few branches in the industrial Midlands (which may say more about the pattern of the Federation's influence than the real distribution of fish friers) and implausible outposts at up-market resorts like Folkestone and Torquay. Wales had six branches, all in the southern industrial belt, although the trade also had a long pedigree in North Wales. So the early heartlands of the trade still predominated on the eve of the Second World War and many of the additional strongholds were in northern mining areas.[73]

But a full picture of the rise of the fish and chip trade in Britain has to take account of the distinctive experience of Scotland and Ireland. The big difference here was the prominent role played by Italian immigrants. Chatchip was startled and annoyed by their high profile in Scotland when he visited Aberdeen in 1932: 'What in the world have Scotsmen been doing to let these foreigners predominate in what is pre-eminently a British institution?'[74] This pattern began to emerge at the turn of the century and the Italians seem to have been in at the start of the fish and chip trade in Scotland. Their numbers increased from about 750 to over 4,500 between 1890 and 1914 and they moved into the 'fish restaurant' business after beginning as vendors of statuettes and later ice-cream. Almost all of them came from villages around Barga, in Tuscany, and Picinisco, in the Val di Comino in the province of Frosinone. Most migrants to England came from elsewhere in Italy, but it is likely that many of the Scottish Italians would have passed through the Italian colonies in London and come into contact with the fish and chip trade there. Wherever the idea came from, it caught on quickly and soon spread among the Italian communities, first in Glasgow, then in Edinburgh; many Italians ran businesses that combined ice-cream parlours with fish restaurants, sometimes on the same premises. There was some Italian involvement in the trade in England and especially in the Welsh mining valleys; but Scotland was unique in the scale of activity and the extent of Italian domination.[75]

In Glasgow, particularly, the fried fish trade was practically originated by Italians. Already in 1906 the Sanitary Inspector was complaining about 'further complaints' of offensive odours from fried fish shops, which were run 'mostly' by 'foreigners'.[76] By 1914 there were said to be more than 400 fish restaurants in Glasgow, selling about 800,000 fish suppers per week. Although the President of the Fish Restaurant Keepers' Association was the very un-Italian sounding Mr James Watson, the Italian community clearly dominated the trade numerically.[77] From Glasgow, the Italian vendors of fried fish and ice-cream extended their activities down the Clyde, following the development of Glasgow's holiday resorts, and into the surrounding industrial towns.[78]

In Edinburgh, on the other hand, if a local newspaper reporter is to be trusted, the Italians moved into an already-established fish restaurant trade in the early twentieth century:

> A striking feature of the chip shops in recent years has been the gradual taking over of them by Italians, who now practically monopolise the trade in Edinburgh. The wily Italians found out that there was much more money in this class of shop than in the ice-cream variety, and so they have gradually wormed their way into the business, and ousted the Britishers, who are now in the minority.[79]

The fish and chip trade was also well established by 1914 in Dundee, Perth, the Fifeshire coalfield and even St Andrews. Although it never became exclusively an Italian concern, it was always dominated by immigrants from two small upland districts of the peninsula. Even in the early 1930s, when home-grown Scots were moving into the trade in earnest, one well-informed contemporary could assert that 80 per cent of all Scotland's fish friers were of Italian origin.[80]

The fish and chip trade in Ireland seems to have been Italian-dominated from the start. A survey in 1909 found 20 or so shops in Dublin – a small number in a population of 290,000, when compared with cities of similar size in industrial England – and 'the majority of these' were in Italian hands. Belfast was described, with frustrating vagueness, as having 'comparatively few fried fish shops' and no mention was made of Italians. As in Liverpool, oysters and shrimps were still more popular than fried fish.[81] Contrary to later legend, chips rather than peas were sold with the fish in both cities. What is most puzzling, however, is the suggestion that Dublin had primacy over Belfast in the development of the trade and especially the Italian side of it. Dublin's Italians, who still 'totally dominate' its fish and chip trade, almost all come from a single small district of six villages, Casalattico in Latium, not far from Rome, just across the valley from Picinisco. They found their way to Ireland by way of Paris and Scotland or various southern English resorts, by-passing London. At some point on their travels they came across the fish and chip trade, adopted it and brought it with them. The puzzle lies in the probability that the migration chain to Dublin would run through Scotland and Belfast; but Belfast, despite its strong industrial base, provided inhospitable soil for Italian fish friers in the early twentieth century and it was Dublin (and probably Cork) that saw the earliest developments on any significant scale. It is a remarkable, even a romantic story but we must not give it too much emphasis, for fish and chips did not become a major institution in urban Ireland as it did in England, Wales and Scotland. Nor was it easy to export it to more distant lands.[82]

The failure of fish and chips to emulate association football as a great British cultural export was not for want of effort in the inter-war years. H. T. Reeves was optimistic about the prospects in 1933:

> Imitation, it is said, is the sincerest form of flattery, and so it is not surprising that foreign countries, having noted with satisfaction what a substantial aid the frying trade has been to the British fishing industry, have set about establishing it on English lines. . . . and the results have been very encouraging.[83]

The greatest successes were achieved in the English-speaking white-settler colonies of the Empire. Reeves himself cited the case of an emigrant from Cardiff to South Africa who ordered a range from Preston and Thomas of his native town and set up a fish and chip shop in Cape Town. The venture was said to have been a great success, although Reeves was only able to confirm the export of two additional ranges in its wake.[84] More convincing evidence came from North America, where there were said to be large numbers of fried fish restaurants in the United States and Canada in 1919, although the only specific references involved Vancouver and Seattle. Whatever the truth of this, new attempts to conquer the United States for fish and chips were being launched, apparently into a vacuum, in the mid-1930s. Gerald Priestland remarked plausibly in 1972 that: 'It would surprise me if, during the past fifty years, there had not always been some bright young man frying away in the English style somewhere in America.'[85] But the efforts of Canada's Marine and Fisheries Department, which in 1921 was urging the encouragement of the expansion of British-style fish and chip shops from, apparently, a small bridgehead in Montreal, seem not to have borne lasting fruit.[86] The most convincing evidence of a successful transplantation of fish and chips comes from Australia and New Zealand. In 1936 the Australian Gas Light Company was busily trying to persuade the Sydney fish and chip friers to modernize their equipment, claiming that the Sydney friers alone used 50 million cubic feet of gas per year.[87] And in 1925 William Pott of Hadfield was busily investigating the prospects for the frying trade in New Zealand, where fish and chips were later reported to be 'just like home', according to Gerald Priestland.[88]

Outside the influence of a recognizable British expatriate culture, the record was even more unconvincing than this rather chequered picture. William Loftas reported on a rapid expansion of the fried fish trade in Germany during the later 1920s: he had been invited to give a lecture tour on the subject in 1926 and two years later he was commissioned by the German Director of Fisheries to report on the country's fried fish shops. The well-established German fried fish industry, as it existed in 1919, fried herrings (especially), haddock and eels on a large scale for retail distribution and home consumption, however, and the introduction of the British version of the trade seems to have come from an entrepreneurial response to the presence of the British army of occupation on the Rhine: 'The khaki boys presented a demand that had to be satisfied, and enterprising caterers were compelled to meet it.'[89] Efforts by companies to introduce fish and chips into France, promoted by fishing-boat owners, had limited success in the mid-1920s and the *pommes frites* of France and Belgium continued to be sold without a fried fish accompaniment.[90] In 1933 Reeves reported an attempt to introduce the trade into Norway, but his confidence that: 'Ultimate success is, however, assured' was not borne out by events.[91] Most poignant of all was the failure of the trade to transfer itself to Italy, despite the Italian dominance of fish frying in Scotland and Ireland. In Barga, where most of Glasgow's Italians originate, fish and chips is apparently eaten once a year, cooked by Glasgow veterans who have returned home for the annual feast of the mules, but there has never been any question of its becoming a regular item of mass consumption.[92] Despite the optimism of the trade's evangelists in the inter-war years, it remained resolutely and enduringly a British preference and did not cross borders or cultural boundaries at all convincingly. Despite Gerald Priestland's cheerful chronicling of fish and chip shops in exotic and improbable places in more recent times, this remains the case.[93]

Fish and chips may have failed to become one of the great British cultural exports of the ages of Industrial Revolution and Empire, but its importance in twentieth-century Britain is undeniable. Its ubiquity and vitality spawned a whole range of supporting industries and its capacious demand for fish was essential to the expansion and transformation of the British fishing industry. The relationships between the fish and chip trade and its suppliers, from trawler-owners and merchants at the ports to oil-refiners and restaurant-engineers, deserve a chapter to themselves.

3 Fish Friers and Other Industries

Contemporaries were well-aware of the importance of the relationships between the fish and chip trade and other industries on which the friers depended
and for which they provided valuable and (in some cases) essential markets.
The most obvious and intimate interdependence lay between the fish friers and
the fishing industry itself, which would have been hard-pressed to find markets
for increased catches and to sustain increasing investment without the working-
class appetites that were tempted and tapped by the fish and chip shops. As
Chatchip pointed out in 1913, the trawler-owners, skippers, crews and merchants were only part of the story here. He listed a range of interests who might
be regarded as sufficiently affected by the demand for fish and chips to be likely
subscribers to and supporters of the proposed National Federation of Fish
Friers. They included ship- and boat-builders, marine-engine builders, sail-
makers, rope- and net-manufacturers, ship-chandlers, barrel- and box-makers
and ice manufacturers.[1] Beyond the fishing industry itself, broadly conceived,
the *Fish Trades Gazette* listed, as early as 1907, a large number of other trades to
which the fish-frier 'gives employment':

> [The frier] proves a very important customer to those who deal in potatoes, oil,
> vinegar, dripping, flour, *etc.*, to say nothing of stove, range, marble fitments, and tile
> decoration manufacturers, and of the thousand and one accessories necessary to his
> full equipment.[2]

An estimate of the weekly expenditure of an unpretentious back-street fish
and chip business in 1930 suggested that, out of £8.80 laid out, £1.75 would go
on rent, rates and depreciation. Of the rest, fish would account for just over 53
per cent and potatoes for just over 10 per cent. Dripping, perhaps surprisingly,
was expected to cost more than the potatoes, making up 16 per cent; paper, salt,
vinegar, soap and soda together added up to 7 per cent. The rest of the money
went on gas for cooking and on electric light. There is no way of knowing how
this notional breakdown might have to be adjusted for a different frying
medium or cooking agent, and gas prices varied widely from place to place; but
this informed reconstruction of a frier's budget does demonstrate that the trade
did not live by fish and potatoes alone. There were other weighty items to
consider.[3]

Quite clearly, however, the most important industry to depend on the fish and chip trade for its long-term prosperity and basic well-being was fishing. Strictly speaking, the catching, marketing and distribution of white fish, which is at issue here, was only part of a wider fishing industry; but it was a separate and distinct set of activities from the herring and other fisheries and its heart beat to a different rhythm. For convenience, I shall continue to refer to it simply as 'the fishing industry'. From the 1880s onwards the growth of this industry marched in step with that of fish and chips and from the turn of the century onwards their mutual dependence increased. The relationship demands further investigation.

The emergence of a white-fish industry, as such, and its concentration into a handful of specialized ports was already well under way by the time the fish and chip trade began to develop in earnest. Humberside, in particular, came to the fore in the later 1830s and 1840s, as trawlers from Brixham migrated by way of Thanet to discover prolific fishing grounds off the Dogger Bank. The rise of Hull and Grimsby in the early railway age was a spectacular industrial success story, although it was achieved at terrible human cost, especially for the 'apprentices' from distant workhouses who provided the cheap labour that underpinned the impressive mid-Victorian growth from small beginnings. The railway companies invested in docks and encouraged development. For the first time fresh fish could be distributed to the growing industrial populations inland as well as being brought to London's Billingsgate market to feed the metropolis. The manager of the Manchester and Leeds Railway, Captain Laws, pioneered the trade with Manchester and the textile districts. During 1841–2 he organized a joint scheme between three railways to create a through fish traffic between the Yorkshire coast and Manchester, where special retailing arrangements were provided. This was a great success, and by 1845 the manufacturing towns around Manchester were sharing the benefits of the scheme, as were other towns along the route. As the railways built on this development, a nationwide distribution network resulted. From the 1850s, especially, 'the railways helped to open the working-class market for fresh and lightly-cured fish' throughout England; between 1841 and 1871 the number of fishmongers known to the census enumerators trebled.[4] By 1877 Hull had 440 fishing smacks and Grimsby 505. 'In that same year the railway carried 44,000 tons of fish out of Grimsby's docks.'[5]

These early developments were accompanied by important innovations. Ice was increasingly used to preserve the fish that were landed dead on the deck by the trawl nets. A 'fleeting system' was introduced whereby large numbers of boats would fish together for weeks at a time, ferrying their catches to a carrier vessel that daily took the fish to shore. At first these carriers were sailing vessels but steamers soon took their place. These developments provided a firm basis for further growth; Jeremy Tunstall has rightly described the years around 1880 as 'a watershed in the early history of the industry'.[6]

The great innovation of the 1880s was the steam trawler. It came in at a time of increasing difficulty in the North Sea ports: the established fishing grounds were yielding smaller catches, fears of over-fishing were being expressed in some quarters and labour disputes were arising, especially as the owners tried to extend the dangerous, unpopular fleeting system to the winter months and to cut the take-home pay of the trawlermen by increasing deductions.[7] Steam trawling came in first on the Tyne in the late 1870s when tugs were adapted in a period of trade recession, but purpose-built boats were soon introduced, spreading rapidly in the major trawling ports during the 1880s.[8] A parliamentary return of 1900 showed that Grimsby had nine steam fishing-vessels registered in 1883, 50 in 1890 and 419 by 1899, while the corresponding figures for Hull were 10, 79 and 376.[9] The introduction of steam enabled new, more distant fishing grounds to be opened out, with vessels going as far as Iceland from 1891 onwards. The capacity of the fleet was greatly increased and ownership began to be concentrated in fewer hands, although this was not yet an overwhelming trend. It was, above all, the coming of the steam trawler that revolutionized the capacity of the fishing industry: it made long, highly productive voyages possible and brought back growing quantities of relatively low-quality fish that needed to find a less affluent and discriminating market than had hitherto prevailed.[10]

Meanwhile, new, specialized fishing ports were developing. Aberdeen arrived firmly on the deep-sea fishing map as it joined the steam revolution: its catch increased from 9,000 tons in 1887 to 63,000 tons in 1902. The west-coast trawler ports of Milford Haven and Fleetwood expanded rapidly around the turn of the century, with encouragement from their railway companies. Milford Haven emerged from nowhere to have 36 steam fishing-boats registered in 1899 and Fleetwood had 32 trawlers in operation by 1903.[11] The exploitation of these new fishing grounds roughly doubled the hake catch between the early 1890s and the early 1900s, while the widening range of the North Sea fleets nearly doubled the cod catch between 1889 and 1901. It nearly doubled again in the spectacular year of 1902, when the total recorded catch for all fish species in England passed 10 million hundredweights for the first time.[12]

It was at about this point that demand from fish friers started to be visibly important to the fortunes of the industry. The great increases in take were concentrated into species that were to become overwhelmingly friers' fish, although the trend in haddock landings (another great friers' staple) was much less pronounced. At the turn of the century, however, it was still assumed in official fishery circles that friers took undersized fish that were otherwise unsaleable – or what the Grimsby fishing magnate, Harrison Mudd, called 'offal fish, such as haddock'.[13] Mudd also pointed out that the local 'longshore people' used to eat the 'small stuff from the Humber', which could apparently now be marketed elsewhere.[14] But clearly the fish and chip shops were already providing markets for species that had hitherto been thrown away or used for fertilizer, as well as finding a home for undersized fish of more conventional sorts. Plaice, for example, had been given away at the dock gates at Hull but was now acquiring a market value; in 1909 it was remarked that hake and skate had not been valued until comparatively recently and had frequently been thrown overboard to avoid the trouble of landing them at the docks.[15] The friers' role in helping to soak up the rapidly expanding fish supply of the late nineteenth century remains disappointingly obscure, but must have been growing steadily in importance.

The decade or so preceding the First World War saw unprecedented expansion both in the fishing industry itself and in the importance of the frying trade. Between 1902 and 1913 the cod catch in England and Wales more than trebled, with Icelandic fish accounting for an ever-growing proportion, while hake more than doubled and skate was not far behind.[16] In London, at least, the friers' role still seems to have involved using up the fish other consumers did not want. A *Fish Trades Gazette* correspondent who sought advice on what to fry when plaice was not available in the metropolis was given a list of generally unglamorous alternatives:

> There are many kinds of fish which can be used to advantage in the pan trade, such as small haddocks, roker, whitings, monks, hake, small codlings and dabs, while many friers consider megrims the best substitute for plaice.

The same issue corroborated this impression when reporting on price trends for the week:

> Whitings were very depressed some days . . . and they came in useful to many friers . . . North Sea plaice was plentiful, and the smaller sizes were well within the range of friers.[17]

In the industrial north and midlands, however, working-class customers were beginning to express firm preferences for particular fish species and friers were not as willing to shop around for cheap varieties as they were (and continued to be) in London. Hull, which pioneered distant-water fishing and was beginning to provide more down-market fish than Grimsby, was emerging as a friers' port in the early twentieth century, with a specialism in small haddock, while Fleetwood received an unequivocal testimonial in 1907:

> A very large proportion of the fish landed at Fleetwood is eventually disposed of to friers; in fact a salesman for one of the largest firms of steam trawler owners declared to a *Fish Trades Gazette* representative that on many days things would be in a poor way but for the consistent demands of the friers.[18]

This was in Fleetwood's formative years and most of the fish (small hake and haddock) went to Lancashire and West Riding friers. Not that the other ports ignored the trade: Grimsby supplied the Southport friers in 1906, despite the migration of many of the area's fishermen to Fleetwood, and it had plenty of outlets elsewhere, while Aberdeen was well to the fore in providing Glasgow with its haddock.[19] Demand from friers seems to have been particularly important in providing markets for fish from newly exploited distant waters: fish from the Faroes and Iceland was strongly associated with the frying trade and friers were recommended to try plaice from the even more distant 'White Sea' fishing grounds as soon as it appeared on the market.[20]

Spokesmen for the frying trade were increasingly assertive about their contribution to the fishing industry. Chatchip was clear about the friers' success in unlocking working-class demand: 'fish friers have taught the people that fish they despised are both nutritious and palatable'. As late as 1920, indeed, he argued that: '. . . if it were not for the fried fish shops one fish meal per week would be the Northern workman's limit'. And the *Fish Trades Gazette* endorsed this outlook in 1909:

whatever antipathy to fish exists among the poorer classes . . . is due to the abominable cooking and the waste that go on in the average labourer's kitchen, although the state of affairs among a large proportion of the middle classes is not much better. The poor have one advantage – that they do not despise professionally fried fish, and those fish friers who conduct their business properly have done a lot of spadework which deserves recognition.[21]

As we have seen, the war made a considerable difference to perceptions of the fish and chip trade; the growing and eventually predominant influence of the fish and chip shop on the demand for white fish in the inter-war years is well-documented. This trend emerged under difficult conditions for the fishing industry, although the catch was much higher than in pre-war years and there were some prosperous years, especially in the later 1920s and above all in Hull. It was Hull, in fact, which did best out of the changing conditions of trade, which favoured lower-quality cod for the frying market from the distant waters of the Arctic Circle. It was Hull, too, that showed sustained growth and profitability during the 1930s when other industrial fishing ports were faltering as the depression hit demand; and it was Hull that contrived to put together the newest and most impressive trawler fleet as investment faltered elsewhere. The Hull trawlers brought back the lion's share of the landings from the Norwegian coast, the Barents Sea and Bear Island, which were very small in 1913 and remained unimportant until the systematic exploitation of these distant waters increased the take to nearly three million hundredweight between 1929 and 1935. Iceland fish, mainly cod, reached its peak landing-level of nearly four million hundredweight (out of a total of fourteen and a half million) in 1932. By 1935 these 'distant grounds' together accounted for 45 per cent of the British white-fish catch, while landings from the North Sea itself had been falling since 1923. Alongside these trends, trawler ownership became more concentrated and the hold of the big industrial fishing ports tightened: in 1935 85 per cent of the quantity and 79 per cent of the value of the British white-fish catch came to the big five ports: Hull, followed in order of magnitude by Grimsby, Aberdeen, Fleetwood and Milford Haven.[22]

Table 3.1 shows the growing dominance of Hull in the inter-war fishing industry at a time when its consuming interest in cod from distant waters made it the most important source of cheap fillets for friers who could no longer afford to indulge the local tastes for particular fish varieties that had become apparent in the industrial districts in Edwardian times. Cod never drove its rivals out, but the balance tilted heavily in its direction during the 1920s and especially the 1930s; Hull, above all, was the driving force and beneficiary of this trend.

Hull apart, the other ports in the top five ran into trouble in the early 1930s. Fleetwood and Milford Haven suffered from the serious decline in the hake catch which began in 1927 and was sharply accentuated in 1931, while Aberdeen suffered from its distance from English markets and from high railway freight rates for coal as well as fish. Like Grimsby, it failed to re-equip its trawler fleet or to go systematically in search of cod in distant waters. Grimsby tended to concentrate on high-quality fish of various species from the North Sea; but in 1935 it was still despatching fish by rail to nearly 3,000

Table 3.1   British white-fish landings in thousands of hundredweights by port, 1913–35[23]

Port	1913	1925	1928	1931	1935
Hull	14	23	26	42	53
Grimsby	32	33	30	35	31
Aberdeen	19	15	15	17	16
Fleetwood	7	10	9	11	11
Milford Haven	4	6	6	7	5
Other ports	35	31	30	27	22
Total	111	118	116	139	138

stations daily and many of these provincial customers must have been fish-friers or wholesalers dealing with them.[24]

By the 1930s, indeed, the fish and chip trade was taking a greatly increased share of a substantially expanded market. And it was not just a matter of cheap cod from Arctic waters. 'Kit Haddock' proudly proclaimed in 1923 that the friers had traded up and had brought their customers' tastes with them, so that there was no going back to the small chat haddocks and whitings, too tiny to fillet, with which the trade had begun: these were the fish that now went to the manure works, helping to distort official figures for average fish prices.[25] The friers were buying mainstream fish rather than rejects, important though cheap fillets were to the struggling small businesses in the distressed areas. And in the West Riding of Yorkshire, especially, customers developed high expectations about fish quality. This was the land of the jumbo haddock, fried in dripping. 'The Chipper' in the *Fish Friers' Review* emphasized that the friers of the Leeds and Bradford area were good buyers of expensive fish: 'Frying here is a good trade, and the friers are proud and careful of their trade'.[26]

So during the inter-war years the fish friers became essential pillars of the fishing industry. The trawler owners recognized this and it lay behind their investment in new vessels and new fishing grounds in the late 1920s. The message was passed on to a government committee in 1929:

> The (British Trawlers') Federation have informed us that there is a large and increasing demand in industrial areas, particularly Lancashire and the West Riding, for fish of the commoner types, such as have been taken in abundance on the Bear Island grounds.[27]

The ensuing depression undermined this optimism, but during 1929 and 1930 158 new trawlers were launched at a cost of over £2.5 million.[28] Each new trawler was said to give permanent employment to 30 men, afloat and ashore.[29] Without the fish and chip trade, many of the 21,000 sea-going personnel in the fishing industry would have had no work, nor would many of the far more numerous workers in supporting roles on the shore, from filleters to publicans and prostitutes. By 1934, too, the industry supported more than 1,500 whole-sale merchants at the five biggest provincial ports – 729 at Grimsby alone – as well as 230 full-scale wholesalers and a much larger number of bummarees, 'who deal in split quantities for the smaller buyer' at London's Billingsgate, where there were also 1,100 fish porters.[30] On top of this was an unknown number of wholesalers and dealers in the inland centres: Bradford alone had 12 in 1929 who specialized in meeting friers' requirements.[31] Over and above the fuel they used themselves, too, the friers indirectly sustained the demand for the 3.5 million tons of coal the trawlers used in the mid-1930s.[32] And then there were the railways. The Great Central found the traffic important enough to design two classes of special locomotives for the express fish trains and complaints about the rail services, which became particularly bitter in the inter-war years, should not mask the value of the fishing industry to the companies, especially as they also did well out of taking coal to the ports for the trawlers.[33] Indeed, once we try in earnest to pursue the ramifications of the fish and chip trade into the contingent development of the fishing industry and its implications, the task soon becomes impossible by virtue of its sheer complexity.

Easier to cope with – though not as straightforward as it might seem – is the development of a specialist engineering industry to cater for friers' special needs and demands. The manufacture of fish and chip ranges and a remarkable assortment of ancillary equipment was an obvious spin-off from the development of the trade beyond its do-it-yourself origins; but the sheer scale of the industry as it reached its apotheosis in the 1930s still has power to surprise.

The fish restaurant engineering industry seems to have begun in earnest in the 1860s and firms were multiplying and diversifying their products by the late nineteenth century. The most important and expensive item came to be the 'portable' frying range, which gradually began to displace older homemade constructions involving cauldrons heated by a furnace encased in glazed brick. These could be erected cheaply by jobbing builders but they counted as fixtures and could be claimed by the landlord when a frier wanted to move on. Small, simple portable ranges were certainly on offer by 1890, when one appeared in the catalogue of a Warrington firm; but it seems clear that similar items were already being made in the Manchester area in the 1860s and 1870s.[34] Meanwhile, potato peelers were being introduced, perhaps beginning with 'Collins' patent potato peeler', invented by a Sheffield frier, and 'Owen's dolly', an adaptation of a familiar domestic washing implement, which featured a five-legged agitator with nutmeg-graters on each of the legs to abrade the potato skins. In the 1870s the 'Wonder Potato Peeler', engineer-designed, would peel up to 30 pounds of potatoes at a time, but depended, exhaustingly, on human muscle power for its operation. In the 1880s the first of a new generation of 'rumbler' peeling machines appeared, probably derived from similar equipment in foundries, which was used for cleaning metal castings; at the same time the first commercial chipping machines came on to the market.[35] This flow of invention and speculation reflected the growing opportunities that this expanding trade clearly presented to the entrepreneur; and the pace of development quickened as the frying trade itself gathered momentum in the new century.

By the Edwardian years the fish restaurant engineering business was already generating substantial firms who set the pace and operated on a large scale. A contender for market leadership was Mabbott and Co. of Manchester's

Phoenix Iron Works, who were given an enthusiastic write-up by the *Fish Trades Gazette* in 1904:

> A few years ago Messrs. Mabbott and Company Limited employed less than a dozen men in every department, and the site of the works, offices, etc., did not cover more than a space of 30 square yards. Town End Foundry, which is now almost entirely employed in the production of the firm's castings, has buildings covering nearly one acre of land, and is fitted up with the newest and most modern plant. Here the castings are made and passed on to the Phoenix Iron Works, where the various ranges and appliances are built. The Phoenix Iron Works are modern and up-to-date in every particular, and capable of turning out an immense quantity of the firm's productions. They comprise the following departments: Stores, tool shop, fitting shop, coppersmiths' room, urn making department, van building department, painting department, warehouse and stock room. Stock is kept ready for delivery, including practically all the goods illustrated in the firm's catalogue, a book of 116 pages . . . Mabbott and Company Limited have also show rooms in Manchester [City], Liverpool, Birmingham, Newcastle-on-Tyne, Cardiff, and London.[36]

We saw in Chapter One that by 1910 Mabbott's were employing 150 people and had an ancillary factory at Chapel-en-le-Frith in Derbyshire. They did not manufacture solely for the fish and chip trade: they had sold large quantities of their potato-peeling machines to institutions of various kinds, for example, and in 1913 they were offering bread-cutting machines, water boilers, tea-measuring machines, stock pots and an enormous range of other machines to the general hotel and catering trades.[37] But the fish and chip trade was at the core of their initial success and remained an important aspect of their business operations throughout the Edwardian years.

The years around and just after 1904 saw a steady extension of the influence of the specialist range-making firms. Companies from the Manchester area were selling ranges in the Potteries and Nottingham and in 1905 the only fish and chip shop in distant Andover had a Mabbott range.[38] Burnley and Gloucester, for example, still had their own distinctive local styles of range, however, and firms like Sandersons of Sheffield were kept afloat by local custom.[39] Practical friers such as Mr Outram of Chester might still build their own ranges and there was plenty of scope for inventors like Albert Travis of Ashton-under-Lyne, who had devised a new kind of brake for railway wagons while conducting his fried fish business, to apply their talents to their trade.[40] But the two dozen or so major firms made increasing headway, boosted by the competition to maximize efficiency while minimizing odour at a time when local authorities were beginning to take a serious interest in 'the fish frying nuisance'. Several firms claimed to have solved the problem in the years around 1910; in 1913 Acme of Holbeck (Leeds), a rising star in the industry, proclaimed that its Hygienic range

> marks an absolutely new Era in the fish-frying trade. Steam-emitting vile-smelling Ranges now superseded . . . The fumes arising from the pans are automatically drawn into the fire, and thus fish frying can be carried on under conditions of comfort.[41]

Meanwhile, a whole new array of friers' requisites was coming on to the market and firms were taking an interest in the appearance as well as the internal workings of their products. Elaborate tile patterns, gleaming brass and copper surfaces and decorative illustrations of maritime scenes all combined to express the fish and chip trade's new-found self-confidence and a desire to communicate prosperity and expertise as well as a reassuring sense of cleanliness to customers who were no longer drawn from poverty-stricken back streets and late-night revellers.[42]

These trends became more accentuated after the First World War, as befitted a trade that was steadily propelling itself up-market. Acme Engineering of Holbeck took up the running and in 1930 it was claiming to be 'the largest fish friers' engineers in the world'. In 1933 its managing director became Lord Mayor of Leeds.[43] But Acme had plenty of rivals and by the 1930s the industry was no longer so closely concentrated into the Manchester area. In 1937 the industry's Association embraced 28 firms, although some of the London manufacturers held aloof. There were five in Leeds, which had become in many ways the centre of the fish frying trade: the National Federation's offices were well-established there by this time. Two more firms were based in nearby Halifax and two in Huddersfield. The cotton towns remained important, however, with four firms in Manchester, two each in Oldham and Preston and one each in Rochdale and Bury. In the light of the industrial profile of Birmingham and the Black Country, it is surprising to find only two firms in that area; and apart from the two London establishments, there were outposts at Blackpool, Nottingham (with two firms) and the well-known firm of Preston and Thomas at Cardiff.[44] The affinity with the northern textile manufacturing districts, the heartlands of the frying trade itself, is not surprising: there was a lot of engineering expertise here to be turned to account. It was entirely in character that Faulkners of Hollinwood should develop a steam-extraction system based on a suction-fan principle that had originally been used in the ventilation of cotton mills.[45]

This was one of a string of innovations in range technology and design during the inter-war years, especially in the 1930s. Gas became more widely used and heating controls more sophisticated, although electric ranges made only limited headway and the so-called 'draught breeze range' revived cheap coke in some areas as an alternative to gas.[46] By this time, too, stainless steel was revolutionizing range-making in various ways, although it did not obviate the cleaning problems that were leading companies into providing new de-greasing agents aimed specifically at the frying trade.[47] The exhibitions of the early 1930s put a remarkable range of competing ranges and other devices on show, featuring endless novelties that were enthusiastically discussed and compared in the trade press.[48] And, in recognition that the purchase of fish and chips was a public act of consumption that often had close affinities with the leisure industries, the presentation of shops and ranges became ever more important. Range design embraced the imposing, the opulent and, at times, the frivolous. Stainless steel ranges could and did emphasize a utilitarian neatness and an emphasis on hygiene; but alongside them in the late 1920s came the Preston and Thomas Fitzhammon 'Marble-de-luxe' range, featuring 'white Sicilian marble', and in 1930 Rouse of Oldham's 'Terrace de-luxe', which offered a vision of solidity and honest worth by looking like the gable-end of a house, complete with imitation brickwork. In 1932 Preston and Thomas exhibited at Manchester 'a range done in what is known as the "impressionist" or "futurist" style of decoration' in yellow and black opalite, itself a self-consciously new and rather daring material.[49] During the 1920s ranges tended to emphasize solidity, sometimes coupled with a reassuring domesticity: as Ray Batcheler put it, they 'ponderously resembled a middle-class sideboard writ large, or an apprentice piece by a monumental mason'. Chatchip picked up this theme, expressing his preference for 'the . . . "piano" or "sideboard" designed range rather than the "writing bureau" design'.[50] But during the 1930s Batcheler detects a spreading Art Deco influence, echoing cinema organs and cinema decor generally. This marked the new acceptability of the relationship between fish and chips and enjoyment. Batcheler treats these developments convincingly but with appropriate caution:

> I am not suggesting that the manufacturers of frying ranges *consciously* decided to ape cinema art deco – though they may have done – but rather that, from about 1930 onwards, this festive style carried with it the right messages of modernity, cleanliness and fun and that these messages were understood, even if they were seldom acknowledged.[51]

All this demonstrates that the fish and chip trade not only called into being an important engineering and hardware industry to minister to its needs: it also created a climate in which inventiveness and vitality flourished among its suppliers. Fish restaurant engineering was a highly competitive and innovative industry and this says much for the receptive and enterprising attitudes of the friers themselves. There is no evidence of entrepreneurial failure or a 'decline of the industrial spirit' in this neglected but by no means insignificant sector of the British economy, whatever might be said about the traditional staple industries. Friers might reflect their customers' conservatism regarding fish species and they certainly had trouble in dealing with inflexible customer attitudes to the price of their product; but the evidence of the fish and chip restaurant engineers indicates a widespread willingness to keep abreast of change on the part of enough friers to keep up a simmering interest in improvement and novelty among their suppliers. There is room for more research in this area.

The friers' relationship with their other cognate trades and industries was less positive and dynamic; but it was also less direct and encompassing. Important though the fish and chip trade was to Lancashire's potato growers, for example, they could be accused of growing inappropriate potato varieties and forcing the Lancashire friers to look elsewhere for their supplies.[52] Seed-crushers and oil- and dripping-refiners were important to the friers but had other markets for their products: the standard history of seed-crushing, an important industry in Hull and Liverpool among other places, has nothing to say about the fried fish trade. Margarine and cattle feeds were much more important.[53] Firms like Crosfields of Warrington might produce special compound frying media for the trade, but this was one minor activity among many: a line worth developing, but not a crucial one. Outside the fishing industry itself and the various ramifications of fish restaurant engineering, the suppliers were more important to the fried fish trade than vice versa, apart from a few small specialist firms. Even so, the cumulative impact of the fish and chip trade on several sectors of the British economy should not be underrated. In the next chapter, however, we introduce the main theme of this book: the social impact of the fish and chip trade. We begin with the friers themselves.

4 The Friers and their Fortunes

Britain's fish and chip shops depended on distant sources of supply, complex technologies and marketing arrangements and impressive levels of capital investment, especially on the part of the big trawling and engineering firms. In their turn, they became a major industry, with a wide range of spin-off effects on the economy and society in which they operated. In the main, however, they themselves were remarkably small-scale and unsophisticated concerns: the overwhelming majority continued to be run as family businesses. More than most kinds of retailing activity, the fish friers remained largely unchallenged by the rise of multiples and the Co-operative movement. Even the biggest individual outlets, like Harry Ramsden's famous restaurant on the outskirts of Leeds, were family run. This makes the trade particularly interesting to historians of the lower middle class of independent traders, the 'petty bourgeoisie'.

Chains of fish and chip restaurants were set up from the earliest days of the trade in the late nineteenth century but they never amounted to much. The Sam Isaacs chain, which was operating in London in the mid-1890s, must have been one of the first and London continued to be in the forefront of such developments.[1] Small fish frying multiples emerged in the provinces in the early twentieth century. At Bristol in 1905 some of the 150 shops were 'worked on the tied-house system, wholesale dealers having a number of shops, and the tenants only being able to buy fish, potatoes and oil of them'.[2] More usual was the more straightforward arrangement whereby one person owned several businesses, most or all of which were looked after by managers. Such shops were sometimes supplied with fried fish from a central depot, to be re-heated on delivery. By 1909 Mr A. Potentier had a chain of shops in Leeds, by-passing the local wholesalers and getting his fish direct from the coast.[3] A chain of five shops was reported from Wolverhampton in 1906; W. H. Bellwood had three in Luton in 1911; Frederick Duckett, a Carlisle frier, had three in Dumfries in 1913, which he ran through a local manager with an assistant in each shop.[4] In the Manchester area in 1911 there were several chains, including seven or eight shops under the same ownership in Salford.[5] Small chains run by Italian families were common in Scotland, where fathers set up their sons in nearby shops after they had learned the trade.[6] And at times we encounter evidence of real panache and entrepreneurial flair. Thus S. W. Snaith of Tynemouth, opening his third fish and chip shop in 1921, overcame a petition against his venture, organized by a local solicitor, in style: he invited the Mayor and Corporation to his opening night, where they duly tucked in to the standard fare. This was claimed as the first civic opening of a fish and chip shop and was a publicity gesture worthy of Sir Thomas Lipton.[7]

But there was never to be a Lipton of the fish and chip trade. This was not because the possibilities were not envisaged. As early as 1910 a feature in the *Fish Trades Gazette* advocated the establishment of a company with a large share capital to emulate the restaurant chains of J. Lyons and the Aerated Bread Co. by establishing 'a network of up-to-date, well-fitted and attractive fried fish shops in various quarters', with 'smart, civil employees' to lift the industry on to a higher plane 'and secure the sympathy of the middle classes'.[8] In 1919 an entrepreneur called Quilliam conducted a sustained newspaper advertising campaign in the hope of establishing a network of fried fish shops 'to fry up and distribute the left-over fish from his company's wet-fish shops', thereby incurring the scorn of Chatchip for assuming that the fried fish trade could still subsist on sub-standard or elderly fish rejected by fishmongers and their customers.[9] Fears of the spread of tied shops and multiples were regularly expressed in the *Fish Friers' Review* in the 1920s and 1930s but, despite their opportunity to buy in bulk and deal directly with the ports, the promoters of multiples never made any real headway in the industry.[10] In 1932 'Utility', writing in the *Fishing News*, could find only two or three chains of fish and chip shops with as many as 15 or 20 outlets, although there were plenty of twos and threes.[11] This was borne out by the pattern of registrations for the White Fish Authority's regulatory scheme on the eve of the Second World War. The first 22,376 friers to register (who would certainly include all the multiples) operated only 23,629 shops and 660 vans between them.[12] And the Census of Distribution in 1950 found that 'of 16,354 organizations, only 442 had more than one establishment, and 22 five or more establishments', and that, 'Only 704, 4.3 per cent of the organizations were without working proprietors.'[13]

From time to time attempts were made to explain the limited headway of the multiples in this superficially attractive industry. Chatchip was clear that direct personal supervision was the only way to make a fish and chip shop pay. There was too much scope for hidden losses in the preparation and frying processes:

> Multiple-grocers' shops, *etc.*, where you can weigh, measure, or count everything in, and check sales against stock, and so on, may be all right from the speculator's point of view, but as a speculation fried-fish shops, without the speculator's personal attention and energies, are worse than ancient eggs.[14]

This explanation found ready support elsewhere and the trade was widely seen as something that successful people passed through, using it as a stepping-stone to higher things rather than developing their interests further within its confines.[15]

It is perhaps less surprising that the Co-operative movement, the other great bugbear of the independent small trader, did not take up fish and chip retailing on any significant scale. Apart from anything else, much of the Co-op's leadership may have been too self-consciously respectable to want to sully the movement's hands with this enduringly controversial trade. But even here some initiatives can be found in the late 1930s. There were Co-op fish and chip shops at Rushden and Irthlingborough in Northamptonshire at this time and another was established in Ipswich in 1939.[16] By 1950 there were 14.[17] And here and there, other large organizations dipped their toes in the water. In 1931 Father Murty of St Gerard's Roman Catholic Church, in Bristol, applied unsuccessfully for permission to set up a fish and chip shop. The church's scheme was that an unemployed member of the congregation would provide the capital and receive a guaranteed wage from church funds, with profits over and above the wage to go to the church. The city's Health Committee rejected this optimistic initiative after local protests and I can find no similar project elsewhere.[18] The only other example I have found of a fish and chip shop being operated for the benefit of a voluntary organization and its members is the purchase in 1948 of a business in Tranent by the Berwick and East Lothian constituency Labour Party, aided by a loan from the Co-op. Profits were to go towards a hall for 'socialist and other activities'.[19] In general, however, the fish and chip trade remained overwhelmingly in the hands of small capitalists and family businesses. Alternatives were conceivable, but they made little impression on the established way of doing things.

Fish and chip frying was anomalous in more than just its unusual degree of resistance to the rise of the multiples and the Co-op from the late nineteenth century. It combined production with retailing to an extent that was rarely found in the small shopkeeping sector: the range and the preparation equipment constituted a manufacturing plant of increasing scale and sophistication. Moreover, fish friers straddled the notional boundary between what Neil Griffiths called the 'professional shopkeepers', who were prosperous members of trade associations operating specialized businesses for which they had undergone an extended process of training, and the 'small' or 'working' shopkeepers who operated precariously on limited amounts of often borrowed capital and drew their trade from the surrounding locality, drawing on limited expertise and dependent on the careful management of customer credit.[20] In the early years of the trade they approximated more to the second of these types; some were closer to the small-scale businesses of barrow-boys or 'penny capitalists' whose importance in working-class life has been strongly emphasized by John Benson.[21] But as the trade expanded and developed, growing numbers of its members came to display more of the characteristics of the 'professional shopkeeper', at a time when the older trades in this category were coming under increasing pressure from the competition of the Co-op, the multiples and the department stores.[22] These demarcation lines are far from clear-cut: individual shopkeepers in differing environments displayed a bewildering diversity of business practices, attitudes, values and social standing.[23] But the distinction between 'professional' and 'working' – or as Hosgood calls them 'domestic' – shopkeepers will still help us to approach an understanding of the fried fish trade as we explore the important questions of who ran these businesses and how successful they were.

We know remarkably little about what sort of people became shopkeepers in Britain beween the late nineteenth century and the Second World War, or about what their aims and aspirations were. At the bottom end of the scale, retailing as a form of 'penny capitalism' was essentially an additional tactic in the struggle for survival, though Benson suggests that it might also be perceived

– presumably by romantic optimists – as 'a dream, a possible escape route from poverty and drudgery'.[24] A few rungs higher up the ladder, historians dealing with the 'working' shopkeepers who met the day-to-day purchasing needs of working-class neighbourhoods have assumed that they were themselves recruited largely from the ranks of wage labour, without really probing any more deeply into the question. In terms of motives and attitudes, there is an interesting difference of emphasis between Hosgood and Crossick. Hosgood sees these shopkeepers as being very much involved in the working-class communities from which their customers – who were also their neighbours – were drawn, though they were distanced from the male world (usually) of factory or workshop and disproportionately attached to the female domain of gossip, social evaluation and informal mutual assistance. Crossick recognizes the validity of aspects of this portrayal, but is also at pains to emphasize the pressures on some shopkeeping families to withdraw from neighbourhood life into a secure cocoon of private domesticity, out of which, presumably, a new middle-class identity might eventually emerge.[25] But before we go much further we need to know more about the actual origins and careers of shopkeepers in order to move beyond the broadest and blandest generalizations with any confidence. A survey of the social origins and careers of a substantial number of fish friers will contribute to this wider agenda as well as helping us to understand the changing workings of the trade itself.

To begin with, evidence from biographies, lawsuits, bankruptcy reports and advertisements in the trade press enables us to form an impression of how much it cost to get started in the trade and how the resources might be put together. The trade began at a decidedly 'penny capitalist' level, although Benson does not deal with it under this heading. Chatchip commented that: 'Probably in the whole history of trades and professions there is none which has had so humble and unpleasant a beginning as the fried fish trade'; and in his introduction to the first practical manual for fish and chip friers he went on to quote Mayhew's description of the early days, in *London labour and the London poor*, which was published in 1861:

> The fish fried by street dealers is known as 'plaice dabs' and 'sole dabs', which are merely plaice and soles – dab being a common word for any flat fish . . . The supply is known in the trade as 'friers', and consists of the overplus of a fishmonger's store, of what he has not sold overnight, and does not care to offer for sale on the following morning, and therefore sends to the costermongers, whose customers are chiefly among the poor . . . Many of the 'friers' are good . . . but some are very queer indeed, and they are consequently fried with a most liberal allowance of oil, which will conceal anything . . . the fish is cooked in ordinary frying-pans . . . The fried fish sellers live in some out-of-the-way alley, and not infrequently in garrets; for among even the poorest class there are great objections to their being fellow-lodgers on account of the odour from the frying . . . A gin-drinking neighbourhood, one coster said, suits best, for people haven't their smell so correct there.[26]

This was a very small-scale trade, involving gambling on making a profit out of reject materials and requiring little fixed capital: on Benson's definition, a classic example of 'penny capitalism'.[27] Moreover, the growing importance of fixed retail outlets and increasingly elaborate – and expensive – technology and fittings did not lead to the extinction of this lowest grade of fish frier. Hawkers of cold fried fish continued to annoy established shopkeepers right through the inter-war years, sometimes offering their cheaper wares to intending customers at the shop door. In 1928 an angry trade journalist thought that their numbers were actually increasing.[28] And for a long time basic frying technology remained remarkably cheap, even if the frying pan itself was no longer an option. In 1912 Codner and Callander of London, EC, were advertising primitive-looking 'fish friers' portable stoves' from £1 1s each and the second-hand price of such an appliance would have been even less daunting.[29] In 1913 a single-pan gas fish frying stove could be had, new, for £3 15s.[30] This would be within the range of street traders like Mr Winton, who told Neil Griffiths that:

> We only had £1 to lay out – we hadn't a clue what it would be like. We'd buy five cases of oranges at 4s a case and if you opened a case and saw clouds of smoke, we'd go back and we'd get no money back . . . So you took a gamble.[31]

Even as late as 1913 it was possible to enter an actual fish and chip shop amazingly cheaply. Eliza Lovell of Peterborough sold her fried fish shop to Thomas Briggs for £6, but the down-payment was only £3 and she had to sue to obtain the rest of the money.[32] This was a uniquely cheap purchase but there may have been many more transactions at this level that did not find their way into the trade press: it may well have been unusual to go to law over such a small amount. This solitary example may thus carry more significance than appears at first sight.

The bottom end of the fish and chip shop market, as presented in the trade press, required a level of capital investment that would need to come from sustained saving on the part of a working-class aspirant, or from access to loans, usually from family or friends rather than a formal financial institution. There is a good run of evidence from the Edwardian years; apart from Eliza Lovell's remarkable bargain offer the cheapest opportunity I can find is the £16 2s 8d which Mrs Lizzie Fowler appears to have paid for a fish and chip shop in Grimsby which, on her showing, turned out to have practically no trade. This was disputed by the vendor, who made the predictable but successful allegation that Mrs Fowler had lost her customers by offering miserly portions of under-cooked fish.[33] Mrs Fowler's shop was probably on a similar scale to the one acquired in Rochdale by Gracie Fields' grandmother, 'Chip Sarah', who (we are told) set herself up in the trade with £15 in savings and the proceeds from selling the stock of the barber who had previously occupied her shop.[34]

For the most part, however, Edwardian fish and chip shops started at £20 or so. This would buy the range and other fittings and such goodwill as the shop could command. Rent and rates would be additional outgoings: only a small élite among the trade owned the freehold of their shops. But a £20 fish and chip shop would not be exactly palatial. In 1905 the *Fish Trades Gazette*'s roving reporter was unfavourably impressed with most of the fish and chip shops in Stockton-on-Tees:

> Some are doing a very nice trade of from 60 stones of fish and ten bags of potatoes, but it is a wonder that some of them do any trade at all, so dirty looking are the surroundings . . . The frying trade seems to be an industry in which anybody with

£20 to £25 can buy a business, including fixtures and goodwill, but some of the establishments I have seen would be dear at that.[35]

Shops at this level of the trade seldom featured in the advertising columns of the *Fish Trades Gazette* and the north-east of England was already a relatively cheap area in which to set up in business. But even in London a corner shop in Hackney Wick, with four rooms and a yard and 'close by large factories', could be entered for £20, with a rental of 13 shillings per week, in 1907.[36] Here the high rent was probably more of a deterrent than the capital outlay and the same probably applied to the five-roomed shop in London SE which was being 'sacrificed' at £25, with a similar rental, a year later.[37]

At this level of the trade, just as higher up the scale, the threshold of entry was lowered by the widespread practice of accepting a deposit and the payment of the remainder by instalments. Thus a Middlesbrough shop changed hands for £30 in 1913, with a down-payment of £15 and the rest due in 10-shilling weekly payments.[38] Even quite a substantial business could be entered for £20 down, although in this case the advertisement gives us neither full price nor location for a suspiciously enticing 'fish, chip, tripe, pea, supper room . . . well decorated, inverted incandescent lights, large mirrors, bright showy shop . . .'[39]

On the other hand, however, the advertised or offered price for a fairly cheap shop could be only part of the story. In 1917 Francie Nichol of South Shields paid £40 for a run-down corner fish and chip shop, the price of which was probably affected by wartime inflation. But she described the interior graphically:

> Only three teeny little boilers. No proper pans or friers or anythin'. Tatey peelin's all over the floor. Two cats squabblin' over some fish in the back. No vinegar or pickles to be seen. The salt pot was dirty. The holes was closed up with grease, and it was empty into the bargain. The lino was worn away so ye could see the holes in the floorboards. Mice, almost certainly. Dead flies like blackberry jam in the little cracked window which was steamed up, and the fly-paper hangin' over the frier had too many flies in it. The counter was greasy and scruffy. Surely them walls weren't really yellow?

So the total cost of setting up included an extra £60 'to put in new counters, big windows, friers, condiments, and to do the place out and stock it'.[40] William Loftas' reminiscences about his initiation into the trade in Manchester at the turn of the century referred to an expenditure of £43 to buy the business, augmented by £10 spent on 'a course of practical tuition by an experienced frier'; in addition, like a great many fellow friers, he did all the wallpaper and wood fittings himself.[41]

To judge from the advertisements in the trade press, what might be called a mainstream fish and chip business would cost between £40 and £80 in the early twentieth century, not including subsequent embellishments and improvements. But this source is certainly biased towards those larger businesses that were worth advertising at national level. Even so, there was clearly a substantial stratum of these middling businesses, which required a considerably greater initial financial outlay. In 1907 £45 would buy into a 'wet, dry and fried' fish shop in Rickmansworth, with 'good stabling' as well as what purported to be a well-fitted shop.[42] A year later, £75 was asked for a fried fish shop in Acton ('splendid position, surrounded by laundries'); £50 bought a shop with living accommodation in central Wolverhampton, rent unspecified, with profits allegedly (but implausibly) running at £4 per week; and in 1909 a fish and chip restaurant in a market town in southern Scotland was offered for £55, with the profits put this time at £3 per week and an offer to teach the business.[43] There were plenty of other businesses in this bracket, at which taking a fish and chip shop imposed a similar initial investment to that involved in taking a pub in a working-class district. Thus in 1911 Harry Ramsden, before he moved into fish and chips, paid £68 for the fixtures and stock of the Craven Heifer in Bolton Road, Bradford, including bar, piano, glasses and an incomplete set of dominoes.[44] This was a run-down pub with hardly any regulars but many front-parlour beershops with minimal amenities would have come cheaper than this and it is interesting to see the drink trade overlapping with fish and chips in terms of initial capital requirement.

Just as the upper levels of the licensed victualling trade soared upwards into the stratosphere of the big country inns and city-centre hotels, so the highest strata of the fried fish trade shaded upwards to embrace some remarkably opulent and financially exacting establishments. Advertised sale prices of £100 and more were not uncommon in the Edwardian years and some shops went far beyond this asking price. A business with 'good living accommodation' and a nearly new four-pan range, on a 'main thoroughfare' in central Leicester, was on the market at £125 in 1904.[45] In 1910 two contrasting businesses came up at £150: a two-pan shop with a supper room in north-west London, whose price was considerably augmented by the 'good house' which came with it, much of which could be let off to leave only a minimal net rent; and an interestingly complex concern at Peterborough, which combined fish and chips with a fishmonger's and rabbit-dealer's business, including market stalls and a pony and cart to go selling on a round in the surrounding rural area.[46]

But fish and chip businesses were quite capable of generating higher asking prices than this without the benefit of additional sources of income. A 'bold corner shop' in London EC, which was said to take between £32 and £34 per week as a specialized fish and chip concern, was offered at £200 in 1910, the price no doubt boosted by the current owners' 27-year tenure.[47] Even this was not the ceiling. As early as 1890 William Daniels' father paid £240 for a fish and chip restaurant in London's Holloway Road, and the son bought it from him for £425 in 1901.[48] Several other fish and chip restaurants in London and Brighton were offered at well over £200 in the early twentieth century and in 1905 a fried fish shop and house in an unspecified 'seaport town' was on sale at £450, although (unusually) this included the freehold, which would have considerably inflated the price.[49] Unfortunately, no price was listed for the most tempting advertisement of all, which indicates just how far up-market a provincial fish and chip business could go in an unexpected corner of south-west England: 'The Devonian FISH and CHIP SUPPER BAR . . . splendid dwelling house; two conservatories, vinery, garden, fruit trees, *etc.*' This remarkable establishment was in Barnstaple and it would be fascinating to learn more about the economics of the business and the way of life of those who ran it.[50]

The great disparity between the highest and lowest levels of the fish and chip trade was still apparent in the inter-war years, bearing out John Stephens' comment in 1933 that: '. . . the trade to-day is a very mixed one, having men in charge who are so different in capacity, experience and outlook. By mixed I mean so many styles of shop, so many different standards of work, and so big a variety in articles for sale.'[51] As several commentators pointed out, the cost of setting up in the trade at a basic level was much greater after the war than before it, as the inflation of the war years was greatly augmented by the cost of meeting the rising expectations of customers and sanitary authorities. In 1919 an intending fish frier from Leamington was advised that £150 or more would be needed to buy 'a really decent fried-fish shop in these days'.[52] Chatchip went further, asserting that £150 would be the minimum price for merely fitting up a fried fish shop according to his (rather exacting) requirements. He advised an aspiring frier from Willesden that his £250 capital 'if judiciously laid out, is sufficient to make a fairly decent start in the fish frying business'.[53] 'Macte Animo' of the *Fish Friers' Review* was less exacting and probably provides a better guide to what was really happening in the lower reaches of the trade. He reckoned in 1929 that £100 per shop would be a low average for the cost of fitting up. Two years later he illustrated the rising initial cost threshold more graphically:

> Where formerly £20 to £30 were thought sufficient to start a Fried Fish Shop, this could not purchase to-day what would cover a few yards of the floor space.[54]

Even in the down-market and generally depressed North-East of the 1930s, J. Conelly of the Cleveland and South Durham Fish Friers' Association could assert in 1935 that:

> To-day it cost in the region of £150 to equip a fish-frying business, compared with the pre-War outlay of about £25.[55]

A more general assessment of the cost of entering the trade came in 1931, when a *Fish Friers' Review* contributor remarked that £100 would now buy (at most) 'a run down established business', while a *new* shop, 'to meet the modern public requirements, and the Public Health Acts, could not be done for much less than £300':

> . . . a modern 2-pan range of ordinary capacity would cost at least £100. Almost all new shops are required to tile their walls, and lay a Terrazzo floor, which would account for another £100, the rest of the capital would be quickly swallowed up by counter fixtures and fittings, chipping machine, electric peeler (which is practically a necessity in these days), ice box, porcelain sink for fish washing, and containers for potatoes, cutting table, *etc.*[56]

The second-hand market and the surviving older shops in the back streets continued to make the trade more accessible to people of limited means than these comments suggest, enshrining as they do the up-market assumptions of an articulate élite of highly aware and improvement-conscious friers. In 1920 there were advertisements for a second-hand fish and chip stove for £8, for a range, chipper and potato cleaner for £25 and for a complete set of basic fish and chip equipment for £27.[57] In 1923 a Halifax man bought a fish and chip business for £75 and there must have been a lot of trading at this level that went unrecorded in the trade press.[58] Entry to the trade was still being made easier by hire-purchase and deferred payment arrangements; in 1932 Chatchip commented critically on the range-makers' generous hire-purchase arrangements, which, he alleged, encouraged under-capitalized people into the trade to compete with established shops. This in turn led to repossessions that augmented the market in second-hand ranges, spreading the chance to enter the trade to a further circle of impecunious aspirants: 'who have neither capital, experience or ability. All they have is a desire to do something to stop the rot in their homes . . .'[59] This perception of the continuing availability of the fish and chip trade as a refuge from the dole and the means test was substantiated by the evidence of the north-eastern fish friers to the Sea-Fish Commission in 1935. They complained that selling prices were being driven to uneconomic levels by newcomers from the dole, with minimum capital expenditure and overheads, in towns like Bishop Auckland. There the depression had bitten deeply and the local authority had not taken up the offensive trades legislation and could not impose minimum standards.[60]

In some parts of the country, then, an almost penny-capitalist version of the fish and chip trade persisted into the 1930s, using the cheapest of second-hand equipment and occupying the most basic of premises while making use of every possible capital-saving device. At the other extreme, especially in London, entry costs at the top end of the market could be far heavier even than Chatchip's recommendations. In 1920 a double-fronted shop in Brighton was on offer at £950 for 'freehold premises, fittings and utensils', while a fish and chip restaurant and dwelling house in an 'East Coast fashionable resort' was advertised at £1,450, presumably also freehold.[61] Two years later a fish and chip shop 30 miles from London, with six rooms and a scullery, a Ford van, a carrier bicycle and all utensils was available for £1,500.[62] In 1929 William C. Daniels spent £1,200 on an *extension* to his restaurant in Kentish Town Road, one of his two London businesses. It featured teak furniture and fitments, tinted plate glass, armchairs and a lift to bring the food down from the Catering Department on an upper floor.[63] And in 1932 bankruptcy proceedings against Samuel Morris, a fish caterer in Whitechapel, revealed that his shop was part of a complex of buildings under his ownership, which included three flats and 12 workshops. It had cost between £10,000 and £11,000 to build.[64] At this level, fish and chips was really big business and a far cry from its insalubrious back-street origins. But the contrasts within the trade were clearly widening as it continued to develop and diversify.

How did fish friers raise the capital to enable them to set up in the trade? As initial costs rose, it was more likely that savings would have to be augmented by loans. Relatives were a common source: fathers sometimes set up their sons in the trade and families would rally round to keep ailing businesses afloat during hard times. Thus a Nottingham turf-and-loam dealer bought a fish and chip shop in a bid to find work for his unemployed son; a London omnibus driver secured what must have been considerable financial support from his family when he bought a business for £240 as early as 1890; and in the early 1920s a

Rotherham frier, who had begun in 1914 without capital of his own, was kept afloat by interest-free loans from relatives and friends, as well as by borrowing from moneylenders. When on the verge of bankruptcy in 1924, he transferred the business to his brother-in-law in part settlement of his debts: an arrangement of which the Official Receiver was extremely suspicious.[65] Arrangements of this kind were not always cosy, as Francis Nichol found when she went into partnership with her mother-in-law in 1916: arguments immediately developed over the division of labour and the financial arrangements, so that the partnership ended in a blazing row.[66] Friends might also support a new venture, although the same hazards might apply. When William Loftas began his fish frying career, his capital came from the sale of half his house, with a topping-up loan of £26 from 'a boyhood friend'. In this case, at least, this turned out to be a good investment.[67]

More formal sources of capital were already in evidence before the First World War. In 1910 a Sheffield widow used £40 of the compensation money for her husband's death in an industrial accident to buy a fish and chip business; a year later we find a cotton-spinner using industrial compensation money to buy a shop in Oldham from his sister-in-law. This venture ended acrimoniously in a lawsuit for misrepresentation and it was said that the ill-fated purchaser knew nothing of the price of either fish or potatoes.[68] This use of compensation payments was common enough in the inter-war years for a judge to venture a generalization about it in 1931 when adjudicating a dispute over a fish and chip business at Swinton:

> There are several people who come before me who have been awarded £50 and £80 or so under the Workmen's Compensation Act and who are anxious to take a business. The idea of being in business seems to be a wonderful one . . . [but] it is better to be a wage earner.[69]

The flow of compensation recipients into the trade was augmented in the immediate postwar years by the returning ex-servicemen with Ministry of Pensions grants about whom so many fears were expressed in the early 1920s; but such sources of capital must in reality have been the preserve of a small, if conspicuous, minority.

More orthodox and familiar sources of finance also began to appear as the trade gained in respectability. In 1912 a Merthyr Tydfil man took out a £90 bank loan to supplement his £20 savings and bring a fish and chip business within reach. Two years later he was bankrupt with a deficit of nearly £200, of which £67 was owed to the bank; but it is interesting that credit of this kind was already being made available to friers and this case is the tip of an iceberg of uncertain size.[70] Similarly, we do not know how many friers were able to emulate W. H. Howe of Otley, who used a building-society mortgage to acquire his business for £600, only to fall behind on the repayments, get into debt with finance companies and sink into eventual bankruptcy in 1935.[71]

In general terms we can identify a range of possible sources of initial capital for fish friers, without being able to say with any confidence what was typical at different levels of the trade, or whether the pattern changed over time. It seems likely that institutional finance became more important as time went on, especially at the more sophisticated and capital-intensive end of the trade, and that family and friends remained important at the lower end of the scale. But it is still impossible to go beyond these broad, speculative impressions.

We can say a good deal more about the social backgrounds from which fish friers were recruited. Contemporaries had their own ideas about this, although opinion outside the trade continued to make assumptions about the low status of friers that derived from the trade's seedy origins long after the friers themselves had begun to stake a confident claim to respectability of background as well as business. 'Sand Dab' in the *Fish Friers' Review* was particularly annoyed when a *Fish Trades Gazette* contributor in 1930 asserted that friers were 'drawn from window-cleaners and whitewashers'; Chatchip had been claiming for a generation that most friers came from the ranks of respectable skilled labour.[72] In 1922 he urged that for the past 20 years the trade's 'phenomenal growth and progress' had been fuelled by recruitment from 'sober, intelligent working people'. In 1935 'The Unofficial Joker', writing in the Manchester friers' monthly magazine, asserted that most friers were recruited from the skilled and supervisory trades, such as bricklayers and spinners.[73] As 'Kit Haddock' remarked in 1927, this was a view from a postwar perspective: the trade's status had been much more problematic in Edwardian times and it had taken the food crisis of 1917 to raise the frier's status and establish the importance of the industry. But the columnist emphasized the thrifty, independent outlook of newcomers to the trade in the 1920s, who were attracted by 'the "Refined and Prosperous" appearance of the modern frier and his establishment'.[74]

Biographical evidence bears out the notion that, from Edwardian times at least, the fried fish trade recruited extensively from the ranks of skilled labour and above. Of 54 friers for whom some sort of occupational history is available, 23 fall within a broadly-defined category of skilled craftsmen, mainly in industry. They include two cotton spinners and four other textile factory workers; six engineers and metalworkers; four in the building and woodworking trades; three coal miners; two glassworkers; a hosiery worker and a chef. There were also seven recruits from other trades, some of higher standing than others: two publicans, a draper and tobacconist, a tailor, a grocer, a man with a milk-round and the keeper of a common lodging-house. Six friers had grown up in the trade and built their careers in it in adulthood. So two-thirds of the biographies reveal backgrounds in the skilled working class or (in various guises) the petty bourgeoisie. Of the rest, a further eight had some claim to be more exalted still: two senior non-commissioned officers in the Royal Navy and an unspecified 'Captain', a commercial traveller, a colliery under-manager, a local government administrator, an organist and professor of music, and a Bachelor of Arts who, according to Chatchip, took up the trade and remained in it because 'he could knock up a more comfortable living for his wife and children that way than . . . by any of the other ways he had previously tried'.[75] The unskilled comprised a long-serving 'other rank' in the Army, a bus-driver, a butcher's assistant, a vanman, an unemployed man and three labourers, adding up to less than one-seventh of the total. Two men were particularly difficult to categorize. One had worked in several trades before settling down to a career in fish frying; the other was Harry de Grey Firth of Leeds, who had spent nearly 30 years dissipating a £4,000 legacy he had inherited at 21. He had spent five years abroad studying art and then set up in business as a money-lender, manufacturer's agent and (eventually) a shop-owner. His fried fish shop in Meanwood Road, run on a slack rein by a manageress, seems to have been his last throw when everything else was on the verge of bankruptcy; but it did not save him from disaster.[76]

Harry de Grey Firth's career was utterly exceptional; the bare occupational details otherwise make the sample look *less* 'respectable' than it actually was. The labourers, for example, included James Haworth, who came of 'a respectable working-class family' and held a steady job with Ramsbottom Urban District Council for several years while acting as secretary of the New Jerusalem Sick Society, before moving to Fleetwood and the fish and chip trade in 1913.[77] The bus-driver had put together £240 to enter his business in 1890 and the chef was a Frenchman, Monsieur Henri Etienne Bernard (as his obituary described him), who had been chef in a leading London hotel before being gassed in the First World War and settling down to fish frying in Morecambe and then Leeds with his Yorkshire-born wife in the 1920s.[78] Several obituaries mention strong religious affiliations, with various branches of Methodism especially evident, and by the inter-war years an impressive roll-call could be compiled of fish friers who were also local councillors and elected members of Boards of Guardians. And there were several men with really remarkable careers, whose complexity and interest cannot be conveyed by simply categorizing them according to the most recent or longest-lasting of the occupations they undertook before entering the frying trade. There was E. B. O'Neill, born in 1851, who began as a builder in Dowlais and for 15 years acted as organist at Dowlais Parish Church before taking up the post of Director of Music at a college in New Jersey between 1897 and 1903; he went into the fish and chip trade after returning home on the death of his father.[79] In a different idiom was A. Renshaw, who before becoming a fish frier in the early 1930s had served for four years on Ossett Urban District Council and had 'occupied many positions in the Miners' Federation', especially on 'the Educational side of the Miners' Welfare'; or Jack Barrow, who had been a mill worker, a 'manager of a concern with 800 men under him', and a parliamentary candidate before running a fish and chip shop with his wife.[80] Perhaps George Chamberlain has the strongest claim to the status of most distinguished fish frier, however, from a remarkably challenging field. He had several parallel careers before becoming a fish frier in 1933, when still in his mid-forties. He had been an engineer, with 18 years' service on the railways; an active member of two trade unions; a leading official in a Friendly Society; a committed campaigner and organizer of demonstrations in support of improved legal status for the blind; a long-serving member of Warrington County Borough Council and the local Poor Law Guardians; an advisor at national level on Poor Law policy and a prospective parliamentary candidate. Not surprisingly, he soon became a highly-regarded official of the National Federation of Fish Friers.[81]

The fish and chip trade thus came to draw upon a wide constituency of skilled craftsmen and tradesmen, including a leavening of the independent-minded and self-taught. It contained within itself an élite, a kind of trade aristocracy, which reflected and perpetuated the best working-class traditions of organization and self-respect. But there is no doubt that my biographical evidence overstates the importance of this strand within the trade as a whole. The biographies I have found are strongly weighted towards those leading figures in trade organizations, or highly successful businessmen, or articulate survivors with interesting reminiscences, who tend to feature in profiles or obituaries in the trade press. To some extent this built-in bias is counter-balanced by evidence from reports of court cases, including bankruptcy proceedings; but there is not enough of this material to give the sample any pretensions towards representativeness. It has no statistical validity whatever. Above all, it is biased towards relatively substantial businesses that were operating in the 1920s and 1930s. Biographical evidence for people from the lower reaches of the trade is not only thin on the ground: it is also short on detail. So we can recover little of the backgrounds of the lesser friers in the back streets, many of whose businesses were short-lived and unsuccessful; the further back we go, the more unsatisfactory the evidence becomes. We have no satisfactory way of reconstructing the careers of the sort of people who were described in the *Fish Trades Gazette* correspondent's report on Stafford in 1906:

> Some of the dealers here, as elsewhere, are of a 'rough-and-ready' type, and their vocabulary is stocked with words and phrases which would fairly make any ordinary individual's hair stand on end.[82]

This stratum of the trade, which was predominant in late Victorian times and steadily declined in relative importance in the twentieth century, is the least accessible to biographical enquiry.

The biographical dossier also leaves out the Italians and Jews. The Italians played no part in the administration of the National Federation of Fish Friers, although they were beginning to join some of the branches in the 1930s, and more generally they tended to keep themselves to themselves. Recruitment was largely by chain migration and family connections, with children and new migrants gaining experience in established shops before setting up on their own. So the Italians came from a distinctive background of impoverished upland farming and, once in Britain, street-selling and catering: they were set apart from other fish friers by more than just the obvious differences of language and culture. And they had their own trade organizations, beginning with the Società di Mutuo Soccorso in 1891, which provided loans to assist Italians who were starting in business in the Glasgow area. Jewish fish friers, who were in at the start of the trade in London and were important in Leeds, with and in other provincial outposts in places like Sheffield, also had their own separate culture and institutions, and (unlike the Italians) catered largely for their co-religionists. Their numbers were augmented by the new immigrants of the late nineteenth century from Eastern Europe: thus in 1909 Wolf Cohen of Limehouse, a Russian immigrant, was doing well as a fried fish dealer and tailor and promised to find work for his newly-arrived brother-in-law.[83] Family connections became increasingly important in the fish and chip trade generally as time went on; but among the Italians and the Jews they were clearly the dominant influence on recruitment throughout the period.[84]

The other obviously under-represented group in the biographical sample is the women, whose importance as independent traders in the fish and chip world was systematically played down by the trade press, which preferred to view fish frying as a craft cast in the same masculine mould as the skilled trades from which so many friers were recruited.[85] The only woman to feature in the sample in her own right is Francie Nichol, who left a remarkable autobiography without which her story would have remained completely unknown.[86] But the biographies of several men who became stalwarts of the trade reveal they were drawn into fish frying through businesses that were originally run by their wives. This was true of E. B. O'Neill, the builder and musician; of J. Lewis, an ex-miner whose introduction to fish and chips came through a business conducted by his wife and her sister-in-law in a wooden hut, using the concessionary coal he received from the pit; and of Tom Smith, a painter and decorator, who joined in his wife's business when he married her.[87] In fact, many women ran fish and chip businesses, some on their own account, some with support from their husbands. Always, a minority of the fish and chip shop proprietors listed in the trade directories were women. As many as eight out of 22 were female in Preston in 1885, although 10 years later the proportion had fallen to 14 out of 93; by 1913 it was 12 out of 133. The same firm of directory compilers gave 12 women out of 103 fish friers in Blackburn in 1894, but only four out of 28 in Accrington, one out of 25 in Darwen and none of the 19 chipped-potato dealers in Church and Oswaldtwistle in the same year. These variations are interesting, but probably reflect differing attitudes and practices among canvassers in the different districts.[88] Kelly's *Directory* for Cumberland showed a much higher striking rate in 1910, with 17 women among the 62 fish and chip dealers it listed; but this was for the whole county and must have been only a fraction of the total. Ten years earlier Bulmer's *Directory* for the same county had listed hardly any women at all. All this reminds us of the vagaries of directory evidence, even in the heyday of these useful local listings.

    With all its limitations, this evidence does show that a significant minority of fish and chip shops were publicly assigned to female ownership in the late Victorian and Edwardian years. Many more may well have been effectively run by women while theoretically belonging to their husbands. This was a source of persistent complaint among the organized friers, who argued that shops run by women with working husbands – and therefore merely augmenting the domestic budget – provided unfair competition for the full-time friers, threatening standards and bringing prices down. The United Kingdom Fish and Chip Friers' Federation, a precursor of the National Federation, was clear on this point in 1909:

> The great drawback to the trade was felt to be the very many small shops in the back streets of the large towns and cities, managed by women whose husbands are at work.[89]

Thirty years later the *Fish Friers Review* was still inveighing against 'pin-money shops' that siphoned trade away from serious friers and threatened the reputation and well-being of the trade as a whole.[90]

    But female fish friers did not disappear during the inter-war years. Some, including independent women as well as friers' wives, were active on local executives of the National Federation in the 1920s and 1930s. And the criticism of women running shops to augment their husbands' wages might have been muted if the critics had reflected on the experiences of those respected colleagues who had been drawn into the trade in this way. In many cases, no doubt, this pattern of working reflected one of the most common motives for going into fish frying: the need to generate additional income while the children were small without incurring child-minding costs. The trade could also be a useful way of sustaining a reasonable standard of living for widows, especially if they had young children. It is not clear into what category 28-year-old Jane Grady of Newcastle fell when in 1919 she was fined £10 for running a fish and chip shop while drawing out-of-work benefit, after pleading that this did not constitute 'employment'.[91] But we do have the example of Francie Nichol to provide some sort of guide, however idiosyncratic, to the motives that might pull women into the frying trade. Francie had just lost the tenancy of the lodging-house she had been renting and the little shop she had been running had been finished off by the depredations of rats. Her new husband had given up his job and gone to look for another and another child was on the way. Under these circumstances, a shop of some kind was an obvious way of making ends meet: the offer of a flourishing fish and chip business seemed a godsend.[92] From this perspective, the fish and chip shop as a survival strategy in the face of unemployment and the poverty cycle is well-illustrated, from the woman's point of view, by Francie Nichol's story.

But there were other ways of looking at this episode. The man who sold the fish and chip shop 'had all he wanted out of it, and was goin' to retire'. The business thus offered the promise of independence and security, which the National Federation of Fish Friers was keen to emphasize as the due reward for hard work in the trade on the part of thrifty refugees from wage-labour. They sought to present it as the dominant motive for entry into the respectable echelons of the trade. As Francie's fish frying career developed further, however, it came to illustrate a further general theme in the recruitment of fish friers: the popular notion of the fish and chip shop as a potential gold-mine, a route to a quick and easy fortune. When Francie escaped from partnership with her mother-in-law and acquired her second fish and chip shop in 1917 (with her husband safely out of the way), the story becomes an object lesson in the possibilities for the upward social mobility the trade might offer. By judicious investment and sheer hard work, she accumulated profits and savings hand over fist and reinvested some of her gains in improvements to the premises, only to have the fruits of her labours taken from her by the return of her husband, who assumed ownership of the business and proceeded to drink a large proportion of the profits.[93]

Neither the story nor its outcome would have pleased the Federation's spokesmen, who were eager to establish the masculine, craft-orientated credentials of the trade and to stress the hard work and respectable lifestyle on which hard-earned success would have to be based. Thus 'Kit Haddock' in 1927 asserted that most recruits to fish frying were 'past thrifty workers out of employment, seeking some investment for their precious hard-won capital, and a living, independent of the present fickle labour market'.[94] This definition was capable of embracing the thrifty unemployed and those who were driven out of their original trade by illness. It could also include the occasional black-listed trade unionist, in whose ranks William Loftas was to be found. He had worked as a national organizer for his trade union, had resigned (with characteristically combative adherence to principle) after a dispute with the executive and found himself branded as an agitator and unable to work at his trade.[95] A leavening of industrial militants who were impatient of the constraints of wage-labour helped to give a radical tone to some of the rhetoric – and policies – of friers' organizations, as we shall see.[96] But what 'Kit Haddock' emphasized above all was the theme of going into the trade in search of an honest living, independent of employers, rather than a pursuit of upward social mobility through a quick killing and a comfortable retirement. For many of the most articulate friers, this kind of independence was more important as a value than fortune-hunting; but it was the independence of the peasant proprietor or artisan rather than that of entrepreneurial competitive individualism. These were the heirs of Victorian 'respectable radicalism', steeped in a work ethic but deeply suspicious of the threatening machinations of capitalism red in tooth and claw.

People of this stamp were particularly offended by the persistence of the myth that the fried fish trade was a quick and easy route to riches, which attracted the wrong sort of recruit and gave the trade as a whole a bad name. This stereotype was already being combated in the Edwardian years. In 1904 'A London Fish Frier' was warning readers of the *Fish Trades Gazette* that: 'There are no quick fortunes made in the trade these days, as was once the case', and urging the virtues of 'perseverance, cleanliness and an article of good quality.'[97] Three years later the *Daily News* investigated the fried fish trade, starting from the premise that: 'There is a popular idea that every proprietor of a fried fish shop is a potential millionaire. The delusion, like the odour, is all-pervading . . .'[98] The report went on to paint a gloomy picture of the trade's real circumstances, laying particular stress on the rising prices of its staple commodities; but in spite of such jeremiads, popular expectations remained high. Even in the depths of the First World War, Chatchip was arguing that: 'Many people had an idea that they could make enough at fish frying to retire in a few years, and some of the merchants had done their best to develop this belief, and would endeavour to crowd the trade in any case.'[99] And during the post-war boom the same writer came up with a plausible explanation for the enduring popularity of this perception:

> . . . many people get it into their heads, because they see crowds of folk in a fried-fish shop, that the proprietor must be making money so fast as to be piling it away on 'edges'. They do not see such crowds in the ironmonger's, the grocer's, the butcher's, and so on, and they do not recollect that all of these tradesmen have usually twice the fish-frier's hours to do their business in, and that generally one customer in any of these other shops will spend at one time as much as a score or more customers in a fried-fish shop.[100]

These attitudes persisted into the 1930s. A representative comment came from the Assistant Official Receiver at Halifax Bankruptcy Court:

> There seems to be something of magic about the fish and chip business. Some of you

seem to think it is a matter of going in and putting on a white apron and making a fortune.[101]

In 1934 the *Daily Express* was still publishing absurd statements about the ease of setting up in fish frying and the lucrative nature of the business. In the autumn of 1937, with the trade in serious difficulties from high fish and potato prices, 'the gold mine myth' was far from dead. A *Fish Friers' Review* columnist blamed well-publicised propaganda from the trawler owners, using low fish prices in time of glut to give the buying public the impression that they were being systematically rooked by unscrupulous money-grubbing friers.[102] By this time it was becoming difficult to sell some shops in places like Preston and the gilt was perhaps beginning to wear off the gingerbread; but the persistence of a widespread belief that a fish and chip shop was an almost instant passport to riches clearly did help to draw into the trade a highly speculative, ambitious, often under-capitalized and always over-optimistic element who were viewed with grave suspicion by the organized friers.[103]

Any attempt to assess how successful fish frying was for those who entered the trade has to take account not only of these widespread inflated expectations, but also of the variety of goals and motives which propelled people into the trade. There were those who sought to use the trade to make ends meet, as a refuge from misfortune or to halt a downward slide in the family's living standards. There were those who sought an independent living, free from the externally imposed routines and constraints of employment in factories and workshops. And there were those who sought to use the trade as a means of rapidly accumulating wealth, whether to finance a comfortable retirement or to generate capital for a more lucrative and prestigious business venture. There was some 'trading up' to improved premises and some limited multiplication of outlets, within the trade itself, but Chatchip asserted convincingly in 1912 that it was rare to find in the fish and chip trade the pattern, common elsewhere, of 'men who began years ago in a very small way now running establishments of a similar nature, but of much larger and more pretentious proportions'. When friers succeeded, he thought, they tended to move on to something else: the fried fish trade was usually 'a stepping-stone to some other ideal'.[104]

Contemporary commentators within the trade were pessimistic about the fortunes of most friers. There was plenty of support for Chatchip's contention that most recruits '. . . invariably [sic] lose their modest accumulated capital in much less time than they acquired it, and then return to the business they *do know* something about, in order to procure a living'.[105] In Birmingham in 1906: 'on the part of not a few, "flitting", as the sudden removal of furniture is described, is a . . . frequent occurrence, and houses change hands from other causes at short notice'. 'Rambler' described the situation in Edwardian Burnley, where large numbers of shops had been opened by speculators and sold to unsuspecting novices, who soon found out how limited the trade really was, with the result that many shops changed hands three or four times a year as successive recruits came face to face with the realities of the lower levels of the trade.[106] The litany of doom continued through the inter-war years, even though 'Macte Animo' admitted in 1928 that the old dictum that 'five years in the frying trade was about the limit human energy could withstand' no longer applied in an age of greatly improved technology and conditions.[107] A few months earlier the same commentator, starting with the assumption that 'you entered the trade with an ambition to improve your station in life', was very pessimistic about the current state of the trade:

> I am constantly having cases brought to my notice of Friers who are in difficulties. They have been forced down and still further down until their savings, which they had worked hard for over many years, had entirely gone, almost destitute, forced out of the trade which had been their living, 'before being crushed out'.[108]

Comments in this vein were reiterated even more forcefully in 1931, as the depression bit deeper; they were given poignant illustration by the reported suicide note of a Colne frier who had been losing money for the last 12 months and found himself hopelessly in debt:

> Too old to get a job, and not able to draw the dole. The future is hopeless . . . They are *opening a shop in opposition* at the bottom of the street, so the last hope is gone. No work, no job, no hope.[109]

At the end of the year the parlous state of the trade in Sheffield generated debate on the letters page of the *Sheffield Telegraph*; evidence was provided of friers closing because they could not meet their bills. One had allegedly sold up for £50 when his range alone should have been worth £150.[110] Similar laments were the staple fare of the trade press throughout the 1930s.

A less apocalyptic variation on this theme emphasized the low returns fish friers and their families received for long hours, hard work and the stressful nature of the business. Thus in 1913 a 'chipper' told Blackburn County Court that he made a net profit of between 22s and 23s per week, which was no more than a labourer's wage, on a turnover of more than £5.[111] In January 1930 'Macte Animo' attempted to reconstruct the budget of one of the many shops in industrial areas that he thought to be taking £10 per week or less. Fish was the largest item of expenditure, accounting for £3 15s per week, and total outgoings, including an allowance of 5s per week for wear and tear on plant, but nothing for wages or insurance, came to £8 16s per week, leaving £1 4s to live on. This would have been uncomfortably close to the poverty line of Edwardian England and it was certainly not enough to support a family in the inter-war years, suggesting that such a shop would only be viable if one member of the family was in full-time paid employment.[112] In 1935 'The Unofficial Joker' directed his comments more specifically at full-time friers with family businesses when he pointed out that, as ex-trade unionists, they were 'scabbing' on themselves by working 70 hours or more per week, without any overtime agreement, and exploiting the labour of their wives at less than the going rate per hour for an unskilled labourer.[113] On this basis, a poorly-paid survival in the trade was the most that the average frier could hope for; fish frying as a route to prosperity or upward social mobility was a delusion.

It is not quite so straightforward, of course. The evidence from the trade press is highly subjective, reflecting the fears, prejudices and recruitment propaganda of the leading lights of trade organizations. But evidence on how long people lasted in the trade, comparing entries in trade directories over time and assuming that success required a career of several years, while an early exit was strongly suggestive of failure, also leads to pessimistic conclusions. A study of the expansive late Victorian and Edwardian years in Preston shows what seem to be low survival rates. Fifty per cent of the directory entries for 1885 were still trading in 1889; 41 per cent of the 1889 newcomers survived until 1892; and the corresponding figures for 1892–5 and 1895–8 were as low as 24.5 per cent and 32.9 per cent. Over longer periods, 23 per cent of the 1885 entrants lasted to 1895 or beyond; but the figures for 1889–98, 1892–1904 and 1895–1907 show only 9.1, 5.7 and 8.6 per cent of newcomers lasting the distance. This makes the Preston friers more volatile than most other kinds of shopkeeper and far more short-lived in their businesses than seaside landladies at Blackpool, where the costs of setting up were broadly similar, the backgrounds of recruits were on a par and the precariousness of the trade was worsened by seasonal fluctuations in demand on the grand scale and high rents, rates and other overheads.[114] It is conceivable that some of the short-lived friers made money hand over fist and retired, or moved on to greater things, within a few years. It is more likely that some of the businesses were used to tide families over a difficult stage of the poverty cycle and given up when times improved. But the circumstantial and contextual evidence strongly suggests that fish and chip shops were more often destroyers of savings than creators of fortunes and that the best they could normally offer was a fairly basic living in exchange for long hours and hard work.

There was, of course, always a leavening of success stories, which probably made more impact on hopes and expectations than their numbers or representativeness warranted. In 1894 a minor scandal arose when James Macgregor, a West Hartlepool Justice of the Peace, was fined five shillings and costs for selling fried fish during prohibited hours: at 3 a.m. on Christmas Day and with his own hands, it was alleged. His magisterial status survived the ensuing fuss and he was a pioneer among many fish friers who held prominent positions in local government.[115] They included the suitably-named Bristol frier Sidney Fry, who in 1919 was re-elected to Kingswood Urban District Council for the fourth time and was vice-chair of Warmley and Keynsham Guardians after 14 years' service; or the London activist John Lyon, who found time to become a Bermondsey borough councillor as well as operating three fried fish shops and maintaining a high profile at national level in the NFFF.[116] At a more materialistic level, the trade press was capable of acknowledging that some friers were able to use fish and chips as a route to prosperity. Thus the *Fish Trades Gazette* correspondent on Blackpool in 1906:

> More than one fried fish dealer who commenced in a humble way has 'made his pile', and there can be no doubt that, if managed properly, the business may be made a lucrative one.[117]

And the friers who built up, or bought into, the big businesses which were described earlier in the chapter, along with such famous public figures as Harry Ramsden, were visible embodiments of the opportunities the trade provided for a favoured few. At a lower level than this, too, there are intimations of more modest but genuine comfort. Thus a Huddersfield frier in 1934 employed two domestic servants whose duties extended to waiting-on in the café attached to his house; but the emphasis was clearly on the domestic aspects of their work.[118] And in August 1937 the Leeds branch of the NFFF organized a motor rally, suggesting that at least one emblem of middle-class consumerism had become commonplace in fish frying circles.[119]

The Leeds motor rally did not pass without complaint from one member who pointed out that it excluded those friers who did not own cars, who seem to have been in the majority. The episode calls to mind an earlier controversy over friers and motor-cars. In 1919 trawler-owners and oil- and fat-merchants were widely quoted in the national press when they accused friers of profiteering, using as evidence the fact that some friers were now car-owners. As one trawler owner revealingly put it: 'Even the humble fish frier may be seen taking his trip in his motor-car.' Chatchip emphasized that this applied only to 'one or two' friers with an enormous volume of trade, but he also responded angrily to the implication that fish friers had no business to aspire to the glories of car ownership. Why should fish frying not be seen on a par with other trades, with the same scope for the successful to prosper legitimately and display the symbols of that prosperity? Why should the frier be 'humble'? But the underlying attitudes were deeply engrained, reflecting the unassuming, precarious nature of most friers' lifestyles.[120] This was a business in which success was measured in terms of retirement to run a Blackpool boarding-house. This was the fate of James Haworth of Fleetwood, who moved to Read's Avenue (a relatively high-class part of town, admittedly) in 1929, 'seeking a change from the strenuous life of a frier': a perception that would itself have been indignantly rebutted by Blackpool landladies themselves.[121]

Throughout the period, in fact, it is clear that most friers struggled to get by and that many fell by the wayside after only a short stint in the trade. The report of the Sea-Fish Commission in 1937 is as pessimistic as the trade press on this issue and deserves to be taken seriously. It found that:

> The fried fish trade cannot be regarded as economically healthy. Its units are on a small scale and are largely concentrated in areas of low spending power. There is, therefore, intense competition for custom, and the resulting pressure on prices militates against remunerative and satisfactory trading.[122]

These comments apply more obviously in the lower reaches of the trade than higher up the scale: to the 'working' shopkeepers rather than to the articulate minority with 'professional' aspirations. But we shall find out a great deal more about the status of fish friers and the nature of their trade if we look more closely at how their businesses worked. This will be the theme of the next chapter.

5 The Nature of the Business

What struck contemporaries most forcibly about the fish and chip trade was the small scale of most of the businesses. After several decades of steady expansion in investment and turnover, a National Federation of Fish Friers spokesman was still able to startle the members of the Sea-Fish Commission in 1935 by estimating the turnover of an average fish and chip shop at between £15 and £20 per week. This provoked murmurs of surprise from a body whose chair had just been probing aggressively into the extent of fish friers' liability to pay income tax, only to be told that perhaps one per cent might pay just a little. But although the friers were pleading poverty and seeking special treatment from the Commission, this estimate was in line with contemporary comments in the trade press that were not intended for outside consumption.[1] Mr Manville of Portsmouth was quick to point out that Mr Rose's figure, based on experience of Leicester, might be just a shade on the low side, but he corroborated the main thrust of his colleague's evidence, amplifying his earlier remark that: 'This business is very much a man and wife business.'

The notional 'average' fish and chip shop of the mid-1930s was probably very similar to the one described by a Bolton weaver, born in 1916, who reminisced about her childhood for a local oral history project:

> Well actually it was only an ordinary house, like a four roomed cottage, same as we lived in, it was only further down the street and they had the front place made into the shop and then the back place of course they did all the peeling of the potatoes and preparing everything for the shop and they kind of lived upstairs . . . this one in particular was a very good chip shop and the people themselves were very clean and they used to be queueing and they would be all round the counter and out and all up the street.[2]

No doubt the second part of this description was less representative than the first: it would probably have been envied by many struggling back-street friers. But even on the eve of the Second World War the overwhelming majority of fish and chip businesses were still being conducted in this decidedly 'cottage industry' manner, and the discussions of changes in the trade that sometimes loom large in the rest of this chapter should not be allowed to obscure this important basic continuity.

Contemporary perceptions from within the trade were increasingly coloured from Edwardian times, and especially in the inter-war years, by a strong consciousness of improvement in technology, hygiene, presentation and status. This affects some of the retrospective views offered in the trade press on the ways in which businesses were operated in the misty and disreputable years of the later nineteenth century. Mayhew's lurid descriptions of the haunts and practices of the earliest London fish friers were grist to this mill. As early as 1910 Chatchip quoted them at length in the process of creating a Whig interpretation of the rise and progress of fish and chips.[3] He went on to offer 'a personal view of the past':

> It is only a few years ago that landlords were very unwilling to let their premises for the purposes of the trade, and when most people with any claim whatever to respectability looked upon fried fish shops and fish friers as abominations to be shunned . . . Can we wonder at it, when we recall to mind the fish frier and his shop in the days of the trade's infancy? Almost invariably in those days the frier was drawn from the ignorant classes, and he made no pretence to cleanliness and paid no regard whatever to the laws of sanitation, even if he knew them . . . His appearance in the shop, too, was often revolting, the same greasy old clothes being used from day to day, with nothing . . . to protect him from the dirt and grease . . . The frying-pans in those days were . . . constructed on the old clothes-boiler plan, with ordinary brick fronts . . . Those who have never seen them in operation can only imagine the delightful odour they created for the frier, his neighbours, and the passers-by.

But now:

> The fish frier to-day is almost invariably a respected business man, who conducts his business on business-like plans, is cleanly in appearance, wears washing apparel for appearance sake and to protect his ordinary attire from dirt and grease, knows the laws of sanitation and puts them into practice. He now has the help of specially constructed machinery for the preparation of his fish and chips . . . The frying-pans are now constructed on the most scientific and approved plans, and they carry away all steam and any disagreeable odour likely to arise from almost any sort of cooking.[4]

This was, of course, a piece of propaganda, strongly flavoured in the second part with wishful thinking. Chatchip himself had plenty of subsequent criticism to offer to his fellow friers and he had to come to terms with uncomfortable revelations about their practices from time to time. In 1919 he was suitably horrified by the evidence given by Bradford's inspector of fried fish shops when a frier was fined for a breach of the by-laws:

> The steps leading to the cellar in which the work was done were covered with mud, the floor below was two or three inches deep in potato peelings and refuse, and the air was foul with the smell of decaying fish offal and potatoes. A tank half full of water exuded a smell which suggested that it had not been cleaned out for a long time. The walls had not been limewashed and were festooned with cobwebs.[5]

He would have been even more unhappy had he known about the house in Castle Cary that sold wild fruits, wet fish and potatoes to the locals, and throughout the 1930s opened as a fish and chip shop on Saturday evenings, frying in rendered-down bacon fat and using a wood-fired boiler in which laundry was done for the rest of the week.[6]

Such examples were becoming exceptional, but Chatchip was not alone in taking an unduly rosy view of the spread of improvement in the trade at times, and this frame of mind distorted perceptions of the past as well as the present. Contributors to the *Fish Friers' Review* in the 1920s and 1930s would look back, in anger or nostalgia, to the 'bad old days' before the First World War. Thus a report from the Food Council in 1927, which opposed attempts to limit competition and urged the frying of herrings (which was seen as an affront to the fish frier's craft), brought a furious response couched in terms of fearing a return to 'the old set-pot brick range, dismal lighted shop, with a perpetual steam-laden atmosphere, frying the dregs of the fish market salved from the manure works'.[7] A few years later 'Macte Animo' provided a more circumstantial vision of the lower depths of yore:

> At one time a Fried Fish Shop could scarcely be found on a principal thoroughfare, they were mainly to be found in back streets, often dismal places with one gas-jet giving out a most miserable light, made more dismal by the steam from the open pans, and the condensation dropping round you, making one feel as if they were waiting in a turkish bath, if it had not been for the sticky, greasy vapour which clung to your clothes.[8]

This was certainly part of the story, but contemporary descriptions and reminiscences give a less Dickensian emphasis although they combine to reinforce the impression of long hours and hard work that 'Progress' gave when he reminisced about 'Pioneer Days' in 1929:

> getting up at 6 o'clock in the morning and having two miles to push fish on a sack barrow before breakfast, then standing outside to clean it and cut it up in all kinds of weather, then to start cleaning potatoes, under the old system of scrubbing them with a yard brush in the old trough.[9]

In 1932 a London fish frier looked back in detail on his daily routine in 1890. The day began at 5 a.m. with a visit to the stables to pick up a horse and van, which were hired from a wood dealer for two shillings per morning. He then went to Billingsgate to buy the day's fish supply, although the destination might be changed to Shadwell if the touts who met the buyers at King William Street said that fish was cheaper there. Twopence was charged for this information. A break was taken for a 'cup of tea and a slice' at a coffee shop and the frier returned from market at 9 a.m. for breakfast and a look at a newspaper. Preparation and work in the shop occupied the time until 3 p.m.; then there was a break until 6.30 p.m. for dinner, sleep and tea. Then from 6.30 p.m. to 12.40 the next morning he worked in the shop, frying and serving customers until after the pubs closed at 12.30 a.m. The shop was supposed to close at midnight, so the constable on the beat had to be 'squared' and a watch kept for sergeants and inspectors. All this added up to something like a 16-hour day, although it was spiced with variety and differing intensities of work.[10]

Other accounts from about this time confirm the pattern of the fish frier's day while providing additional details and minor variations. Mrs Jennings, whose father kept a fried fish supper bar in Shepherds Bush, remembered getting up at 4.00 a.m. to go to Billingsgate on her father's horse-drawn van and then going on to the King's Cross potato market for 'a couple of sacks of potatoes'. Between these transactions: 'we'd always have a cup of tea at a pub with a drop of rum in it, and I very often used to have a hot roll and butter, and I used to have a little drop of rum in my tea'. But '. . . my days was very very hard . . . I was up sometimes at 4, never went to bed till 12 at night'.[11] A voice from the provinces, that of Mrs Beddoes, who was born into the trade and then married a frier, also emphasizes hard work and long days. Mrs Beddoes' father, Thomas Lord, began in Birkenhead in 1883 and introduced fish and chips to Wrexham in 1885. He built his own brick ranges and was a pioneer in the peeling of potatoes for chips, using one of the early lathe-type peelers. Even so, the working day began long before school opened and continued late into the night. The Beddoes themselves, running a fish and chip shop in Manchester from 1894, expected to be open until 1.30 on Sunday morning, serving after the pubs closed.[12]

These reminiscences present a more down-to-earth and credible world than that of the propagandists and retrospective apostles of improvement. They show us lives in which small pleasures and relaxations were fitted into a hard, unrelenting daily round and give an insight into the range of social networks into which a frier might be drawn in the course of a day that took him far beyond the preparation room and the frying range. They speak of a late Victorian fish frying world not as far removed from that of the Edwardians as Chatchip's version of the trade's history might suggest. The Beddoes emphasized the liberation that a gas-powered potato peeler brought to their lives, in terms of shorter and less strenuous working days. But Edwardian reminiscences and descriptions do not present a remarkably different picture from these of the 1880s and early 1890s. The late Victorian memories may well come from the upper levels of the trade – both the London friers had access to horse-drawn transport, for example – but the apparent continuities should still give pause for thought.

The most atmospheric – and sympathetic – reporting from the Edwardian years comes from Olive Malvery, a 'lady journalist' who took a week's work with an East End fish frier as part of a more general programme of investigation into the lives of 'the masses'. Miss Malvery worked for a 'big, good-tempered, good-natured widow', who began her day at 4.30 a.m. with coffee laced with gin, 'of which she took quite half a cupful', before the inevitable trip to Billingsgate on a cart driven by an employee, a 'sleepy, surly youth'. The journalist was most impressed with the bustle of the fish market and the complexity of the transactions, which involved payments to a 'minder' for the horse and a porter to bring the fish to the cart. After breakfast, preparation began in earnest, for this was a shop with a lunch-time trade:

> With the assistance of the surly driver, the fish purchased at the market was sorted, cleaned, and cut up into small pieces. Then several baskets of potatoes were scrubbed and washed. After this they were put in a machine that cut them up into small slices. Then followed a general clean up of the premises. This completed, fires had to be lit in the furnaces, over which the frying pans were soon to be set. The fish was fried in a specially prepared oil. Each piece of fish, before frying, was dipped into batter.

After the lunch-time customers had gone, cleaning and preparation for the

evening took until 4.00 p.m., when three hours of 'much-desired rest' inter-
vened. At 7.00 p.m. frying began again and 'between the hours of 8 and 10 it
was scarcely possible to fry fish fast enough for the buyers who crowded in and
waited at the counter'. The shop eventually closed its doors at midnight, after a
working day of at least 16 hours. Miss Malvery mentioned the smell of the trade
and the distinctive atmosphere of the shop, but only in passing. Her main
impression was one of sheer, sustained hard work:

> How any human beings can long stand the wear and tear of such a life is beyond my
> understanding. I must say that I never had a harder week in my life.[13]

This was a big shop with an impressive trade but the daily routine seems little
different from that of the 1890s; Chatchip's protestations of improvement seem
at best unconvincing.

Chatchip himself offered a reminiscent view from retirement of the daily
routine of a family-operated fish and chip business in the early twentieth
century. This was drawn directly from personal experience and gives convincing details that cannot be found anywhere else. The day began at 5 a.m. in
London but an hour later in big provincial towns where markets were more
accessible. Friers in smaller places had to go to the station to meet their fish on
arrival, or make expensive arrangements with carriers. Fish was a daily purchase but potatoes and other vegetables were bought on Mondays. While the
husband was buying, the wife would be cleaning the shop, polishing the brass
fitments and seeing to the children. After breakfast, the potatoes would be
washed and peeled and the fish cut up into portions. After the midday meal the
potatoes would be 'eyed', and an hour's rest might be possible before the
children returned from school. After tea, the husband lit the ranges and
brought in the prepared material, while the wife made the batter. Between
6 p.m. and 7.15 or 7.30 p.m. the husband would fry while his wife served at the
counter; during the slacker period between then and about 9.00 p.m. the
husband was able to carry on alone while his wife put the children to bed. Then
both worked together during the second busy period from 9.00 to 11.00 p.m. or
(on Saturday) midnight. On Fridays Chatchip would also open at lunch-time,
but he missed the Saturday early evening session so that his wife could get out
to the shops. The regular routine was: supper at 11.35 or 11.45 p.m., bed at
12.15 a.m. and up at 6.00 the next morning. And many shops also opened
regularly at lunch-times. The work was so hard that 'nine out of every ten
people who came into the trade got out of it again as quickly as ever they could':
a characteristic exaggeration but perhaps a pardonable one.[14]

The memories of a Barrow-in-Furness frier's son suggest that not everyone
worked as hard as Chatchip, however. Mr M7B's father brought up eight
children on the income from the fish and chip trade, beginning in 1893. Mr
M7B himself was born in 1897 and remembers that sustained work began at
9.00 a.m. or a little earlier. The day's fish, which was ordered by telegraph from
Aberdeen or Grimsby, had to be fetched from the station at 5.30 p.m., but this
job was done by each of the children in turn. The children also called in to help
with the potatoes during the school lunch break but there is no evidence that
Mr M7B's mother took an active part in the business. Opening times were
similar to those described by Chatchip but Mr M7B's father was able to take

Saturday afternoons off to play football for a local team, although this regular escape was made possible by his team-mates who came round and helped with the shop work on Saturdays, 'getting tidied up so that he could play football for them'. Mr M7B reminds us of the hidden economies of a fish and chip business, too. His father bought household groceries in bulk from the provision merchants who supplied the flour and potatoes for the shop and the children ate a lot of fish and chips themselves, taking any fish left over from the night before on 'outings'. This is a much less work-ethic-ridden, treadmill existence than that described by Chatchip; it reminds us that even in the Edwardian years the fish frier's lot was not necessarily either sweated labour or hand-to-mouth poverty.[15]

Nevertheless, the status of the fish and chip trade was much higher after the First World War than before and its practitioners became better-off and more self-confident. This was not just a matter of the flagship businesses at the top of the scale, like Harry Ramsden's: it extended through most of the trade. Fish frying technology was becoming more sophisticated, more visually impressive and more effective in saving labour and liberating friers for non-business activities. Friers were paying more heed to the appearance and cleanliness of their premises and beginning to reap their reward in praise from Sanitary Inspectors and Medical Officers of Health, who had been prominent among their pre-war critics. In many cases, prices had increased in step with improved standards, as had the volume of trade and even the social standing of the customers. A new self-confidence was abroad in the 1920s, stemming in large part from a widespread perception of the friers' importance to the war effort. When the trade's National Federation returned to using the label Fish Friers, after a brief flirtation (mainly at the behest of the southern branches) with being Fish Caterers, the editor of the *Fish Friers' Review* expressed his views with forthright confidence:

> Some friers are humbly apologetic when stating the nature of their business to outsiders. Why? they should [*sic*], is an enigma to me. Personally I glory in the cognomen; and am totally unashamed! The name fish frier is preferable to 'snob'. Snobbery does not enhance dignity; it has rather the reverse effect.[16]

Some insecurity remained, however, even when friers' organizations began to pride themselves on having an influence on civil servants and policy-making. In 1939 an eagerly awaited radio broadcast on the fried fish trade was greeted with mixed feelings because the use of Lancashire dialect in a dialogue between a frier and his customers was held to compromise the status of the trade – and especially because the piece had ended with sounds of unseemly revelry ('the entry of bibulous revellers recently ejected from the nearest pub') which revived unwanted associations with drink, violence, late hours and low company.[17] There were still large numbers of small shops in slum districts and depressed areas to set against the widespread evidence of improvement. Moreover, the 1930s saw paradoxical trends in the trade: a sustained crisis and agitation over rising fish, potato and other raw-material prices, coupled with a persisting improvement in the standards of most of the shops and the aspirations of many of the friers. These issues will come clearly into focus if we look more closely at specific aspects of how fish and chip businesses operated, before moving on to investigate the attitudes and activities of the trade's organizations and pressure groups in Chapter Six.

The fish and chip trade was above all a domestic craft industry of independent producer-retailers, developing in this way at a time when other manifestations of this pattern of work were generally in terminal decline. As such, fish and chips usually engaged the joint, collaborative labour of husband and wife in a recognizably pre-industrial working relationship: the kind of integration of home and work which Leonore Davidoff and Catherine Hall see as having ended for the substantial bourgeoisie, the town-centre traders and professionals, between the late eighteenth and the mid-nineteenth century.[18] Lower down the scale, it persisted through the nineteenth century and beyond, in other trades as well as fish and chips, especially among the 'working' as opposed to the 'professional' shopkeepers.

In many cases, domestic relations in the business were complicated by the husband having paid employment outside the home, in the manner of Robert Roberts' father, a skilled engineer who liked to call himself a 'master grocer'.[19] But in the overwhelming majority of fish frying households, participation in the business was a shared responsibility, although the actual division of labour varied according to the size of the business (and whether paid labour could be bought in), the age and number of children and the values and expectations of both partners.

Shops like the one in which Olive Malvery worked, big enterprises employing several people and presided over by widows or other independent women, were undoubtedly rare; but it was rather more common for women to shoulder most of the responsibilities of the business while their husbands did other things. In Francie Nichol's case this kind of relationship became parasitic. Her husband bought the fish from the quay in the morning, 'but he would walk around with a bottle of rum while he bargained' – and took the horse into the bar with him. Then the serious drinking began and continued through the day:

> I would be servin' in the shop and you could hear the click-clickin' and the pop-poppin' as the [bottle] tops kept comin' off, with him swearin' at them all the while. It wasn't good for business, you know. People could hear full well and you could see them lookin' and wonderin' what was goin' on. And this sort of thing went on year in and year out, me doin' the workin' and worryin' and him doin' the drinkin'.[20]

More common was the situation denounced by the secretary of the Bolton fish friers in 1919:

> There are a great number of fried-fish shops controlled by women while their husbands are on other employment earning a decent wage, some as spinners, *etc.* These are the whole-time friers' most serious competitors. They are demanding six hours per day with an increase in wages; their extra spare time they will devote to assisting with their businesses . . . It is high time the N.F.F. pointed out to the trade unions this growing nuisance . . . let the trade unions tell their members that they cannot serve two masters, they must quit one or the other, and by one man having one job it will prevent unemployment to a great extent.[21]

This syndicalist solution was not adopted, although it is interesting that it was suggested. The Bolton secretary's fears proved unfounded but we cannot know what proportion of businesses were organized along these lines, with the husband participating after his return from a day's work. A substantial number of the shops listed in the directories under male names may well have fallen into this category.

The National Federation, on the other hand, sought to present the norm as being a partnership between man and wife, organized in the manner described in Chatchip's reminiscences, with the man doing the buying, the heavy preparatory work and the actual frying and the woman doing the cleaning and most of the serving of customers, along with most of the child care, housework and domestic shopping. This pattern of working echoes pre-industrial practice, as dignified by Mary Prior with the title of 'the Jack Sprat principle of the division of labour': the husband works at his trade, at which the wife assists in a subordinate capacity while doing the domestic work of the household.[22] It is not surprising to find that the trade's spokesmen saw fish frying as a craft and laid great emphasis on a formidable combination of experience, 'knack' and technical expertise as the essential qualities of a successful frier. Thus 'Macte Animo': 'Fish frying is an art. It cannot be learned in a day.'[23] The trade press contained much discussion of the technicalities of working the increasingly complicated machinery, especially in the 1920s and 1930s, adopting a mode of discourse that tended to exclude women from the mysteries of the trade. Fish frying did offer scope for the skilled worker to apply his expertise to the improvement of machinery in his own shop. An article on refrigeration in the *Fish Friers' Review* in 1928 is a classic example of the encouragement of this do-it-yourself mentality: its author remarked on the way in which individual friers accumulated little inventions by trial and error.[24] The trade could thus become hobby as well as work, reinforcing a masculine culture of domestic craftsmanship.

In keeping with these attitudes, spokesmen for the trade were often patronizing in their discussion of women's contributions to family businesses. 'Macte Animo' was happy to write in praise of 'The Woman Behind the Counter' and her essential contribution to the frier's work and household management, but he assumed that 'the frier' was her husband.[25] In 1934 'The Chipper' was more subtle:

> There are certain things about the shop that women notice better than a mere man, and if there are any ideas for new features to be picked up, then the women are the first to notice them and try them out. Perhaps some day the trade will realise that the growth of the frying industry . . . has been largely due to women . . . They have, in most cases, given shops that homely and friendly atmosphere that means so much to the comfort of customers when they are waiting for the fish to be ready.[26]

But this left the real business of buying, selling and frying as the man's job; and like 'Macte Animo', 'The Chipper' was clear that women should have no part in the serious business of the National Federation. Their role was to keep up morale and sustain sociability by organizing whist drives and the like; if they did more than that there might 'be more discord than business at the usual monthly meetings'.

Alternative attitudes emerged in the 1930s. In 1937 a Bradford contributor to the *Fish Friers' Review* praised the competence of the local secretary's wife when she deputized for him because of illness. He also admired the trade knowledge of another local lady:

> It made me think that the day is not far off when Mrs Fish Frier will be on the Executive Council of the N.F.F.F. – and why not?[27]

In practice, no aspect of the trade had ever been beyond the reach of women. When in 1917 the Board of Agriculture and Fisheries' representative at a conscription hearing argued that fish and chips was 'as an occupation a one-man job, but it was too heavy to be done by a woman or old man', he was in error, as Francie Nichol could have told him.[28] The spread of powered machinery for potato washing and preparing reduced the terrors of the heaviest part of the work and there is ample evidence of women frying alongside the men. One illustration comes from a Preston man's memories of his parents' brief, unsuccessful foray into fish frying:

> Mother having done cooking in service thought she would be an expert at chip making and the frying of fish. This is not so as you have to know the 'nack' [sic]. Poor old dad had no idea. He got blamed for everything that went wrong, and plenty did. 'Look at your dad,' mother would say, 'he's putting the fish in the fat the wrong way and it's too hot.' When dad did the fish they always came out like potato crisps, all curled up. He hated it all.[29]

This was a far cry from the image the trade's spokesmen sought to propagate. More positive evidence comes from the results of the fish frying competitions held from time to time during the inter-war years. The first of these, held at the Deep Sea Fishing Exhibition in Islington in 1922, seemed likely at one time to attract more female than male competitors – to the chagrin of Chatchip, who had admitted to the belief, often enunciated to his wife, that women could not fry fish as well as men. In the event, a Catford woman won the bronze medal and three others (with 19 men) won certificates of merit.[30] At Olympia in 1930, with 500 entrants competing at preparing and frying a stone of mixed fish, Mrs Bell from Attercliffe (Sheffield) won the second prize and the 43 winners of prizes or certificates included six women. A second competition a year later saw 16 women winning awards and a year later in Manchester the women also made an impressive showing.[31]

A few intimations of domestic tensions over the running of businesses and the division of the spoils also began to surface. Chatchip tells us of a friend whose wife was defined as an assistant under the Shop Hours Act of 1912 and therefore had to be given a weekly half-holiday, whereupon the husband decided to take one himself; but as Chatchip pointed out, he could have avoided the issue by making her a joint proprietor of the business, which he chose not to do.[32] Significantly, the *Fish Friers' Review* in 1927 contained a long feature on the laws relating to husband and wife, and it may be that Francie Nichol's grudging but complete acceptance that her husband had the right to take over her business was not as common a frame of mind outside South Shields or after 1918.[33] Chatchip's wife was apparently unusual in 1911 in wanting to be paid a money wage for work done in the shop but in 1922 he reported that wives were beginning to rebel against counter work.[34] These are tantalizing glimpses of a kind of domestic conflict that must have been inherent in the nature of fish frying as domestic manufacture, with the enormous calls it might make on the time and energy of wives and mothers who also had conventional domestic responsibilities. The 'double shift' of housework combined with engagement in the labour market was not just a problem for female factory workers: it might apply just as strongly to fish frying and to other family-based retail and domestic manufacturing trades. But under these conditions only strong characters like Mrs Loftas were able to translate their work in the family business into pounds, shillings and pence earned as individuals in their own right.

Not all fish and chip businesses involved the labour of the wife in this way. This was not just a matter of big businesses like Harry Ramsden's or the comfortably-off frier who enquired about his income tax liability in 1933:

> My wife does not assist in my business but is employed part time by a dressmaker and receives £39 per annum . . . The profits of my business were £240.[35]

It might extend to concerns like the shop in Dalton Road, Barrow-in-Furness, which had no gas or hot water upstairs but provided a living for husband, wife and eight children without the wife needing to work in the shop: fish and chips was apparently her husband's sphere, while she did the domestic cooking.[36]

But this was clearly a measure of success, and the ideal was that the fish and chip trade should provide a decent living from the combined labours of husband and wife. Thus the president of the Preston fish friers in 1936:

> In many shops, a man and his wife were employed, and in a number of shops, the business was 'just keeping them'. That was not good enough. If the business employed two people, it should provide two decent wages.[37]

Most people were content with less than this, to the irritation of the friers' spokesmen and leaders. 'Just getting by' was a widespread aspiration: only an ambitious, articulate minority seems to have wanted more than that. And in many cases, 'just getting by' entailed exploiting the labour of children as well as their parents.

From the earliest days of the trade it was generally assumed that fish friers' children would help in the business as best they could. Fish frying was not unusual in this respect, but the enduring importance of young children's work outside the regulated factory and workshop sectors of the economy is still worth emphasis. Mrs Beddoes began work for her father in 1884, when she was nine years old; her 'main job' was 'to clean hundreds of pieces of plaice before she set off for school in the morning'.[38] Two prosperous fish friers of the 1930s, R. Pye of Portsmouth and Henry Youngman of Leeds, were introduced to cleaning fish and potatoes at about the same age around the turn of the century, although it does not seem to have put them off.[39] Mrs Jennings, whose father kept the shop in Shepherds Bush, remembered a real extended family operation:

> I left school at 11 and I used to chop the potatoes and my grandmother used to lift the bucket away as I chopped the potatoes which we served in the shop.[40]

In 1919 Chatchip thought that the employment of young school-age children in the peeling and eyeing of potatoes and other 'backyard work' ought no longer to take place, even when the proprietor's own children were at issue. It was of questionable legality and the necessity for such help, which might reasonably have been claimed before 1914, was no longer there.[41] But some years later he argued that fish friers should train their children to follow in their footsteps:

> Teach them [the business] until they realise that there are as many technicalities connected to . . . the frying trade as there are with the medical profession. And I am not joking.[42]

Teenage children would certainly be expected to lend a hand, like Mr D2P, who helped behind the counter and with the chipping of potatoes in the late 1920s.[43] And the query in 1927 from a frier who wanted to know whether he could put down wages (and a bonus) for his two daughters on his tax form, without paying health and unemployment insurance for them, provides some confirmation for the assumption that fish friers' children continued to be seen as economic assets to the business – although from a later age than at the turn of the century.[44]

More generally, child labour was attractive in a business that involved light, repetitive tasks and errand-running as well as heavier labour. But legislation continually reduced the scope for this. In 1934, for example, the West Riding County Council adopted as a by-law a clause in the Children and Young Persons Act of 1933 that forbade the employment of children under 14 in the kitchen of a fried fish shop.[45] Two years later, when a Gateshead frier was fined £2 for employing a 16-year-old boy after 10 p.m., the prosecuting counsel commented on the 'prevalence' of such offences by fish friers.[46] A particularly interesting and revealing case arose at Sunderland in the same year, when James Fasey was prosecuted for employing three girls under 18 in his shop after 10 p.m. and not keeping a record of the hours they worked. He pleaded ignorance of the law and the police were not unsympathetic. Superintendent Cook said that the girls had not complained: they were 'happy in their work and had plenty of leisure during the day'. The defence counsel argued that the fried fish trade was a special case:

> It was extremely difficult to get girls . . . over 18 to work in these shops, and the Employment Exchange had sent married women . . . It is far more fitting that married women, especially if they have children, should be in their homes after 10 p.m., than young people.

The girls worked for about three hours during the day, then from 7.00 to 11.00 p.m. 'They get a good wage and would rather be there than in domestic service.'[47] This case raises a lot of issues about attitudes to women's and children's employment, especially in north-east England, which cannot be pursued here. What it also reveals is the tip of what must have been a considerable iceberg of adolescent labour in fish and chip shops, which normally remained hidden from official sources.

Fish and chip shops also provided waged employment for adults. The job advertisements in the *Fish Trades Gazette* in the years before the First World

War show that at the highest level there was a national market for skilled fish friers, some of whom could aspire to becoming shop-managers or buying into the business. Youth, respectability and smartness were much in demand and in nearly one-third of the advertisements mention was made of the desirability or necessity of abstention from alcohol. Clearly, some employers realized that fish frying was thirsty work. Levels of payment were hardly ever mentioned, but the plum job (location unspecified) appeared to be this:

> Young man and his wife wanted to manage fried fish shop; must be a good frier, quick, and very clean; house, gas, coal free; wages 30s. per week.[48]

This was a skilled man's wage with impressive-looking perquisites, but it was right at the top of this particular ladder. Jobs as managers were few and hard to come by. A more usual level of payment is indicated by the case of Sam B. Cordwell, a Plaistow frier who sued his employer in a dispute over whether his wages should be £1 or 24s per week: an unskilled labourer's income.[49] But a lot of female labour came much cheaper than this. Olive Malvery, who was being taken on as a general assistant rather than a frier, was offered five shillings per week plus meals, and it is clear from the discussion that in this, as in other shop trades, some assistants lived in on the premises.[50]

After the war the labour market seems to have tightened, although this cannot always have been the case in depressed years and areas. In 1920 we find a shop-owner in Cromer envisaging the possibility of a female manager, and a manageress was employed in Leeds in 1924.[51] In 1922 it was alleged that the low status and relative discomfort of the trade meant that friers had to pay more than other retail traders to attract and keep staff. In 1934 Councillor Derricott regaled the appreciative North Staffordshire friers with the story that he had advertised for a female assistant for his florist's shop and secured 14 applicants, whereas a vacancy in his fish and chip shop brought only one enquiry.[52] In 1939, as the 1934 Shops Act with its restrictions on working hours began to bite, complaints of shortages of female labour were being made from places as far apart as Tyneside and Cardiff. At the NFFF's annual conference, Mr Bright of Newcastle alleged that girls could obtain a medical certificate to say that the trade was unsuitable for them and go back on to unemployment benefit after they had accumulated enough stamps to make this possible. A Cardiff delegate claimed that there were 1,600 girls on the books of the local labour exchange, none of whom were said to be suitable for work in the fish and chip trade.[53] These complaints seem decidedly suspect, especially in the light of the apparent popularity of employment in James Fasey's Sunderland shop; but it does seem that at times, and in places, there were genuine recruitment problems.

Evidence from London suggests that wages were far from princely, however: between 50s and 70s per week in 1939 for cleaners, cutters and friers of fish, who were adult men, and between 25s and 40s per week for the women who cleaned the shops and served at the counter.[54] But most waged employment in fish and chips almost certainly involved female part-timers working evenings only, as in Portsmouth in 1930.[55] And friers tended to prefer to intensify their own labour rather than go to the expense of hiring assistance. 'Utility' exemplified this attitude in 1932 when he calculated that one person could look after

three pans if two were being used for chips, but not if two were being used for
fish: in the latter case using a two-pan range was preferable to hiring an extra
frier.[56] Certainly, only a few friers sought to emulate J. W. Wooler, who
managed to employ two men, their wives and four girls in his Redcar shop
before the First World War.[57] The Manchester friers who gave evidence to the
Sea-Fish Commission in 1935 reckoned that the average shop required the
labour of a man and a 'lady assistant' or 'a girl', though it is not clear where the
wife fitted in.[58]

Under all the circumstances it is not surprising that there is no evidence of
trade-union activity among friers' employees, although there was some speculation about the possibility in 1919–20.[59] It is quite clear that most friers'
assistants were recruited locally, informally and often through direct personal
contacts, as 'Landancee' indicated when giving advice to potential employers in
1931:

> Do not engage helpers who live very near, they may have too many friend customers
> and it is surprising how much these pals get for their money . . . Never set relations
> on if it can possibly be avoided, you will be asking for trouble if you do. When trade
> falls off you do not feel like stopping them, and if you want them to pull a bit extra out
> they think you are turning their blood to water.[60]

Beyond the family basis of the fish and chip trade, it is obvious that there was
a labour market of considerable dimensions for everything from managers to
cleaners. The friers' employees are a shadowy army, but their existence is a
reminder that friers were petty capitalists, just as their pre-industrial forebears
in domestic manufacture were. In this respect, as in many others, there are
plenty of precedents for the ways in which the friers organized their businesses
in broad outline, however peculiar to the trade some of the details may have
been.

The friers' activities were, however, increasingly regulated by national and
local government: one of the key aspects of this, which affected employment
patterns, was the question of opening hours. Friers who depended on their
business for a living opened for long periods anyway, partly through fear of
missing out on potential custom and partly through fear of competitors. In
Manchester in 1935 many shops were still opening for five dinner-times, six
tea-times and six supper-times per week, a total of 43 cooking hours per week
on top of at least 30 hours' preparation time.[61] Preston's friers were outdoing
them in 1937 by opening for 48–50 hours spread over 17 sessions, although the
chair of the local friers' association thought this to be unusual as well as
undesirable.[62] Within this framework of sustained pressure to open for long
hours, two issues aroused particular controversy. These were the law on closing
time and the rights and wrongs of Sunday opening.

In the formative years of the trade it was generally believed that if a frier had
no refreshment licence 'he could serve for both inside or outside consumption
until 10 p.m., and after 10 p.m. he could go on indefinitely serving for outside
consumption only'. With a refreshment licence a frier could 'keep open for all
purposes until the public-houses of the locality close, but . . . must then shut
up'.[63] So most friers did not take out a refreshment licence: most of their trade
was for outside consumption and a lot of it came from drinkers after closing

time, with a leavening of night workers, such as dockers and miners, coming off the late shift. But in the years before the First World War this system came under pressure. The police in some parts of England began to prosecute, or to threaten prosecution, when a customer in a shop without a refreshment licence was seen to eat a single chip while still on the premises after 10 p.m. In 1912 the Appeal Court endorsed this view of the law and friers in South Wales (in particular) began to feel uneasy about staying open late.[64] In Scotland, meanwhile, a full-scale crusade was being launched against the late opening of fish restaurants and ice-cream parlours. The campaigners were 'joint committees representative of the churches, religious, philanthropic and temperance bodies in the city'. They were worried about young people of both sexes staying out late in each other's company beyond the reach of parental supervision and they were also upset about Sunday opening (which included staying open after midnight on Saturday). A conflict of several years' standing came to a head in 1913, when the Scottish county councils introduced by-laws requiring fish restaurants to close at 10.30 p.m., while the party of restriction on Glasgow Corporation went for 10 p.m., with an extension to 11.00 p.m. on Saturdays. The Glasgow fish restaurateurs fought the restrictions head-on before the Sheriff and got the weekday 10.00 p.m. closure changed to 10.45 p.m., with the proposed imposition of Sunday closing replaced by approved opening hours of 10.00 a.m. to 8.00 p.m. Elsewhere – at Uddingston and Dundee, for example – restaurants opened separate take-away outlets for after-hours sales. This seems to have been perfectly legal, with the result that in Dundee it became:

> quite common to see young men and women in the central thoroughfares of the city walking along with parcels of chips in their hands and a bottle of lemonade stuck in their pocket.

This was not exactly what the reformers had envisaged but they had nevertheless succeeded in restricting the scope of Scotland's night-life, imposing shorter working hours on unwilling fish friers in the process.[65]

There seems to have been no similarly overt public morals campaign against English fish and chip shops, and the Italian influence in Scotland may have made the trade seem particularly suspect there. But before the war the uncertain state of the law and its interpretation led growing numbers of friers to take out refreshment licences, and 11.00 p.m. closing became much more common. Wartime restrictions brought earlier closing still: a standard time of 10.30 p.m. was imposed in 1918. Experience of earlier closing, which had hitherto been thought impracticable, brought widespread support for the practice. Bolton's friers resolved unanimously in 1919 to keep the 10.30 closing time even after the order imposing it had been rescinded. Chatchip put forward the arguments in favour:

> the same amount of business . . . has been done. Customers realise that if they do not want to go to bed supperless they must procure their suppers within the prescribed hours . . . The saving of fat and fuel . . . is very considerable, and more than compensates for . . . the inability to cater for the stragglers . . . The concentration of the frying hours has allowed more time for relaxation and recreation . . . where assistants are employed the business has been more attractive. Consequently there

has not been the same inclination to abandon the trade for other spheres . . . no real hardship can accrue to any individual frier, as his competitors would all be on the same level.

This point of view generally seems to have carried the day. Some towns continued to make special arrangements to allow some friers to open late, especially on Saturdays; but the First World War effectively killed the 'open all hours' mentality that had prevailed hitherto; it made friers realize they need not be the slaves of their customers in this respect and that the law could actually be useful in imposing shorter hours and restraining competition. As Chatchip put it, '. . . a concentrated trade of four or four and a half hours each evening is better than a spasmodic trade extended over six or seven hours'.[66]

Attitudes to Sunday closing took longer to resolve, and it was still a live issue at the start of the Second World War. An early friers' association had tried to get rid of Sunday opening in Blackburn in 1905, but a prosecution had foundered because a fried fish shop serving hot food for the consumption of the poor was held to be exempt from the Lord's Day Observance Act. This ruling haunted the trade thereafter.[67] Local initiatives for the introduction of municipal by-laws seem not to have come to much and it was not until 1930 that any semblance of a national campaign began.[68] As articulated by 'Macte Animo' in the *Fish Friers' Review*, the opposition to Sunday opening had (as before) nothing to do with religious scruples and everything to do with working hours and restraint on competition. Outside seaside resorts in the season, there was no need for Sunday opening: it merely transferred customers who came two, three or four times a week from other days, increasing overheads and working hours to no purpose.[69] A sustained agitation by the NFFF followed and in 1937 the Sunday opening of fish and chip shops was formally prohibited, except in resorts during the summer months. The organized sector of the trade was well pleased: 'Sunday trading was a growing evil, not because the majority of Friers who opened on a Sunday desired to do so, but more frequently because they felt bound to do so' for fear of competition. The law turned out to be far from watertight and persistent evasions were reported; but it removed the spectre of a seven-day week from most friers and their families. To one Dewsbury frier, things were bad enough anyway: he complained of 'slaving six days a week with only a typical "BBC Sunday" left for family enjoyment'.[70]

The friers may have worked long hours – and they may well have used labour-saving technology to open for longer periods rather than or as well as to give themselves more free time – but the work itself was varied and required a wide range of skills and attributes to be done well and successfully. In the first place, they had to decide on what kind and quality of raw materials to buy and how to go about it. With regard to fish, the range of possibilities was limited by customer preference and conservatism, with particular places developing and sustaining strong preferences for particular species. The origins of these local traditions are obscure but they were well-established in the early twentieth century in some provincial towns. In Bury, for example, sprag was preferred, but nearby Heywood also had a taste for plaice and Radcliffe showed a strong preference for hake. Hake was also coming to the fore in Manchester and

Ashton-under-Lyne, but in Birmingham and Walsall it was merely tolerated as a cheaper substitute when plaice was expensive. Haddock was first choice over much of the industrial West Riding but in Nottingham nobody would touch it, however cheap the price. Only in London and parts of the south did the range of acceptable species go beyond two or three local staples. Weymouth's friers were able to offer a varied menu and Londoners were particularly catholic in their tastes, with a widespread preference for skate that was rare in the north and midlands.[71]

Thirty years on, a government retail fish survey found that local and regional variations were still enormous, although some of the details had changed. In London the market was fairly evenly divided between skate, rock salmon, cod, haddock and plaice, whereas in Glasgow haddock was overwhelmingly predominant and hake was hardly less so in Manchester. Cod and haddock dominated in north-east England but hake led the field in Birmingham and Cardiff, where a local speciality called an 'elongater' was also much in demand. It was said to be 'something between a ling and a conger' but was so obscure that, as a civil servant gleefully remarked, 'The Fisheries Division could not tell us how to spell it'.[72] These variations certainly owed something to patterns of supply: most of the hake came through the West Coast ports of Fleetwood and Milford Haven, which were important suppliers to parts of Lancashire and the West Midlands, as well as South Wales, whereas Glasgow's suppliers specialized in small haddocks; cod and haddock were very much North Sea fish. Billingsgate generally provided a bit of everything for friers who were not afraid to shop around.[73]

Where preferences were firmly established, friers found it difficult to trade down to cheaper kinds of fish when the local speciality was expensive or in short supply. The friers' tolerance of the conservatism of their customers was a source of frequent complaint in fishing industry circles in the 1930s, for it made life difficult for trawler-owners and merchants who found the flexibility of the market reduced in costly and irritating ways. In 1939 Professor Alexander Gray of Edinburgh, writing in jocular vein to a colleague on the White Fish Commission, blamed both the friers and their customers. He concluded: 'We ought to have a choice of dogs, cats, monks, skate – perhaps even the edible parts of the shit.'[74]

Nothing so exciting came to pass, nor did well-established regional differences in the ratio between fish and chips change markedly over the period. In 1911 Chatchip reckoned that:

> In most places in the North the frier would at least sell a pennyworth of potatoes to every pennyworth of fish . . . Now in London and many places in the South the average is about 'four o' fish' and 'one o' potatoes'.[75]

This follows logically from the notion that chips originated in Lancashire and fried fish in London. It is also further complicated by evidence that the ratio of chips to fish sold was higher in the Potteries than in Lancashire at about this time.[76] Similar contrasts were still visible in the 1930s. In 1932 the high price of potatoes was hitting friers in Glasgow and Lancashire particularly hard, because their business economies depended far more on chip than on fish sales. One informed commentator in 1939 reckoned that the ratio of fish to potatoes in (unspecified) northern areas would be 1:5, in sharp contrast to the situation in London.[77] This helps to explain how the Retail Fish Survey used by the Sea-Fish Commission in 1935 came up with such enormous differences in the amount of fish used by an 'average' fish and chip shop in different parts of the country. The yearly mean for the shops studied was 3,843 stone in London, shading through 1,970 on the north-east coast (where some of the shops in the survey were going up-market) and 1,412 in Glasgow, to 1,033 in Cardiff, 938 in Birmingham and a mere 555 in Manchester, where not only did chips predominate but pies and other alternatives to fish were also particularly in evidence.[78] It would certainly be dangerous to read too much into this evidence in isolation.

Fish certainly remained an important item in the Manchester frier's budget and here as elsewhere there were changes alongside the continuities in the twentieth century. In the Edwardian years, friers gradually shed their reputation for retailing cheap, small fish that had been rejected by the fishmongers. This stereotype was very much alive in 1900, when committee members and witnesses before the Select Committee on the Sea Fisheries Bill were in firm agreement that such fish was a friers' preserve everywhere from London to Dundee. A Broughty Ferry fish merchant was at pains to associate them with 'the Italian chaps that come across to our country, the fried fish shops – the smaller they get them the better'.[79] The smaller, cheaper kinds of fish continued to predominate, but as it gained in respectability the frying trade in general lost its early identification with immature fish: the kind that might be only four inches long and seem to be all bones and batter. In 1909 the *Fish Trades Gazette* explained to its readers that the word 'chat', used to describe small haddock and hake, had been 'invented and adopted by the trade' in response to the 'good market' that had emerged among the friers. This in itself conferred a measure of legitimacy. By 1927 the National Federation was informing the Food Council that there was 'no truth in the charge that fish friers buy the cheaper kinds of fish for cooking'. Only the 'best live quality fish' were used. This was perhaps protesting too much, but the days were certainly long gone when friers took the ageing, tiny, bony leftovers from the market or rejects from the fishmonger and turned them into very cheap, nasty food for the poor. There was a real improvement in the quality of the fish purveyed from around the turn of the century, and this was an important change.[80]

From time to time attempts were made to widen the range of fish types on sale. This was a matter of introducing less popular or attractive species rather than lowering fish quality as such and it tended to be a response to problems of supply or price. In 1905, under such conditions, there was a campaign to develop dogfish as a friers' fish; J. Lawrence-Hamilton of Brighton suggested it was already being widely sold and enjoyed under various assumed names. But in most places it had to remain incognito. In 1935 Henry Youngman of the NFFF, secure under a cloak of secrecy, told the Sea-Fish Commission that it was widely sold when prices were high but 'you do not tell your customer you are serving dogfish'.[81] The outbreak of the First World War forced friers to take whatever they could get: first ling, then catfish, sold under the euphemism 'Scotch hake'. As the crisis continued, coalfish became a staple, although it was disliked for its dark colour as well as its name (the actual flavour and texture were widely agreed to be excellent). At the end of 1917 there was even talk of frying sprats.[82] These expedients were tolerated during wartime but the return to normality after the Armistice involved a return to the preferred, and by this time traditional, fish species. When rising fish prices and low customer incomes forced north-eastern friers to abandon haddock in the early 1930s, there was fierce consumer resistance. Mr Barret told the Sea-Fish Commission in 1935:

> Two years ago if you had asked me to cook slices of black jack [coalfish] I would have cursed you. Today I cannot afford to buy anything else. My customers do not like it, but I have to tell them that I cannot afford to buy anything else, and they have to have that or nothing.[83]

There is an air of wounded pride about this testimony, and it conveys the attachment to traditional species and ways of doing things that had grown up among the friers and their customers and that only the strongest economic pressures were capable of changing.

This conservatism did not extend to ways of preparing and presenting fish. The NFFF forcibly told the Food Council in 1927 that most fish, with 'very rare exceptions', went to the friers headed and gutted and that fillets prepared and dressed ready for cutting into frying portions were 'largely in vogue' and 'increasingly popular'.[84] This development had arisen mainly, but not entirely, since the First World War. Filleted fish was becoming available from Aberdeen by 1905; in Manchester from about the same time friers were able to get their fish boned, headed and gutted at a small charge by specialist workers at the wholesale fish market.[85] In 1919 Chatchip announced a new enterprise at Hull for 'heading, boning and cleaning of all kinds of round fish for fish friers', to be packed for direct dispatch to the user; this was the prelude to a rapid expansion in the sale of fish ready-filleted at the coast. But there was widespread suspicion of this innovation: many friers wanted to know what kind of fish they were getting and expected the ready-made fillets to come from the coarser and less tasty kinds of Iceland-caught fish.[86] So when supplies were good, English friers continued to buy traditional fish, often doing their own filleting; and in Scotland, especially, small, fresh haddock remained popular despite the inconvenience of dealing with it, because it was generally agreed to have a much better flavour.[87] As 'Sand Dab' remarked in 1928, filleting was in itself an unalloyed boon to consumers:

> Our customers in the old days . . . must have approached their fish and chip supper in the same manner that one would expect a fox terrier to approach a hedgehog.[88]

But although ready-made fillets made considerable headway in the inter-war years, they did not sweep the board and many friers continued to prefer to prepare their own fish, except during periods of acute supply problems when the reliability of ready-filleted fish tilted the balance in its favour.

In principle, filleting was a useful development for the trade. It made its products more palatable and made it easier to go up-market. But friers continued to be cautious about the nature and quality of their supplies, even if it involved them in extra work. Basically, the frier's job was to provide good fish of approved species at an affordable price for a clientele which knew what it liked and was capable of discriminating between different kinds and qualities of fish. London friers were already being told in 1904 that their customers could tell the difference between fish bought at Billingsgate and fish consigned directly from the coast.[89] And in 1935 Manchester customers were said to be well aware that cod was substituted when hake was too expensive.[90] So one pre-requisite of being a successful frier was the careful buying of acceptable fish for a relatively discerning and potentially critical clientele.

There were three basic ways of buying fish. A frier could attend the local wholesale fish market if there was one, send a weekly order to a merchant at the nearest market or at the coast, or buy daily by telegram from a merchant.[91] The first method gave reassurance about quality, although in 1908 the Manchester Fish Friers' Association complained that 'a good deal of stuff which is unfit for human food is frequently offered for sale, and occasionally palmed off on unsuspecting dealers'.[92] Small friers might suffer from the machinations of middlemen in the local markets, who broke up the big consignments and, it was alleged, made fat profits by re-selling to friers in smaller lots. There were complaints about this from Birmingham in 1935; in Glasgow the Italian fish friers did not bid for the large consignments but waited for others with more capital to make two or three boxes available to them.[93] Even without these difficulties, a daily market visit was time-consuming and involved a very early start. A weekly order was the more usual method, but the frier did not know the cost until the fish arrived and it was easy to over-order if there was a sudden dip in trade. H. T. Reeves urged friers to specify an alternative to their preferred fish if ordering by this method, because otherwise a shortfall in the catch of that particular species might lead to very high prices while an acceptable substitute might be much cheaper. He also warned against simply taking the cheapest offer. The *Fish Trades Gazette*'s advice to examine fish packages carefully from top to bottom on arrival illustrates the need friers had to build up a good relationship with a trusted supplier, but this had to be set against the need to keep a close eye on price as well as quality from week to week.[94] Friers were terribly vulnerable to wide fluctuations in fish prices and availability and their costs could be heavily inflated in bad weather, especially in the winter months. A closer eye on the situation could be maintained through a daily order by telegram but this was only worthwhile for the larger frier: Reeves was clear that 'it will not prove of much benefit to the small man'.[95]

The ordering of fish was thus a stressful, risky business and from an early stage some friers began to combine in making joint purchases, with a view to sharing risks and making economies of scale. In 1908 the Bradford and District Fish Friers' Union started a cooperative buying scheme for its 110 members; the idea was adopted in several other industrial towns at about this time. The South Wales friers found that they encountered fierce opposition from the merchants when they set up a direct buying company, but by August 1913 they had kept their own buyer at Milford Haven for 16 months.[96] In 1919 a short-lived National Fish Friers' Co-operative Supply Association was set up, but it only lasted until 1921, and the successful organizations were local in their scope.[97] Most friers, however, continued to buy independently, building up experience and coping with fluctuating markets as best they could.

Some friers' cooperative purchasing associations also bought in other basic raw materials, especially potatoes, oils and fats. Potatoes needed to be ordered less often and their prices fluctuated less disturbingly, but some expertise was required here, too. Some kinds of potato were more suited to fish frying than others. So friers bought carelessly at their peril: apart from the need to check for slugs, wireworms and assorted diseases, they were liable to increase their costs if they bought varieties that did not fry well – and they also risked antagonizing their customers. Chatchip expressed the key concerns with characteristic directness:

> In selecting potatoes, therefore, the frier must remember that he requires a potato which will have the least possible amount of waste, be economical in its absorption of fat during the process of cooking, and, when cooked, be both palatable and digestive.[98]

In pursuit of these goals, friers needed to be aware of suitable potato varieties at the different seasons. King Edwards became the frying trade's favourite in the early twentieth century and held their position into the 1930s. H. T. Reeves recommended them in 1933 ('When made into chips, it turns out a "toasty" hue and wonderfully crisp'), but newer varieties then made headway and by 1940 Majestics seem to have held sway.[99] Soil type also mattered: potatoes grown on warp or silt land were a clear favourite for the trade, while sandy soils were not favoured. In 1911 Chatchip recommended buying from produce merchants or commission agents, as 'most farmers are queer men to deal with, and invariably want more money on the ground than you can buy for at the depot'. But a lot of friers continued to make their own arrangements with local growers and in 1942 a civil servant remarked that under wartime conditions friers had been prevented from 'obtaining the cheap supplies which they had been able to get pre-war by private arrangement with the growers'.[100]

Potatoes mattered particularly to friers in northern England and Scotland, where portions were large in relation to fish portions and most of the profit usually came from chips rather than fish. 'Rambler' in 1913 was one of several northern commentators to assume that profits came from potatoes. In 1935 Mr Mills of the Manchester friers admitted that he subsidized his fish trade from the profits on other items:

> I can sell fish at a loss every day this week, but I shall be in pocket at the end of the week because I am only supplying fish to keep my customers to buy the other things, potatoes, peas and beans.

This was a common way of doing business throughout the period.[101]

Important though potatoes were, we must not assume that all, or even most, friers were aware of the full range of issues and complexities ventilated in the trade press. Mass-Observation in Bolton in the late 1930s consulted a local frier, known as Harry, about the niceties of the trade, but all he was prepared to tell them was:

> there is two kinds of potatoe [sic] – long and round. They got more [chips] out of the round than the long – also round ones were always heavier – and the long ones were more likely to be rotten in the middle.[102]

We cannot know to what extent Harry was teasing his earnest questioner but it is interesting – and entertaining – that his professed opinion was completely at variance with that of an expert from the Ministry of Agriculture and Fisheries, who argued in 1926 that since the trade needed chips of even length, between two and two-and-a-half inches long, the ideal potato was flat, elongated and of medium size because round ones gave too many small chips.[103] This is a telling reminder that it is dangerous to base accounts of the working of a trade with endless local variations too uncritically on the views of officials and trade journalists, although their versions of events must necessarily form the basis of any attempt to generalize.

The other staples of the frying trade posed fewer problems in the purchasing. The choice of frying medium was largely dictated by local preferences and practices. Before the First World War the range of choice included cotton-seed oil, nut oil, dripping, compound lard (a mixture of cotton-seed oil and beef stearine) and pure lard. Soya-bean oil became more widely available in the inter-war years and all the frying media became increasingly purified and refined to minimize cooking smells.[104] But, as Reeves pointed out: 'It would be folly to begin frying in oil in a district where for years the public had been used to . . . dripping'.[105] These preferences, as with the attachment to particular kinds of fish, were well-established in the early twentieth century, with dripping predominating overwhelmingly in the West Riding of Yorkshire, cotton-seed oil in most of Lancashire, lard in the Burnley area and vegetable oils in most of London.[106] All the conscientious frier could really do was search for the best possible supplier and take care with the storage of materials which, if neglected, could all too easily become rancid or mouldy.

Once the raw materials had been acquired, they had to be prepared for frying. Chatchip, writing in 1911, was eloquent about what this involved:

> It is really wonderful what a lot of people there are who envy the frier; they seem to think he has all the day for rest and recreation, and only works in the evenings and dinner-times at the week-end. How in the world they imagine the materials are got ready for the shop passes my comprehension . . . If . . . some of these people had just one full week at the business they would find out that the preparation of the trade materials was a bigger job than the frying . . . So if any reader has selected the fried-fish trade with the idea of having an easy time of it, he can at once disabuse himself of that idea, and . . . be prepared for plenty of work – much of it dirty, tedious and monotonous.[107]

Chatchip began with instructions on heading, boning and cutting up different sorts of fish, pointing out useful details such as the need to cut flat fish 'clear to the belly . . . as the belly part . . . is very nasty through the invariable breakage of the gall'. This was generally messy and unpleasant work and it is easy to see why the advent of fillets at affordable prices was widely welcomed by friers as well as their customers. The cutting of fish into portions of the right size to fry at a profit without leading to complaints about short measure was, and remained, an art in itself. Certain kinds of fish, such as roker, required specialist expertise in skinning and cutting. Skate was so costly to prepare that by the early 1930s it was difficult to make a profit on it, although Southampton friers complained that customers who asked for it would take no substitute.[108]

Fish preparation began to attract the concentrated attention of Medical Officers and Sanitary Inspectors in the early twentieth century and it was here above all that impervious surfaces and meticulous cleanliness came to be required. The trade was gradually pushed away from conditions such as those reported in Gorton (Manchester) in 1908, when the Sanitary Inspector complained that: 'The fish is cleaned sometimes in dark and filthy little sculleries, or in the yard in the open or under small sheds.'[109]

The advent of refrigeration was part of a general improvement in hygiene and working conditions. In 1910 friers were being alerted to the virtues of the cold store ('the fish does not deteriorate, though it goes a bad colour') and of mechanical refrigeration – although three years later it was assumed that 'only the wealthy fish frier' would have a refrigerator.[110] Ten years later, the best that could be assumed was that most up-to-date friers would have an ice-box and only in 1928 did an extended – and highly technical – series of articles on refrigeration appear in the *Fish Friers' Review*. Only in 1933, with the advent of the Electrolux soundless electric refrigerator, did real enthusiasm begin to emerge.[111] Friers' suspicions of frozen fish may have coloured their attitudes to refrigeration. They were most unwilling to come to terms with Canadian frozen fish even when the supply crisis of 1917 was at its worst. Suspicions were still having to be dispelled in 1933, when assurances were made that freezing did not discolour fish or affect the flavour.[112] H. T. Reeves regarded some kind of cooling system as essential but he warned his readers that some machines were not only expensive to install, but also to maintain. He provided instructions for making a cheap do-it-yourself ice-box for the small frier. Only in the early 1930s, it seems, was fully-fledged automatic refrigeration technology really becoming an attractive proposition and then only in the upper levels of the trade. But the spread of the ice-box should not be underestimated in its power to reassure friers, reduce waste and provide a better service to customers.[113]

Changes in the washing and peeling of the potatoes made an early and positive impact on the preparation processes. Potato washing had originally been the most physically demanding of the frier's tasks, as it involved 'tipping them by the bagful [then 126 lb.] into a big tub full of water, and then whirling them round and round with a big yard-broom'.[114] A primitive, commercially designed potato washer and peeler was available in the late nineteenth century, but its use required up to 20 minutes of fierce manual effort to rotate 30 pounds of potatoes and the appropriate amount of water until the process was complete. The *Fish Trades Gazette* was still being sceptical about the value of such machines in 1904, although this soon gave way to enthusiastic endorsement.[115] A spate of innovations followed and by 1910 several rival washing, peeling and chipping machines were on the market, powered by electricity as well as by gas. By 1927 it could be assumed that 'every modern Fish Frier' used a power-driven peeling machine.[116]

But the reality was more complicated. Friers in London and the south, using a smaller volume of potatoes, were much less eager to take up these innovations than their northern counterparts. In 1913 Chatchip remarked that such friers remained unwilling to peel potatoes for chips: it made waste and extra work. A range-maker apparently claimed to sell a dozen peeling machines in the north for every one in London and the south. 'Observant', a southern frier, made the same point in 1914 and urged his colleagues to mend their ways, pointing out that the many mechanically-minded friers could easily and cheaply adapt an old motor-bike engine to power a peeler. These blandishments had limited effect. In 1932 Chatchip was still complaining that some southern friers merely 'tub 'em [potatoes] and swirl 'em with a yard brush': it kept costs low in poor London districts where large penny portions were the rule and customers had learned to like potato skins. Few friers in these areas eyed their potatoes, either: this was an activity that Chatchip had wrily recommended as 'a pleasant pastime for your leisure hours', and it was often imposed on children.[117] These differences remind us that 'best practice' differed in differing settings and that the successful frier needed to be aware of the expectations of his or her customers as well as listening to advice from the trade press and its advertisers.

Some friers went in for additional refinements or expedients. Fish-cakes were widely sold – they were a useful way of selling odd bits of fish – and in 1930 a firm was offering pan-ready fish-cake mixture. In 1932 Chatchip, in frivolous mood, urged friers to pursue variety by introducing imaginative moulds for unusually shaped fish-cakes, or going in for corrugated chips instead of boring old straight square ones. This was perhaps an idea whose time had not yet come. More in tune with current preoccupations was a tip that bits of fish trimmings should never be thrown away when they could be turned into 'fish bits for pussies' and sold for a penny a time.[118]

All this was merely tinkering on the fringes. What counted most, perhaps, in the making of a frier's reputation was the frying process itself. In the first place, the batter in which the fish was almost always coated was of the utmost importance. As the advertisers of batter mixes came to realize, batter flavour and texture became crucial issues when customers compared and evaluated shops. As a *Fish Friers' Review* commentator suggested: 'The making of batter is not the haphazard business some people imagine it to be':

> almost every frier has a pet method, the result of experience and experiment, in fact I may term it a secret process, to be jealously guarded and kept in the family.[119]

Hazards included over-fermentation, which resulted in an unpleasant dark, glazed, tough batter guaranteed to drive customers elsewhere. The ideal batter was said to be 'the thickness of real good cream' but there were regional and local variations in taste. Worcester in 1905, for example, was said to favour a thick, highly-coloured batter: various colouring agents were on offer by this time. A thick coating of batter was a useful way of disguising small fish portions and it could cover up a multitude of sins. Best practice, as recommended in the trade journals, was nevertheless very demanding. Chatchip remembered that in the early years of the trade, batter-making was a really arduous process:

> one had to batter and handle some 300 pieces to the £1, all with the aid of very crude tools . . . My own tools at that time consisted of a large earthenware bowl and a large wooden spoon.

But batter-mixing machines and powdered eggs were already coming to the rescue before the First World War and there was a spate of further innovations in the 1930s, including patent batter mixes. The importance of all this is perhaps best illustrated by Harry Ramsden's obsessive concern to get his batter right:

> [the] ingredients were measured with an excruciating care, even down to a specially-made measure for adding precisely the right amount of water to the 3lb. and 6lb. bags of batter-mix. The scales were checked every day and if any measure of any ingredient was 'out' by as much as one grain, great was the wrath of Ramsden senior.[120]

Harry Ramsden was also a keen researcher in pursuit of the ideal vinegar; again, this was no mere obsession with detail.[121] Vinegar was not sold in fish and chip shops: it was made available to customers for them to season their purchases. Because it was free, perhaps, it was often used extravagantly, along with the salt that was also provided. Some friers responded by providing the cheapest kind of vinegar, heavily diluted. A standard recipe for friers' vinegar in the early twentieth century involved mixing one gallon of acetic acid with eight gallons of water and adding 'a few drops of browning' to colour. Chatchip thought this to be unsuitable for a 'good-class trade' and advocated two parts of good malt vinegar to one of water for the discerning customer. But acetic acid kept its devotees and in 1932 they were advised to use brown vinegar bottles, especially where 'the kiddies are fairly heavy on the bottle', to disguise dilution and avoid adverse comment. Only in the late 1930s was there a sustained move towards malt vinegar and later spirit vinegar, partly on patriotic grounds: the vinegar brewers were British and almost all the acetic acid was imported. Harry Ramsden and Chatchip were undoubtedly correct in assuming that vinegar quality would affect popular perceptions of shops; but most friers preferred to economise because their profits were vulnerable to widespread abuse of the free provision of this essential adjunct to their product.[122]

Effective frying was more than just a matter of choosing a range, installing it and setting off with confidence. New friers needed to be taught to manage their ranges, whether by the vendor of the business, a friend in the trade or a representative from the range-maker. Friers had to work out how much to fry to meet demand at different times of day and to gauge how hot the frying medium should be for best results. As ranges became technologically more sophisticated in the inter-war years, some problems became less pressing. Fish and chips could be kept hot until the next influx of customers and temperature gauges removed any element of guesswork about heating levels. This made for a bewildering range of choice in range design and presentation. The problem of which fuel would be most economical and best suited to a particular style of trade remained vexing. From the late 1920s onwards the *Fish Friers' Review* began to report elaborate calculations on such issues as the thermal efficiency of different makes of range; the relative merits of gas, electricity and small coal or coke furnaces were discussed in similar mathematical terms. How far all this appealed beyond a trade élite is debatable and it is significant that range-makers laid emphasis on the attractive, up-to-date appearance of their ranges alongside their technical attributes.

Chatchip at least was more concerned to stress the virtues that came with experience. He urged friers to listen to their pans and to cultivate the 'frying sense' that was worth much more than scientific instruments. The most important thing of all was to know which way up a fish should be fried. Chatchip insisted that boneless pieces of round fish should go into the pan with the side from which the skin had been cut facing downwards, while flat fish went in with the dark side downwards. He did not know why this was so, but offered it as a lesson of experience. It would be more convincing in principle if Harry Ramsden's son did not remember his father saying the exact opposite about the round fish. But the outcome of incompetent frying – the fish curling up in the heated fat – was common enough to have its own distinctive word within the trade: it was known as 'snirping'.

Although the trade's doctors differed on some aspects of best practice, there is no doubt that the actual frying of the fish was a skilled job, if it was to be well done, and one in which experience continued to count for as much as theory and technology. A belief that this was so was central to the self-respect of the many friers who had been apprenticed as craftsmen in their earlier lives; but an awareness of this potentially distorting influence on the sources need not lead us to conclude that they were wrong.[123]

Perhaps the aspect of fish frying that attracted the most obsessively detailed contemporary commentary was the ventilation of shops and ranges. The smell associated with fish frying from its earliest days, especially when low-grade cotton-seed oil was being used, had been the greatest single influence in stigmatizing the trade. Prosecutions for nuisance were regularly reported in the trade press in the early twentieth century and the smell nuisance was one of the main reasons why fish and chips was labelled as an offensive trade after the Public Health Act of 1907. It was not just a matter of amenity, although prosecutions were often based on such grounds: thus a boarding-house pro-prietor in Newbury sought an injunction against the fried fish shop next door on the grounds that the smell had driven all her lodgers away. 'In September she had a garden party, and everyone was obliged to go indoors when the fish started frying.'[124] But there was also a fear that the smell would stimulate disease: a carry-over from the Victorian miasmatic theory of disease trans-mission that may help to explain the hostile attitudes of many Medical Officers of Health towards the trade. George Driver, Bradford's inspector of fish and chip shops, still cleaved to this old orthodoxy in 1913:

> He would point out to them (the Fish Friers' Association) that it would be a very serious blow to the fried-fish trade if a death took place which could be traced to typhoid fever contracted through the smells emanating from the cellars of a fish shop.[125]

The fear was the same even though Driver was speaking of a different source of evil smells.

Friers thus came under strong pressure to reduce their emissions of noxious odours. The Edwardian solution, especially in London, was a hood to collect the fumes generated in frying and carry them away to an outlet at an inoffensive height. The London County Council survey of friers' premises in 1906 found this method adopted in a 'very large majority' of the shops; but most of them were defective in various elementary ways, and the LCC issued detailed advice on appropriate hood and flue design. This rather medieval solution was soon challenged. Chatchip described the hoods as 'hiding places for matter of a most revolting kind which is slowly but steadily becoming putrid' and alternatives involving condensing or 'burning' the steam made rapid headway. Experiments were made in London and Bradford before 1906, and Faulkners of Hollinwood seem to have pioneered the commercial adoption of these systems. Belper's Medical Officer of Health spoke for many when in 1913 he praised a new shop in the town which consumed the fumes 'by passing in pipes through the fire' and added:

> it was high time that the old-fashioned, obsolete, obnoxious abominations should cease. The old fried-fish method of cooking had rendered the atmosphere of the streets sickly in the evenings, and this should be swept away.

By 1919 the *Fish Trades Gazette* orthodoxy was that hoods were out of date – they were too cumbersome for effective cleaning – and sliding pan covers were recommended. But the hood was a long time dying and its pros and cons were still being discussed in the trade press 10 years later. For Reeves in 1933, however, there was no problem: modern condensing technology and flue design had disposed of noxious smells and there was no need for an extended discussion of this issue. This was certainly optimistic with regard to the older shops in the back streets; but it illustrates the way in which a major problem of the early twentieth century had retreated to the sidelines by the 1930s, making it much easier for the trade to lay claim to higher status and a 'better class' of customer. Meanwhile, however, friers had had to find out about ventilation and condensing systems as part of the necessary expertise of their trade – on pain of stigmatization and possible prosecution.[126]

A mundane but more enduring concern, which carried symbolic as well as practical significance, was the presentation and specifically the wrapping of the frier's product. In the earliest days this was not a problem: A. Church remembered that in south London 'people either brought their own dishes or carried the fish home on pieces of string deftly passed through the heads of the fish'.[127] But the trade soon acquired a reputation for wrapping its wares in newspaper, which embarrassed its more ambitious members. In 1904 the *Fish Trades Gazette* was already recommending greaseproof paper because it was cheaper than newspaper and avoided the problem of newsprint getting on the food, although advice was still being offered on where to get newspaper for an outer wrapping and how much to pay for it. The local newspaper office could be expected to supply it for 2s per hundredweight, or the frier could advertise locally for good, clean newspaper at up to a penny for 4lb.[128] Subsequently, however, the trade's spokesmen waged an enduring war on newspaper wrapping, with limited success. The alternatives were more expensive, especially as many friers had their own informal ways of getting a newspaper supply: they would reward children with a portion of chips or a cinema ticket, for example. For a long time friers were aware that other food trades also used newspaper. In 1908 the *Lancet* reckoned that it was used in 'about nine out of ten butchers' and fishmongers' shops, except, perhaps, the very "tip-top" establishments' and similar complaints were still being made in 1926.[129] As the trade began to move further up-market in the 1930s, criticism became less obsessive; but the rising cost of wrapping-paper as war approached drove some friers back to earlier practices. In 1937 a Preston frier blamed other pressures for his reversion to

newspaper and in so doing helped to explain the dismay of some of his
colleagues:

> Some time ago . . . I started using brown paper and parchment for wrappings instead
> of newspaper. But now my trade has dwindled through increasing competition, and I
> am faced with a return to newspaper wrapping. And where do the newspapers come
> from? From houses where cats and dogs have been sprawled on the papers all day.[130]

But this convenient and increasingly distinctive practice has never died out.
Some customers actually preferred it, although others insisted on taking their
own bowls or plates for hygienic reasons. A Bolton oral-history interviewee
gave what was probably a representative account of normal practice in the
1930s:

> they would put them in paper, but at that time it was newspaper, they used to collect
> newspapers and put a small square of greaseproof in the middle and put the chips on
> and just wrapped them up and that was it.[131]

Eating out of newspaper, like eating in the street more generally, put forward
a claim to unpretentiously democratic values and a spontaneity and informality
that were widely prized in some kinds of working-class culture.[132] There is
little wonder that the sustained disapproval of the respectable élite within the
trade was unable to eradicate it. But in other respects, and perhaps significantly,
fish friers who cleaved defiantly to newspaper wrapping were more than willing
to improve their image and their premises.

A spate of advice to friers on cleanliness, tidiness and the presentation of
their businesses began in the trade press in 1910, no doubt in response to the
increasing regulation of the trade by local authorities after the 1907 Public
Health Act. In 1911 Chatchip proposed a daunting regime of regular cleaning
on top of all the frier's other duties. The range should be thoroughly wiped
externally at the end of each day's trading and tin and copper and brasswork
brightened with Vim, Panshine or Brilliant-Shino. And:

> once a week the pan-covers and steam-pipes should be disconnected and thoroughly
> washed in a strong solution of hot water, soda and washing powder. At the same time
> the hot plate should be scraped and scoured with steel shavings and pumice-stone
> until every bit of burnt starch is entirely eradicated.[133]

This merely elaborated on the recommendations of the London County
Council's Medical Officer, who also emphasized the need for daily cleansing of
everything in the preparation area; but the details give some indication of the
amount of elbow-grease required to do the job properly. Personal cleanliness
was also enjoined. Chatchip stressed the importance of clean hands and of
being seen to wipe them before serving customers, who apparently remarked on
how unusual this practice was. He also urged that friers would 'present a much
smarter and more up-to-date appearance' if they wore 'a white grocer's jacket

and apron'.[134] This was still being advocated in 1928 in tones that suggested that it was far from universal. It was reinforced again by a piece in the *Fish Friers' Review* that advised on the best kinds of underwear for friers as well as singing the praises of the white coat, which would involve extra washing or laundry bills.[135]

The white coat might encounter passive resistance but the general standard of cleanliness in the trade undoubtedly improved, although more as a result of sustained pressure from sanitary authorities than through the good offices of trade journalists. By the late 1930s the *Fish Friers' Review* was able to report enthusiastic endorsements of hygiene standards from inspectors in Leeds, Castleford and Coventry in successive months, while the Retail Fish Survey in 1935 gave special mention to the 'spotlessly clean' frying equipment in Glasgow's shops and to the clean, bright shops of Cardiff and the Rhondda Valley, with Italian-run shops singled out.[136] Not that a state of universal perfection had been achieved: Henry Youngman of Leeds admitted to the Sea-Fish Commission in 1936 that people who avoided fish and chip shops were not inevitably snobs, because there were still too many shops that were not fit to enter.[137] But the changing tone of attitudes and comment is highly revealing, especially in a climate of rising expectations about these matters.

Friers were also enjoined to go beyond mere cleanliness and make their premises positively attractive. Chatchip in 1913 asked: 'Why on earth should a fried-fish shop be a dark, dismal place, enough to give one a fit of the blues on entry?' He advocated the use of ornamental tiles featuring 'landscape views and pictures of animal life', although he drew the line at mirrors, which attracted dust and grease, and inset clocks, which reminded customers of how long they had been waiting when the shop was full. He also gave a striking description of how he proposed to redecorate his shop:

The whole of the fixtures will be oak-grained and varnished . . . The walls may be painted from floor to ceiling an electric green, or the bottom half a chocolate colour, with the top half a light terra-cotta . . . To relieve the bareness and add to the attractiveness I intend to paste about three pairs of good pictures on the walls. These I shall surround with oak varnished paper to represent frames.

We cannot know how many friers elected to follow this advice or decided to brighten up their premises in other ways, but there is no strong evidence of widespread concern about decoration, colour schemes and the attractive properties of materials until the 1920s.[138]

Chatchip also emphasized the negative impression that could be given by neglect of details. He advised friers not to leave a scruffy bag of coal on the floor next to a clean frying range; not to show customers the back of the waistcoat while frying; and not to use a 'pint whisky bottle with a split cork' to hold vinegar, or a 'penny tin dredger' to hold the salt.[139] This was all part of a developing notion that friers needed to advertise, both to compete with each other and to hold their own against rival contenders for the popular purse, some of which were being heavily promoted by centralized managements. Properly presented, the shop premises could be an advertisement in itself. So Edwardian friers were advised to take pains over attractive window displays and to put up illuminated signs.[140] As early as 1904 they were also being urged to provide wrapping paper and carrier bags featuring pictures of the shop and to lend out plates bearing the shop's name: an idea that foreshadowed Harry Ramsden's ill-fated decision to put his name on the restaurant's cutlery, which soon had to be reversed because of pilfering on a grand scale.[141] Canvassing and putting out leaflets in the neighbourhood were also recommended. These were enduring themes, although the use of coupons, special offers and trading stamps was generally discouraged.[142]

In the inter-war years the organized sector of the trade began to consider more ambitious, coordinated schemes. In 1927 a proposal from Portsmouth for a national promotion of fish and chips, in competition with other heavily advertised foods, was considered by the NFFF but rejected because it would benefit all friers rather than just the members of the trade association.[143] 'Sand Dab' produced a poem for a 'publicity poster' that would have promoted NFFF shops specifically, but it seems (mercifully) not to have been taken up:

If you wish to preserve your Health
And desire to accumulate Wealth,
Purchase your Fried Chips and Fish
The popular and nourishing dish,
From Certificated Federation Friers
Competent, Clean and all Tryers.
Do not risk your Health again,
It is easier to lose than regain;
Seek the sign of all Bona-fide Friers,
The National Federation of Fish Friers.[144]

This McGonagalesque effusion contrasts oddly with the brilliant poster advertising of the Empire Marketing Board and the 'Eat More Fish' campaign organized by the British Trawler Federation during 1929-31, both of which featured fish and chips on the hoardings and made a great deal more impact than anything the NFFF could have organized for itself. As an adjunct to the BTF scheme, friers organized essay and poster painting competitions in local schools, with prizes for the most effective and enthusiastic treatment of fish and chips. At the local level, too, individual friers or local associations used cinema advertising as well as hand-bills and window displays; H.T. Reeves devoted a chapter to advertising and window-dressing in his trade manual in 1933.[145] But it is hard to escape the conclusion that in so far as the trade was boosted by successful, competitive advertising campaigns, especially when these were most important in the 1930s, the key initiatives came from outside the ranks of the friers themselves, although their representatives played their part in prompting the explicit inclusion of fish and chips in campaigns that were much wider in their overall scope.

In a lot of ways, though, the best advertisement for the trade was a widely held knowledge that its prices were accessible and seen to be fair; pricing was one of the most important skills of the successful frier. But it was not a matter of matching the price of a portion of fish or chips to prevailing market conditions. Rather, it involved adjusting the size of portions and perhaps the nature of what was offered to the expectations of customers. At the lower end of the market, especially, prices were fixed by custom and the limited resources of the purchasers. In many areas they were also held down by competition, not only from rival friers but from other kinds of cheap foodstuffs. This left friers with limited room to manoeuvre, but within a restricted framework it offered opportunities for skilled manipulation to obtain the best possible returns without sacrificing goodwill and credibility.

Before the First World War the ruling price of fish and chips was very low indeed. At the turn of the century Mrs Jennings' father sold them at 'halfpenny and a ha'porth' and Olive Malvery found that children in the East End would buy at this price, although working men might have twopence worth of fish and a pennyworth of chips.[146] The usual Edwardian price appears to have been a penny each for fish and chips, or a penny for fish and a halfpenny for chips, although halfpenny fish pieces were still being widely sold in 1913.[147] The First World War drove prices up sharply and they never returned to pre-war levels. Chatchip reckoned that the standard price in the inter-war years was three-pence for fish and twopence for chips; but in practice there were considerable variations according to location, economic conditions and clientele.[148] On the one hand, friers in depressed areas, especially in north-eastern England, were under severe pressure to keep prices as low as possible; and during the late 1930s campaigns against a return to selling penny fish were undertaken by friers' organizations in Preston and Chorley and over much of the West Riding, as well as on Tyneside and Tees-side.[149] On the other hand, wherever friers catered for prosperous groups within the working class and tried to go up-market, a demand existed for portions of fish at anything up to sixpence. In 1935 the Retail Fish Survey found considerable variation in pricing policies in its sample towns, as Table 5.1 shows:[150]

Table 5.1 Prices, portion sizes and fish species in the fish-and-chip trade in four urban areas, 1935

Place	Price	Portion size	Fish species
Cardiff	2d	3.5 oz.	Hake or elongater
	3d	4.5 oz.	Hake or elongater
	4d	5.6 oz.	Hake or elongater
Glasgow	3d	One small fish and chips	
	4d	One large fish and chips	
	5d	One small, one large fish and chips	
	6d	Two large fish and chips	
London	2d	2½ to 3 oz.	Other than skate
	3d	3 to 4 oz.	Skate
North-east coast	2d	5 to 6 oz.	Cod fillet
	2d to 3d	5 to 5½ oz.	Haddock

In London the most popular fish price was threepence, but a big frying firm in south London sold 32 per cent of their pieces at 2d, 38 per cent at 3d, 20 per cent at 4d and 10 per cent at 6d. This last category was said to be growing in importance and associated with a higher class of customer.[151]

So actual price levels were not the simple matter that Chatchip's broad generalization made them seem. But at any given level of price and quality, customers expected prices to remain constant over long periods of time and made plain their disapproval of price increases. Many friers believed they simply could not increase their prices and retain their customers. But the price of raw materials was far from constant. It fluctuated in the short term, according to the weather and the deal the individual frier had struck with his supplier; in the medium term, according to the seasons and the fortunes of the fishing fleets; and in the long term, where there was an inexorable upward trend, especially after 1914, which was monitored by the friers' organizations with deepening anxiety during the 1930s. Thus in 1934 the *Fish Friers' Review* cited Ministry of Labour statistics purporting to demonstrate that fish prices were now 110 per cent above their 1914 levels in towns of more than 50,000 people and 83 per cent up in smaller towns and villages. The figures for potatoes were 96 per cent and 70 per cent. These trends were completely out of line with other food prices: those of butter, cheese and margarine had actually fallen.[152] The complexity of calculating fish price trends would have generated grave scepticism among the friers had the results not confirmed their darkest expectations, but there is no doubt that there were powerful long-term trends pushing fish and chip prices upwards, which included the cost of fuel, oils and fats, premises and technology.

In the face of these daunting trends it seemed almost impossible to raise prices. This frame of mind was well-established among friers before the First World War. In 1907 C.H. Benfield of Leicester complained that:

> we ought to be able to charge for our fish according to the market's price, especially in winter when everything is dear . . . considering that fried fish is the cheapest supper to be had, I am sure that the public could be got to pay the increased price in the winter time if we could get the trade together.[153]

This was a big 'if', and most friers were even less sanguine. Chatchip might comment that the baker raised his selling price when flour became more expensive, so why should the fish frier not do likewise? And he might challenge the popular notion that penny pieces of fish were necessary to keep the price within reach of the poor, arguing that friers could not afford to be philanthropists. But he had to admit that it was difficult to charge $1\frac{1}{2}$d a piece when competitors were charging 1d.[154] The magnitude of the problem in Bradford, a stronghold of the trade, was expressed by the chair of the local association in 1913:

> They had let the public get such a hold over the trade that the people now demanded hake, haddock or whatever fish they desired for their halfpennies, and went elsewhere if they could not get it.[155]

Customers assessed friers' costs – and profit margins – from the cheap price of low-quality leftover fish in the fish market, not understanding the purchasing system or the other costs involved. The fear of raising prices had reached the point where friers preferred to close down, or stop selling fish, when prices became too high to sell for the customary amount.[156]

There was, then, almost a 'moral economy' of fish and chips: customers had entrenched notions of what constituted a fair price and were most unwilling to go beyond it.[157] This was one of many almost pre-industrial aspects of the trade. This frame of mind persisted through the First World War. In late 1914, with prices soaring, 'The public seemed to think that the fish frier should not advance his prices'; while in 1919 the friers' leader, John Lyon, complained that: 'The public cannot or will not understand the cost of cooking. They only know that fish is cheap compared with 1918, and are already expecting pre-war portions and prices.' Customers never allowed friers to forget that they were charging double the pre-war rate and there were frequent accusations of profiteering, none of which seems to have been substantiated.[158]

Resistance to price increases continued in the inter-war years. In 1929 a Coventry frier, bemoaning the rising price of fish, protested that: 'It is imposs- ible to get the money back from the customers.' In 1937, when local friers' associations across the country tried to impose minimum prices and sought to pass cost increases on to customers, there was widespread opposition and complaint. A leading frier in Newcastle upon Tyne reported that many of his customers had refused to pay higher prices and had not returned to the shop. A Leeds frier commented that: 'The general public will not stand for increases in the price of fried fish portions.' The unemployed simply could not afford to pay more. In this general context T. Reeder of Preston argued that friers were too much dictated to by their customers and too much the slaves of rumours of profiteering and sharp practice. They would even top up bowls of chips if customers complained. 'The Frier must be the shopkeeper, and the customer must be kept in his place.' There was no truth in the story that customers had taken to frying their own chips: hardly any of the necessary wire baskets had been bought locally in recent months. But even the indefatigable researches of Reeder could not overcome the pressure to hold prices down in Preston and pennyworths of fish and of chips continued to be sold in spite of the local association's best efforts. This remained true in many areas of low wages and high unemployment until the Second World War.[159]

So rising raw material costs and overheads could not readily be passed on to customers; even seasonal variations in costs had to be averaged out over the year, with profits in summer balancing frequent winter losses while selling prices remained constant. Chatchip summed up to the effect that the trade operated 'a system of standard prices' coupled with 'a system of basic costs ruled by the law of averages'.[160] Mr Clarke told a meeting of civil servants in 1935 that friers:

> try to keep a level price as long as they can, and they do keep a level price, as a matter of fact. They rather vary the size of the piece, if prices are abnormal. They change the size of the piece, but do not change the price.

This was easier to do because neither fish nor chip portions were weighed: complaints might arise when they diverged too much from the standard or expected size, but portion sizes were a matter of custom and consensus rather than precise measurement.[161]

Edwardian friers were already coping with fluctuations in prices by varying portion sizes, covering up wherever possible with a liberal use of batter. One Manchester frier, during a difficult period in 1906, is said to have remarked that 'he had lately sold almost as much batter as fish, and up to the present his customers had made no complaints'.[162] During the worst of the war it was impossible to disguise the decline in portion sizes. A Tyneside frier, during the potato crisis of 1917, remembered before the war giving a pound of chips for a penny and making a profit; now a pennyworth would weigh only one or two ounces and people were unwilling to buy.[163] But in normal times there was more room for manoeuvre. In 1931 friers were advised on serving chips when potatoes were dear:

> Cut about an inch off the end of the chip servers . . . and you will be surprised how much further the chips go.

Chatchip went further, urging friers to keep a range of scoops of different sizes for different potato price levels.[164] Disguising small fish portions was more difficult, but Mr Clarke described how friers learned to divide a stone of fish into as many twopenny and threepenny pieces as possible, concluding, 'It becomes quite an art.' Chatchip, defending a Bath frier before a post-war profiteering tribunal in 1920, was characteristically emphatic about the skills involved:

> The Bath Committee were evidently under the impression that fish-friers guess the size of their portions of fried fish and chips. There is, however, very little guesswork about it; the experienced frier serves out to a previously calculated return, and the week-end does not see so many coppers between the actual and the estimated returns.[165]

The Bath case was part of a spate of prosecutions under the profiteering legislation of this time; and in later years cynical comments from disaffected customers regularly found their way into local newspapers. Thus a Sheffield contributor to a controversy on the profitability of fish and chip shops in 1932 commented that the cost of fish to the frier was 'not excessive when one considers the minute quantity of fish (mostly batter) that is served out for twopence, and he made similar comments about the chips.[166] But these were minority views. The evidence strongly suggests that, faced as they were by a potentially lethal combination of rising and unpredictable costs, and prices that were held down by custom and the limited purchasing power of many customers, the friers needed all the expertise they could command in portion management if they were to make ends meet.

Chatchip had confined his comments on friers' calculative expertise to 'the experienced frier' and in 1919 he complained that too many friers still estimated their quantities by guesswork and failed to pay themselves for preparatory work in their costings.[167] More generally, critical comment on friers' accounting systems forms a theme running right through the period. Many friers clearly depended on conventional wisdom about the proper relationship between takings and raw materials used. In 1906 a correspondent to the *Fish Trades Gazette* was advised:

nearly everyone engaged in the frying trade has different systems and methods, but as a guide . . . By using 1 cwt. of oil you should take £14. Your fish should realise £6 per stone, and you should take 30s with every half-peck of flour.[168]

Thirty years later Chatchip attacked this kind of 'rule-of-thumb costing'. Northern friers tended to 'double up in their tills on the cost of spuds and fish', while Londoners looked for £1 in the till for every hundredweight of potatoes and stone of fish.[169] By costing on this basis, friers were not taking proper account of vital elements in their budgets, such as fats and fuel, nor were they paying themselves properly for their own labour.

The failure of friers to keep proper accounts was an enduring theme in the trade press. It was being pursued in the *Fish Trades Gazette* before the First World War, but very little headway was made and it took the changing circumstances of the inter-war years to arouse a few flickers of interest. The Huddersfield friers were unusual in inviting the local Chamber of Trade's consulting accountant to give a lecture on the rudiments of book-keeping in 1919, when he emphasized the importance of proper accounts for income tax purposes and as an aid to selling the business.[170] But in 1927 the NFFF leadership had to admit to the Food Council that:

The large majority of friers keep their accounts in a very crude manner, and others keep none whatever. You must understand that it is only the small proportion who are doing well who indulge in the luxury of certified balance sheets.[171]

An enterprising accountant offered 'The Fish Retailer's Simplified Account Book' to the trade for 2s 3d through the *Fish Friers' Review* in 1934, but his success was probably limited. In 1935 a bitter controversy raged about the Sea-Fish Commission's attempt to prepare a detailed report on the financial circumstances of the fried fish trade through an examination of a representative collection of friers' accounts. Loftas argued that the small minority of friers who kept itemised accounts would provide a misleading sample, but others took issue with him. C. Berry of Otley asserted that: 'Twenty per cent of friers have accounts prepared yearly by chartered accountants.' This claim was not supported by any evidence, but it is clear that most friers continued to run their businesses with only the most elementary awareness of their financial circumstances, basing their calculations of costs, profits and margins on instinct or rule of thumb.[172]

Friers were similarly slow to respond to the blandishments of insurance companies. They were already dabbling in this market in 1910, when an enquiring South Wales frier was told that insurance could be arranged with the Globe, the Liverpool Victoria and several other firms, the usual terms being 7s 6d per cent.[173] In 1921 the International Insurance Company directed a full-page advertisement in the *Fish Trades Gazette* at the fried fish trade.[174] But it was not until the early 1930s that insurance began to take a high profile in the trade journals, as companies negotiated with friers' organizations to offer discounted package deals covering fire, illness, injury, food-poisoning damages claims and third-party cover for other aspects of the business.[175] In this as in other aspects of the trade, however, the take-up rate for important innovations was low until a generation after they first became available. Only the labour-saving inventions were taken up with any enthusiasm – and even here the record was, as we have seen, decidedly patchy until well into the inter-war years.

Fire was the most obvious disaster against which insurance cover might be needed; the manufacturers of chemical fire extinguishers eagerly pursued fish friers' custom in the 1930s.[176] During 1935 there were 25 fish and chip shop fires in Leeds alone, evenly divided between over-heating pans and fires in flues, while in 1948 there were 529 fish and chip shop fires in England and Wales.[177] A related disaster was that suffered in 1910 by William Sutcliffe of Hull, who sued his supplier for selling him fat that exploded and blew all the windows out when he tried to use it, burning the plaintiff, damaging his clothes and forcing him to sell his business.[178] Exploding stoves were not unknown, as a case in the Potteries demonstrated.[179] But physical hazards of this sort were only a small proportion of the ills to which this difficult trade was heir.

The friers' problems often began at the very beginning. Many shops were not all they seemed when presented to the intending buyer. In 1927 'Kit Haddock' warned that some shops were 'artificially doctored . . . as traps for the unwary'. Their turnover might be inflated by the sale of large portions at low prices, by 'feeding' the till or by the use of fake invoices. Chatchip amplified this account with stories of fivepenny suppers being offered for threepence and free suppers being advertised on the opening night. A Plumstead frier boosted his apparent takings and made his shop look more attractive to an intending purchaser by leaving money at a nearby sweet shop to be given to children on condition that they used it to buy fish and chips at his shop. These devices were intended to trap people who did not know the shop or the district into buying at an inflated price. It was not only novices who fell for these stratagems: an editorial in *The Frier* in 1923 expressed amazement at how easily 'old friers' might be gulled in this way. The best defence was to insist on a fortnight's trial of the business before buying it. Otherwise, the only hope was to pass the over-capitalized concern on to someone else at as small a loss as could be contrived.[180]

Even if they managed to install themselves in reasonable premises at a fair price, many friers were insecure in their tenancies; despite a successful struggle in the early 1920s to secure legal protection for the goodwill of shops that operated from leasehold premises, the numerous weekly tenants remained unprotected. Problems could also arise over the definition and ownership of fixtures and fittings: the ambiguities and legal uncertainties in this area cast a further pall of insecurity over friers' business activities.[181]

Basic raw-material supply problems also contributed to the uncertainties and risks of the trade. There were regular 'fish famines' in winter when the trawlers could not cope with the conditions. In 1908 the price of small haddocks in London had been 6d per hundredweight one week and 25s the next: a 50-fold increase. Bad fish were also an occasional hazard. Failure to spot them might lead to commercial disaster, as a Balham frier found when his customers brought the offending items back, told their friends and he lost his trade and had to close down. Fish were not the only hazardous items. In 1911 an Essex frier secured £175 damages for loss of trade and goodwill after his suppliers erroneously sent him motor lubricating oil instead of cotton-seed oil and several customers fell ill.[182]

The frier's vulnerability was compounded by his position at the end of a long chain of suppliers and distributors. The trade was threatened by strikes among trawlermen and on the railways; the widespread use of coal as fuel generated anxiety every time the miners downed tools.[183] The First World War was particularly traumatic, as supplies of all kinds were threatened and interrupted. In its aftermath the railways came in for severe, sustained criticism that rumbled on throughout the inter-war years. In 1919 Chatchip pleaded for the development of road transport in the fish trade, to provide a remedy for the incompetence and inefficiency of the railway companies who refused to compensate for late and ruined fish under the rubric that stated that consignments were sent at 'owner's risk'. They would only make a refund when a delivery went completely astray and the frier who suffered had to close for the day. A spate of complaints followed, from various sources, about the unreliability of the railway service for fish friers. One enterprising Manchester fishmonger hired an aeroplane to bring a cargo of fish from Fleetwood, asserting with unwarranted optimism that: 'With the acquisition of larger cargo machines, we may quite readily nail down the coffin of "railway grievances"'.[184] These grumbles were only partly occasioned by the short-term problems of the railways in coping with heavy postwar traffic using run-down equipment. In 1934 even the Scunthorpe friers were complaining of railborne fish arriving in unfit condition from nearby Grimsby. One critic, noting that the railways' distribution charges were still 51 per cent up on prewar levels, despite falls in a range of costs and overheads, described the fishing industry as 'an absolute Klondyke for the railway companies'. But road haulage continued to be shut out from the fish trade and the vagaries of the railway companies continued to generate bitter complaint from friers who could never be sure their fish would arrive on time or in reasonable condition.[185]

Fish and chips was, to a remarkable extent, a seasonal trade and this posed problems of its own. There was general agreement throughout the period that most friers had to make their profits during the summer months, in the hope that this would tide them through the high fish prices and depressed demand of the winter.[186] This made friers particularly sensitive to any influences that might threaten price levels during the favoured period, as we shall see. It also made them anxious about profits even during the weeks when trade was at its best. Insecurity was never far away, compounded by the fear of competition both from rival foodstuffs and from neighbours in the same trade. In the soft-fruit season, friers sometimes expressed mild paranoia about competition from cheap cherries and strawberries for the spare cash in limited budgets at what should have been a good time for the trade, with long, light evenings and the lack of domestic fires, which kept home cooking to a minimum. This was not just a London phenomenon: it was reported from Hull as well, although it is difficult to gauge its full extent.[187] Fluctuations in the prices of more ordinary staple foods also attracted attention: thus it was alleged that a glut of cheap meat in 1909 had adversely affected fish consumption.[188] In 1935 Victor Joseph of J. Lyons and Co. told the Sea-Fish Commission that fish sales had dropped off in the face of competition from cheap eggs, bacon and meat, and this would have been endorsed by many troubled fish friers in the 1930s.[189] The Preston friers' agitation in 1937 against unfair competition from the town's numerous confectioners, who were apparently selling meat pies after official closing hours, was likewise a manifestation of widely held disquiet.[190] Meanwhile, competition within the trade was a persistent obsession and the trade journals devoted an enormous amount of space to the problems arising from too great a density of shops, especially in the older working-class areas, and from cut-throat competition in pricing and quantity supplied.[191]

The trade's spokesmen were also eager to emphasize the health hazards that arose from difficult working conditions as well as from the stresses and long hours of the job. In 1910 Chatchip commented on the damaging aspects of the frying process:

> To work five or six hours every day in a steamy, grease-laden atmosphere is positively injurious to health.

A post-war commentator offered a different emphasis, stressing the time spent in 'the chilly atmosphere of the preparatory room or cellar' and the large number of friers who had to retire as a result of bad health brought on by the sharp temperature variations between the cooking and preparation processes. And in 1935 'Macte Animo' urged the importance of half-day closing, offering a necessary break that would cut down on doctors' bills arising from overwork. The realities behind these perceptions of the trade's unhealthiness are difficult to establish, but the perceptions themselves are interesting and important. A related theme was introduced by Chatchip in 1910, when he suggested that friers use their free afternoons for sport, which would 'relieve the deadness of so many friers' experience, a deadness which, to my mind, is responsible for shops constantly changing hands'.[192]

Any general tendency towards monotony in fish friers' lives was open to disruption from time to time in unwanted ways. This was particularly likely to arise in direct, physical form from customers who wanted a late-night supper after the closure of the pubs had deprived them of a further drink supply. It seems to have been particularly prevalent in the trade's early days. Looking back at Birmingham in the 1870s and 1880s from the vantage point of 1906, a correspondent commented that:

> There are now very few of the 'scrimmages' and 'sloggings' that used to enliven the interiors of some of the shops, and also the public thoroughfares in which they were situated, at all hours of the night.

Not that the Edwardian years were trouble free. Chatchip reminisced about an old friend in the trade who:

> ran a shop in one of the meanest quarters of Manchester, and he always had handy – fastened by a stout leather loop under his counter – an old-fashioned kitchen chair leg. It was a most formidable weapon, and I regret to say it very often had to be in evidence, particularly on Saturday nights after the public-houses had closed.

By 1919, however, the days when a fish frier 'needed to be a pugilist and a bruiser' had gone, although Chatchip issued warning noises about a postwar revival of 'a spirit of rowdyism and hooliganism'. Indeed, his comments were prompted by a case in Ashington where two men were fined for assaulting a fish frier's wife after a late-night dispute over change in which they broke 24 plates and 'threw a lot of fish at the ceiling'. It is not surprising to find similar cases surfacing in the 1930s. Thus a Hartlepool couple were sent to prison for attacking a fish frier after he remonstrated with them for drinking out of the vinegar bottle; and in 1931 three men attacked the owner of a Burgess Hill shop after he asked them to eat outside because it was after 10 p.m.:

> Halls got on the counter and Brown threw a piece of fish which struck witness behind the ear. Then I saw fish and chips flying all over the room, added witness.

A Bradford fish and chip shop had a doorman to control the queue at busy times and in 1931 he was attacked by a woolcomber who tried to jump the queue. It is difficult to imagine any other retail trade, apart from the drink trade itself, which was subject to these risks: the fish frier must have been haunted by the spectre of possible violent assault in all but the most respectable districts, even though the actual incidence of the problem almost certainly declined after the First World War.[193]

Police intervention was welcome on occasions such as these, but at other times the police themselves enlivened friers' lives in unwanted ways. Friers were often kept under close surveillance in case they continued to serve, or allowed food to be eaten on the premises, after the legal hours. There were regular prosecutions on this score, although police practices varied from town to town. In some towns police vigilance and adherence to the letter of the law were said to add up to 'petty harassment' and the situation could sometimes be exploited by the unscrupulous. It would be interesting to know more about the background to the case at Beverley in which two policemen were found guilty of stealing £1 from a fish and chip shop when they dropped in at 11.15 p.m. to play the piano: it is compatible with a kind of jocular intimidation which may have been all too common. As purveyors of late-night refreshments, friers were also vulnerable to police surveillance of drunks and prostitutes. In 1935 a Manchester frier was fined for allowing 'undesirable women' to frequent his dining-room to pick up drunken men as the pubs closed. The *Fish Friers' Review* saw this as unfair, because it was for the police to identify and accuse prostitutes: the frier had every right to serve them provided they were behaving decently. Drunks were easier to identify, although it was usually sound policy to serve them quietly and let them go rather than to risk a scene by asking them to leave. But all this added up to a formidable array of public order problems, without clear-cut solutions, for that overwhelming majority of friers who depended heavily on the late-night trade – and especially for the vulnerable minority who were in close proximity to city-centre entertainment districts.[194]

Friers could thus be deemed guilty by association with a range of more or less nefarious activities, but perhaps the most embarrassing aspect of the trade was one which for many years seemed inherent in its very nature. The smells arising from fish frying had a private as well as a public dimension: the odour of cotton-seed oil, in particular, clung tenaciously to the person as a symbol of occupational identity. In 1906 'A.R.' of Boston was told that: 'There is no preparation that will prevent the smell of fish-frying. The only remedy is

thorough cleanliness.' A Cumberland frier complained that some of his colleagues gave the trade a bad image:

> It is my lot at times to attend a large public market to buy potatoes, and one is often
> made painfully aware – by smell – that other fish and chip friers are near you. They
> are in the same clothes in which both frying and cleaning are done.

In 1913 Chatchip described the sad circumstances of a travelling companion
in the trade who knew that everyone in the compartment could smell his 'odour
of stale cotton-oil and cooking': it permeated the house and all his clothes.
Occasional lawsuits show that neighbours might also complain of similar
contamination. Chatchip had a characteristically demanding remedy for this
problem, insisting that no self-respecting frier should be plagued by it:

> Experience shows that a bath containing some Jeyes' fluid, and an entire change into
> clothing (underclothes as well) which have been laid aside in a drawer with a bunch of
> lavender, entirely rids one of any odour.

Even so, the problem persisted into the inter-war years, compromising friers'
attempts to become accepted in respectable society. A Preston frier's son left a
heartfelt warning to any reader of his reminiscences who might be tempted into
the trade: 'Don't any of you have a chip shop as you can't get away from the
smell.'[195]

Under the circumstances, it is hard to disagree with Chatchip's comment in
1910 that the fish and chip trade had had to 'fight its way to public favour and
confidence through walls of prejudice as thick as those of Jericho'. Alderman
Archibold of Middlesbrough, who declared in 1907 that he 'would put down
every fried fish shop in the country without compunction', had plenty of
counterparts elsewhere, including, as we shall see, significant numbers of
Medical Officers of Health and other public figures whose pronouncements
received widespread publicity. And such prejudices were not without foundation, even as they persisted into the 1930s and beyond, although they did the
majority of fish friers an increasingly grave injustice. They added to the
difficulties of a risky, demanding trade, helping to perpetuate the demeaning
and embarrassing label of 'offensive trade'. To struggle against the prejudices
and problems that bedevilled the trade, it became clear that some form of trade
organization was necessary, although the individualist predilections of many
friers constituted a formidable obstacle to success. But the rise of fish friers'
organizations, the causes they took up and the values they expressed, must form
an important part of any attempt to analyse the trade's development and assess
its significance. It will also provide another window into the attitudes and
aspirations of the British petty bourgeoisie more generally.[196]

6 Solidarity and Suspicion: Organization and its Limitations

The petty bourgeoisie in Britain has never played a prominent role on the national political stage. Its contribution to economic and social change has been less than ostentatious, hidden as it was behind the more spectacular activities of big business, high finance and mass movements. The contribution of small shopkeepers and traders to the Chartist movement, which should have brought this forgotten social stratum into the limelight, was conducted at local level and has only recently been rediscovered in earnest by historians. Their subsequent activities have been unsung and almost invisible. Only a handful of historians and sociologists have ever taken a sustained interest in them, and then the questions asked have sought primarily to explain this apparent quiescence, especially in the light of the much greater prominence accorded to the petty bourgeoisie in the politics of major countries in western Europe, most obviously France and Germany.

Mike Winstanley argues that shopkeepers – especially small ones – have been hidden from history because they have been assumed to be isolated individualists, locked into fierce, sustained competition with each other at the local level, without the time or the inclination to get involved in wider social and political issues. They might complain about rates and taxes, and some of them might organize to defend their trades against government regulation and competition from the multiple stores and the Co-op, but basically they were locked into a private sphere of local concerns and family preoccupations.[1] Winstanley sets out to challenge this assumption by exploring the political activities of shopkeepers and documenting some of the sustained trade organizations and campaigns to which they subscribed. He points especially to the limits to shopkeepers' individualism, to their desire to regulate their trades so as to minimize the risks and threats of untrammelled competition, if necessary invoking government help in this quest. He concludes that shopkeepers were only individualists when it suited them and that various pragmatic calculations might draw them into combination and confederation. But what he does not show is why this did not go further and why the petty bourgeoisie in Britain did not become a distinct, identifiable political force in their own right, as in the case of the German *mittelstand*.[2]

Geoffrey Crossick seeks to explain this wider issue in terms of the values and beliefs that prevailed among shopkeepers and master craftsmen. He identifies two influential strands in petty bourgeois attitudes. First, there was a tradition of shopkeeper radicalism that could be traced back to the late eighteenth century but was still important in the early twentieth. It saw the state as corrupt and oppressive, dominated by the self-interested machinations of governing aristocrats whose mantle in this demonology was inherited by big business and civil servants. The second strand was a populist form of economic liberalism, an ideal of minimal intervention in the market place by government of any kind and an identification of non-intervention with the inherited liberties of the free-born Englishman. These attitudes helped to sustain a 'narrow moral individualism' that Crossick identifies with the British petty bourgeoisie. He illustrates it through the views expressed by the Birmingham toolmaker Joseph Brown, who was convinced that 'the best capital a man can have is himself' and that 'each man's life is a problem of which he must find the solution . . . each man must seek it for himself'. Crossick does not argue that such values prevented shopkeepers and tradesmen from joining together in associations for their mutual support and assistance; indeed, he documents and analyses the work of such collectivities, from organizations of small shopkeepers upwards. But he suggests that these attitudes helped to confine the concerns of shopkeepers almost entirely to their own localities or trades. For him, the dominant values of the petty bourgeoisie consist in an aloof, anxious, family-centred, self-sufficient individualism.[3]

Christopher Hosgood provides a different emphasis. He divides his Leicester shopkeepers into two categories:

> 'domestic' or small shopkeepers, who were firmly grounded within the working-class community, and 'principal' or large shopkeepers, who participated fully in the middle-class world.

Thus shopkeepers should not be lumped together as a class apart: they were 'well-integrated into their respective communities' and each group 'had the ability to assume the class identity of the community which they served'. On Hosgood's showing, 'domestic' shopkeepers continued to share the life and culture of their working-class customers and neighbours: they were not isolated individualists. They might enjoy an added measure of power and respect, as adjudicators of credit ratings and reputations, but their interests were ultimately bound up with those of their customers, whose habits and way of life they defended from the slurs that were sometimes bandied about by social reformers. On this showing, they lacked a distinctive political identity, while being distanced from the masculine industrial world of work and trade unions; Hosgood, Crossick and Winstanley all agree on the difficulty of organizing shopkeepers as a group and the limited nature of their collective concerns. John Benson's comments on the lower levels of retailing, in his book on the 'penny capitalists', run closely parallel to this discussion; ultimately all the recent social historians of shopkeeping share a great deal of common ground, differing more in emphasis and in angle of vision than in essentials.[4]

Shopkeepers began to organize in earnest at local and national level in the 1890s, although the Early Closing Association, founded in 1842, had a much longer pedigree as a national umbrella organization for local bodies formed to campaign on this specific issue. The 1890s saw the development of large numbers of local associations to look after the collective interests of particular trades and of Chambers of Trade which brought together the various trade associations of particular towns. Some trades began to federate nationally, beginning with the Federation of Grocers' Associations in 1891; later in the decade the National Chamber of Trade emerged as 'the retailer's equivalent to the Trades Union Congress or Employers' Federation'. Most of these organizations brought together the more substantial traders, but in 1905 a national organization for the protection of small shopkeepers against their larger rivals, who were pushing for Sunday closing and compulsory early closing, also made its appearance. There were also specific organizations dedicated to campaigning against the growing influence of the Co-operative movement.

In general, these bodies aimed to restrict competition, to limit price-cutting and to oppose intervention by local or national government in the conduct of retail businesses. This was held to lie beyond the legitimate spheres of government activity; and opposition to the state was such that, before 1914 at least, there was little thought of seeking its benevolent intervention to improve the conditions under which shopkeepers operated. This was to change considerably in the post-war years, which have been neglected by historians of retailing, whose studies tend to stop short at the First World War. Retailers' organizations also devoted their energies to campaigning for low rates and taxes and to lobbying for better treatment from suppliers of essential services like gas and water. Beyond this, they sought to safeguard their members' interests on a variety of issues, from railway rates to insurance provision. And we must not forget that they also brought tradesmen together socially, cementing friendships, providing outings and shared entertainments and building a consciousness of the common identity and interests of 'the trade' as a whole. By 1914 almost every trade was organized at regional or national level, although the extent and representativeness of the membership varied enormously from trade to trade and town to town.[5]

These shopkeepers' movements have been discussed in broad outline, but we lack sustained studies of the workings of particular organizations for individual trades, with the idiosyncratic exception of seaside landladies at Blackpool.[6] A study of the fish friers' organizations will not only help us to understand the trade itself. It will also make a contribution, as a case-study, to the deeper investigation of petty bourgeois attitudes and values which needs to be pursued, especially for the inter-war years in Britain. In their turn, the existing general interpretations of petty bourgeois attitudes and organizations will provide a comparative context for an assessment of the fried fish trade itself.

As befitted its lowly origins, the fish and chip trade was slow to organize itself both at local and national level. The first sustained initiatives came after the emergence of the national small shopkeepers' federation in 1905. As with other trades, the friers tended to respond to perceived threats and to protest against proposed intervention rather than to set their own agenda in a positive way. The delayed mobilization of the fried fish trade as an interest group owed something to the limited nature of the threat posed to the friers by the multiples, department stores and Co-operatives which seemed so much more dangerous to so many other retailers. When the friers did begin to organize themselves, their targets were threefold. They sought to reduce the impact of high and fluctuating raw material prices, which were felt to be inflated by speculation and sharp practice on the part of producers and merchants. They mobilized against the threat of government regulation and especially the scope for strict control on working practices that seemed likely to follow the labelling of fish and chips as an offensive trade under the Public Health Act of 1907. And they directed their fire against untrammelled competition within the trade through price-cutting and the multiplication of shops. The second and third concerns were in some senses contradictory, as regulation by local authorities under the offensive trades legislation was a potential weapon against the overstocking of the trade. We shall see that the fish friers continued to face both ways on this issue through the 1920s and into the 1930s. But these three themes were enduring preoccupations: indeed, by the 1930s concern over prices and regulation was gaining an extra dimension. The marketing boards and other regulatory bodies of the new corporate state were seen to be pushing raw material prices up in ways that generated extra profits for farmers and trawler owners, while squeezing friers' profit margins and threatening the future of the industry. Meanwhile the aims and aspirations of friers' organizations continued to broaden, and a variety of political perspectives competed for predominance among the leaders and the rank and file. To develop these themes in greater depth, we need to begin at the beginning.

The first fish friers' association for which evidence survives is the Hull and District Fish Friers' Supply Association, which celebrated its twelfth annual general meeting at the end of 1905. It had clearly begun life as a bulk buying organization which aimed to secure economies of scale and a share of the profits of raw material acquisition for its members. In 1905 it paid a 10 per cent dividend but by that time it was also involved in a wider range of trade protection activities, for it defended a member against a charge of selling fish and chips 20 minutes after midnight on a Saturday.[7]

The Hull friers had no visible parallels elsewhere at the turn of the century, and it was not until 1904 that more general stirrings became visible, as the *Fish Trades Gazette* reported a proposal for setting up a Fish Friers' Co-operative Association. This was intended to buy fish direct from the ports and import Australian dripping while cutting out the middleman, but it was also supposed to provide cheap insurance and supply mortgages while 'bringing together members of the trade in closer union'. Nothing more was heard of this initiative, but its plans for developing outwards from narrowly economic and instrumental initial goals were in line with the subsequent development of friers' organizations in the longer term.[8]

Further initiatives at the local level became visible over the next two years. Local associations came into view in Lancashire towns like Accrington and Blackburn, and in 1906 80 Bradford friers joined together to buy fish at bulk discount direct from the wholesalers.[9] This interest in by-passing the middleman was an enduring feature of friers' organizations, and concern to impose minimum prices among a 'respectable' stratum of the trade also emerged at an early stage. Thus the Glasgow and West of Scotland Fish Restaurant Keepers' Association, founded in 1907, had as one of its prime aims 'to raise the price of fish suppers from 2d to 3d'.[10]

As local associations began to multiply and friers became increasingly concerned about a growing spate of prosecutions for nuisance, proposals for a national organization surfaced. Early in 1907 an Oxford frier, T. C. Bayliss, urged his colleagues to pull together in a National Fish Retailers' Association, whose main concerns were to be collective defence against prosecutions for nuisance, and actions against another enduring source of complaint: the charges and conditions for consigning fish by rail. Two or three letters of support came in, perhaps significantly from areas without friers' organizations of their own, but it took the emergence of a more clearly defined threat later in the year to generate a sustained campaign on these lines. As it became clear that the public health legislation of 1907 was going to incorporate Sir Shirley Murphy's suggestion that fish frying should be added to the list of offensive trades about which local authorities were empowered to make regulatory by-laws, the friers' unease reached the editorial columns of the *Fish Trades Gazette*. A proposal for a national trade organization, primarily to deal with the problems expected from such regulation, attracted immediate support from 'Rambler', who expressed the fear that the prospective controls might mean 'the extinction of seven friers out of every ten in England'. Again, however, no real momentum could be generated and early in 1908 a London frier felt compelled to restate the case for a National Federation:

> Fish friers, from the nature of their business, are specially liable to outside interference, both justified and unjustified. Moreover, the fried fish trade is increasingly attracting the attention of Parliament. Vital legal questions are cropping up, and both for individual protection and for general protection a strong central Association of fish friers is urgently needed in order that their reasonable freedom of action may be preserved. It is useless to let things slide until the industry is on the brink of a precipice.[11]

It is difficult to tell how widely shared this sense of urgency was. As matters were developing, the trade certainly had a visible, pressing need to organize itself – which in this case was not shared by other retail interests. But awareness of the problem had probably not spread beyond quite a narrow trade élite: the *Fish Trades Gazette* reached only an articulate minority of fish friers. And it was not clear how a national organization could be given effective form, without the presiding direction of a charismatic individual with the time and resources to pull friers together over a wide area. This combination of qualities was unlikely to be found in a trade whose members characteristically worked long hours for limited rewards.

It is perhaps not surprising, then, that the first remotely effective moves towards a national federation originated with the local associations whose numbers had been gradually growing. In March 1908 the Lancashire Federation of Chippers made its presence known, as its chair wrote from Bolton with a query about the law on the carriage of fish by rail; in the summer of 1909 this modest body blossomed into the United Kingdom Fish and Chip Friers' Federation. A quarterly meeting in November, held in Bolton, drew delegates from Manchester, Oldham, Blackburn, Burnley, Chorley, Nelson, Preston and Bury; only the apologies for absence from Sheffield and Bradford on the Yorkshire side of the Pennines gave any hint of real influence beyond the Lancashire cotton towns.[12] These origins were entirely appropriate: not only was this area one of the original heartlands of the trade itself, it was also a stronghold of trade unionism in exactly the kinds of skilled and supervisory occupations from which the friers were mainly drawn. The trade union structure in cotton spinning and weaving, in particular, was firmly based on a similar pattern of federations of small organizations that had grown up in response to local problems. But this particular organization was not to match the reputation for strength and effectiveness that came to be accorded, rightly or wrongly, to the cotton unions.[13]

For more than a year, the UKF grew in ambition and spread its area of influence. Its early deliberations focused on the familiar topic of collective purchasing, but attitudes to the 'offensive trade' label and to compulsory Sunday closing were also aired at the outset. On the offensive trade question, the UKF was happy to work with the sanitary authorities to improve the standards of the trade but even so 'it was felt that some of the proposals and suggested restrictions should be resisted'. As more and more local authorities took up the opportunity provided by the 1907 Public Health Act to designate fish frying as an offensive trade, the second set of attitudes increasingly prevailed. In June 1910 the UKF followed the lead of the Manchester friers and appointed a deputation to lobby the Local Government Board for some restraint on the powers provided by the by-laws. Particular concern was expressed at a proposal to require all frying to be done in a room separate from the shop, or to surround the range with glass screens with only a window to communicate with the serving area. This would have greatly increased costs and worsened working conditions. The UKF was still eager to use a measure of regulation to get rid of the 'riff-raff' shops, but not at the cost of undermining the rest of the industry. At the Local Government Board the friers' deputation gained access to John Burns himself. They hoped that the minister's proverbially humble origins would ensure them a sympathetic hearing and they were not disappointed. The threat of separate rooms and screens was removed and the friers were consulted about the drafting of model by-laws. Here at least the benefits of organization were apparent, although these concessions did not prevent an incessant flow of subsequent complaints about the persecution of individual friers by allegedly officious Sanitary Inspectors and Medical Officers.[14]

On the Sunday closing front, the UKF was less successful. In 1912 it tried to get the Sunday opening of fried fish shops prohibited under the Shops Act of the previous year. Philip Snowden proved to be a sympathetic contact in the Labour Party, but the Act itself had been such a political hot potato that it is not surprising that no real headway was made. This was, after all, an attempt to change the *status quo* rather than an effort to protect existing ways of working: as such it would have required more resources than the friers could bring to bear to have a real chance of success.[15]

Chatchip blamed the disappointment over Sunday trading on the UKF's limited influence and resources and although he clearly had an axe to grind on this issue, his comments should be taken seriously. At its peak the UKF had only 2,000 affiliated members, and its claims to represent the United Kingdom rested on the tenuous affiliation of the Edinburgh friers' society. Otherwise it extended no further than cotton Lancashire and the West Riding of Yorkshire. The South Wales association, which was formed at Pontypridd in November 1911, may also have affiliated for a short time, but an organization that embraced less than 10 per cent of its trade could not expect to carry much political muscle. Moreover, the affiliation fees from the local associations amounted to only 3d per member per year; the embittered Chatchip, who had been actively involved in the UKF's inner councils, reckoned that this was barely enough to cover postage costs. The UKF was already in a state of crisis and internal dissension by October 1911 and it does not seem to have seen 1912 out. The roots of the collapse, in terms of internal politics, could be traced back to 'a rumpus' at a meeting in Manchester, at which a personal attack was launched on the secretary and prime mover, Mr Southern of Bolton. The Manchester friers themselves disbanded in the summer of 1911. The friers' first attempt at building a national organization had had its successes but had come to an untidy and unseemly end.[16]

The problems and grievances which had fuelled the drive to organize had not gone away, however, and a second attempt at national federation followed hard on the heels of the UKF's demise. In April 1913 the Bradford association, which had 99 members, was planning to organize a Yorkshire Federation; a month later it succeeded in defeating Bradford Corporation's proposals for stringent regulatory by-laws in the House of Lords. The Bradford friers were so active and assertive, faced as they were with a particularly interventionist local authority, that it is no surprise to find them liaising with the South Wales association in June 1913, using the good offices of the *Fish Trades Gazette* to try to set up a National Federation. The South Wales friers sought a common front on such issues as opening and closing hours, local authority supervision, health and sanitary questions, transport costs and conditions, and fish and potato supply. The last of these had been a particularly contentious matter for some time, as friers had had to contend with unusually high prices that bit deeply into their profit margins. A *Fish Trades Gazette* editorial gave strong support to the idea of federation, for a variety of reasons:

> The fish friers have to fight for their existence. Jacks-in-office, busybodies suffering from excess of zeal, have an instrument made to their hand in the Public Health Acts with which to hinder business or harass those legitimately engaged in carrying it on . . . A Federation would have a great educational force. It would help to eliminate the unfit: it would encourage the survival of the fittest.

And it would bring friers together to discuss the problems outlined by the South Wales association, while also agreeing policy on 'questions affecting labour – National Insurance, Employers' Liability, the Shops Acts, and some day, possibly, the Trade Boards Act . . .' From all angles, a national federation was beginning to seem a good idea.[17]

The National Federation of Fish Friers was actually set up at a meeting in Manchester on 11 November 1913. It grew out of these initiatives but the impetus for the inaugural gathering itself came from the newly revived Manchester association, whose president, Harry Hamer, took the chair. In its beginnings, however, the NFFF spread its tentacles over a much wider area than had the UKF. Despite the venue of the meeting, the only Lancashire cotton towns to send delegates were Nelson, Colne, Oldham and Rochdale, although Wigan was also represented and Glossop, just over the border in Derbyshire, sent two delegates. Blackpool and Liverpool made up the Lancashire numbers, and Yorkshire associations were actually in attendance on this occasion, with representatives from Bradford, Halifax, Keighley, Sowerby Bridge and Middlesbrough. Further afield, delegates came from Hanley, in the Potteries, South Wales and Weymouth but there was no hint of any Scottish connection and the London area was conspicuous by its absence. Even so, the NFFF had much less implausible claims to national coverage than its predecessor. But it soon became apparent that a wide geographical range of affiliated societies created problems of its own.[18]

The delegates at the inaugural conference were happy to agree about their opposition to 'unfair and unscrupulous dealings', the duties of the officials, and the basic affiliation fee, which was to be one shilling per member per year. They were also in broad agreement about the need for some form of local government regulation to raise the standards of the trade and enable it to expand into more respectable areas – although some delegates who had experienced regulation were unhappy about the extent of officials' powers of interference and others were sensitive about the implications of being labelled an 'offensive trade'. Real dissension emerged, however, over the allocation of conference delegates and the size of the executive. Representatives of the Manchester area, anxious to keep costs low, wanted a small executive to be drawn from within a 'reasonable' distance of the headquarters, which were to be in Manchester. Delegates from the more distant associations, such as Middlesbrough, wanted to make sure their views were heard and argued for a larger executive without geographical restriction. The smaller associations also resisted a proposal for delegate allocations to be proportional to the number of members in a local association. To some extent these disputes reflected a suspicion of Manchester which was articulated by a Mr Wadsworth of Halifax:

> The mere fact that the meeting was held (in Manchester) that day had given rise to a feeling in some of their minds that the Manchester Association wanted to carry the whole thing. They did not want to take that impression back to their respective associations.

The advocates of an 'open' executive and one delegate per association won the day, but the tensions which surfaced at this point are revealing. Real financial pressures lay behind the Manchester proposals and the limitations on the Federation's finances are underlined by the general agreement that the one shilling per member affiliation fee was the most that could be asked. Awareness of this difficulty and of the related problems of getting and keeping a substantial rank and file membership was expressed in the delegates' discussions, but this did not prevent them from looking forward to large-scale co-operative purchasing arrangements and planning to set up a Federation periodical. One interesting omission from the agenda may have been due to a desire to minimize potentially damaging dissension. Nothing was said about the fixing of minimum prices, nor about alternative strategies for coping with the rising cost of raw materials, apart from co-operative purchasing. This problem had been the main driving force behind the revival of the Manchester association but it had also led to bitter disputes and resignations from the local executive. There is, perhaps, no wonder that it was kept from the limelight on this occasion, but this did not prevent it from recurring many times in the future.[19]

William Loftas ('Chatchip'), the NFFF's first secretary, expected that 2,000 or 2,500 members would affiliate at the outset, generating an income of about £100 per year. As it turned out, this shoestring forecast proved wildly optimistic. The Federation began with £30 of subscription money as its only resources; by February 1914 it had spent £21 3s 2d as against an income of £36 6s 0d. Fewer than 20 local associations had affiliated and the membership was about 700. The executive went ahead with producing the *Fish Friers' Quarterly Review* but any subsequent progress was disrupted by the advent of the First World War, which brought about the *Review*'s sudden demise and plunged the trade into confusion. Despite a worsening economic situation, little was done in the early years of the war and there was no annual conference in 1915. By the spring of 1916 the Federation was down to 311 members and seemed to be on its last legs. But the events of the next two years were to falsify any such forecasts.[20]

Despite the NFFF's limited resources, efforts were made throughout the first two years of the war to secure government intervention against soaring fish and potato prices and to allow range-makers whose factories had been diverted to war work to perform essential repairs to friers' equipment. By the beginning of 1917 potato prices were posing major problems for friers who had been using chip sales to compensate for the expense and limited availability of fish. On 1 February 1917 the coalition government's Food Controller issued a schedule of maximum prices for potatoes, but there was extensive evasion by producers and local friers' organizations were seriously discussing the possibility of growing their own potatoes on allotments and smallholdings. Existing contacts between the NFFF, civil servants and ministers were strengthened by the sustained negotiations the crisis made necessary. The civil servants themselves continued to be mystified by the perverse behaviour of 'this puckish vegetable', as Beveridge called it, and the friers remained dissatisfied with their treatment. But there were at least kind words from J. R. Clynes, who was soon to take over as Food Controller, and from senior civil servants like H. G. Maurice, who were prepared to recognize the trade's importance as a supplier of cheap, wholesome food to the working classes. The groundwork was being laid for fuller consultation and better treatment when an even more disturbing crisis, this time involving the supply of oils and fats, began to develop in the autumn of 1917.[21]

The shortage of frying media, which threatened to destroy the fish and chip trade completely, emerged as a major problem at the beginning of October, when Mr Mansfield, the senior civil servant in charge of these commodities at the Board of Agriculture and Fisheries, told a deputation of friers that they would have to organize more effectively and provide reliable evidence of their needs before their supplies could be assured. He expressed astonishment that so few friers were affiliated to the NFFF, urging the necessity of a recruitment drive. This was, in fact, already under way, as mass meetings of friers were held in major centres and new branches began to join the national body. By the end of the year the oil and fat supply position was becoming desperate and on 1 January 1918 the Food Controller took possession of all the United Kingdom's oils and fats. Several other industries, from margarine to munitions, were competing for access to these unglamorous but vital commodities. The friers had to campaign fiercely to secure their share, basing their arguments on the ubiquitous importance of fish and chips in working-class diet and the useful way in which the trade channelled consumption away from bread grains towards home-produced potatoes. They were successful, benefiting from the government's purchase of the Egyptian cotton-seed crop and the distribution of a specially blended compound oil, a mixture of animal and vegetable ingredients, at controlled prices. Early in January a special Advisory Committee to the Fish Friers' Trade was established by central government to deal with these issues; its members included friers from all over the country, including two from the otherwise obscure Scottish Fish Friers Association. This desirable outcome may have owed less than the organized friers liked to believe to their assiduous lobbying: readers of the *Fish Trades Gazette* were told that Sir Arthur Yapp, the Director of Food Economy, had been alerted to the trade's problems by a heckler at a meeting on Tower Hill and had begun an investigation on that basis. And the friers' success was certainly not inevitable: the ice-cream trade had already been suspended for the duration of the war because of the sugar shortage. In the end, the friers had made their case for the overwhelming strategic importance of their trade to the war effort. What followed was a sustained drive to register friers for oil and fat supplies, which brought an unprecedented growth to the membership and influence of the NFFF, under whose auspices most of the registration took place.[22]

During 1918 and into 1919 the organized friers asserted their new influence with growing confidence. In the meetings of the advisory committee on oils and fats they criticized the quality and price of the government's standard compound frying medium and pressed (unsuccessfully) for a subsidy for fish friers. They lobbied for an extension of opening hours under the restrictive Light, Heating and Power Order, introduced in March 1918, and they safeguarded the right of friers to buy potatoes at wholesale rates and even direct from the growers, against a threat to have friers classed as consumers and required to buy at retail prices. This latter success owed something to the London friers' threat to stop selling potatoes and to display notices in their shops explaining their decision. The war had brought the fried fish trade a sense of pride and power which would have been unthinkable in former years. It also brought a large number of new members to the NFFF.[23]

The annual conference of the NFFF at the end of April 1919 was remarkable for the geographical range from which the delegates were drawn. Executive Council members came from Eastbourne, Northampton, Norwich, Bristol, Newcastle upon Tyne, Aberdare and Swindon, as well as Rotherham, Preston and Blackpool, while the President was John Lyon from London and the almost inevitable Loftas kept up the Manchester influence as secretary. There was a noticeable South Wales contingent among the delegates and the NFFF had clearly become a national organization. The adoption of London as a meeting place reflected a wish to emphasize this development. Meanwhile, the membership had grown from 1,297 to 3,214 over the past year: this still accounted only for an active, aware élite within the trade but it was an impressive record all the same. Moreover, it was only part of the story, because the NFFF no longer contained all the organized fish friers in England. Most of the Yorkshire friers and some neighbouring associations were now affiliated to a rival association, the Northern Counties Federation of Fish Friers.[24]

The NCF had its origins in the rivalry between Lancashire and Yorkshire, and especially between Manchester and Bradford, which was already evident at the NFFF's inaugural conference. Its secession was partly a matter of personalities: William Loftas was hard-working but opinionated and abrasive and his efforts to take the NFFF down a road of his own choosing generated furious, abusive argument. Above all, however, what counted was access to raw materials. During the crisis over oils and fats, the Yorkshire friers were anxious to continue to fry in dripping. But Loftas was unresponsive and he had enough strategic power as a negotiator to endanger the supply of what was already perceived to be an essential element in a distinctive Yorkshire fish frying tradition. Indeed, Yorkshire's spokesmen were capable of celebrating their attachment to dripping in emotive language whose implications were downright disturbing:

> Animal fat is the food of a dominant people. The cry for vegetable oil throughout the country was for the feeding of an inferior people. Animal fat for the dominant race. Animal fat for the dominant county within that race.[25]

Perhaps this was in some sense a joke. But the commitment to Yorkshire frying methods was real enough and it was the main reason for the damaging split in the organized frying trade that opened and quickly widened during 1918.

From its earliest days, the NFFF's effectiveness had been hindered by the personal rivalry between two of its leading figures, Loftas and William Pott. In September 1917 Loftas also fell out with Mr Pullan of Bradford, the current NFFF president, over his eagerness to affiliate the Federation to a new umbrella organization for the whole fish trade, the National Sea Fisheries Protection Association. Against this background, it is not surprising that his Yorkshire enemies blamed Loftas for an anonymous article in the *Fish Trades' Gazette* in October, which argued that there was such a strong demand for animal stearine for munitions uses that friers and their customers would have to get used to vegetable oils – which were better anyway – or change to compounds that combined animal and vegetable ingredients. This brought about a sustained controversy. Yorkshire suspicions were fuelled by Loftas' privileged position in gaining access to government officials, which his own self-esteem probably led him to exaggerate. Early in 1918 there were conflicting reports at different times over whether Loftas or Pullan had the power to negotiate with officials on the NFFF's behalf: Loftas as (by this time) full-time secretary had a clear tactical advantage. By the end of February Pullan, Pott and the Bradford friers were at the core of a new Yorkshire Federation of Fish Friers, whose exact relationship with the NFFF was undefined but seemed to hinge on whether or not Loftas continued as secretary. When he was re-elected after acrimonious debate at the annual conference in March the die was cast, although the Yorkshire Federation did not turn itself into the NCF and formally secede from the NFFF until July. The dispute was sharpened by mutual accusations of financial malpractice and it undoubtedly weakened the organized friers, damaging their otherwise rapidly increasing credibility in government circles.[26]

The NCF exerted an influence of its own, especially in its first year of activity. Pullan and Pott joined the governmental Advisory Committee to the Fish Friers' Trade and the NCF campaigned particularly vigorously for the exemption of fish friers from conscription. Pott also claimed that: 'With the Ministry of Pensions . . . we prevented an undue rush into the trade of discharged soldiers'; he took the credit for sorting out fish allocations and obtaining equipment repair permits. In 1919 the NCF launched its own journal, *The Frier*, which seems to have been published from Pott's house in Glossop and combined assertive, incoherent and sometimes abusive editorials with extensive reporting on the social life of the local branches, but it remained essentially a Yorkshire organization, with outposts in Durham and Chesterfield as well as Glossop, and a brief fraternal relationship with the Scottish Federation. In March 1919 this body claimed to speak for 98 per cent of the Scottish friers but by July 1920 it had disintegrated and Glasgow, Edinburgh, Dundee and Aberdeen had formed their own separate societies. The NCF lasted rather longer. *The Frier* ceased publication at the end of 1923 when its parent body was absorbed into the new Association of British Fisheries, a further attempt at an umbrella organization for the whole of the fish trade; but some of the branches outlasted the demise of the NCF as a separate entity and during 1925 most of them rejoined the NFFF. But they returned to an organization which had become much weaker in the intervening years.[27]

The NFFF's increased membership helped it to sustain quite a high profile immediately after the war. It campaigned for the continuance of price controls on key raw materials; it lobbied for a measure of security of tenure for small shopkeepers against the machinations of their landlords; it fought to ensure that friers would keep their purchasing status as traders rather than customers, despite the efforts of rival trades to the contrary; and it set up a legal aid fund and a cheap rate insurance scheme. The NFFF was also behind the Corn Sales Act, which was supposed to prevent the giving of short weight, and other abuses by wholesalers. Less successfully, it campaigned against Offensive Trade status, in opposition to the NCF, which preferred to use Offensive Trade Orders to provide a crude but fairly effective barrier to new entrants to the trade in over-stocked areas. The NFFF preferred to go for a special Act of Parliament to regulate the trade as a whole. In 1925, after much discussion, this policy issued forth in a draft Bill to 'Regulate and Control the Fried Fish and Chipped Potato Trades'. This legislation would have abolished all offensive trade labels under the 1907 Public Health Act, while requiring all fish and chip shops to register with their local authorities, at a fee of two guineas per year. Applicants for licences were to show 'at least a rudimentary knowledge' of the public health and safety aspects of the trade, and no new licences were to be granted in too close proximity to existing ones. Minimum hygiene and equipment standards were to be imposed. The whole Bill amounted to an attempt to initiate the professionalization of the trade. It engendered fierce dispute within the NFFF: Blackpool and Leicester, for example, opposed it root and branch. And it was never introduced into Parliament. But it does underline the twin quests for respectability and regulation that lay at the heart of NFFF policy.[28]

The concern for respectability was demonstrated in a slightly bizarre way when the 1922 Annual Conference decided to rename the organization the National Federation of Fish Caterers, with a view to escaping from what was seen as being an unattractive image. This policy was reversed five years later but the initiative was revealing. In keeping with these attitudes, the trade's spokesmen were delighted when the Blackpool conference of 1920 was accorded a civic reception; the precedent was followed at subsequent conferences. To set against this, however, the 1920 conference marked the beginning of a sharp, sustained decline in NFFF membership, which brought new financial problems in its wake. The secretary reported a fall from the 1919 peak of 3,214 to 2,712, although new branches continued to be formed at places as far apart as Nottingham, Colchester and Portsmouth, and Glasgow affiliated later in the year. But the downturn continued inexorably, as membership fell to 1,983 in 1921, 1,469 in 1922 and only 866 in 1923. Bitter comments were made about the prevailing individualism of the trade at large and the disloyalty of those who had joined in order to secure their supplies in the difficult years of 1918 and 1919 and now fell away when the crisis had passed. The failure of the national cooperative purchasing scheme which was introduced in 1919 may also have affected the NFFF adversely, although the Federation itself was never directly involved in the affairs of the ill-fated Fish Friers' National Co-operative Supply Association.[29]

It was in this period of rapid decline that the NFFF came closest to disappearing altogether. During 1923 Loftas, who had become President of the NFFF, agitated for the Federation to become incorporated into the Association of British Fisheries, which had been set up as a result of a government initiative to pull together the various fish-related trades, from trawlermen to fishmongers, into a single organization with a Royal Charter. Loftas had a soft spot for such schemes and he had enjoyed rubbing shoulders with the eminent as one of the three fish friers' representatives on the committee to draw up the constitution. But his attempt to persuade the NFFF to wind itself up and transfer itself lock, stock and barrel to the ABF was thwarted by the new secretary, W.H. Rose, who insisted on taking the proposal to a full delegate conference instead of letting the NFFF's executive decide. The conference voted overwhelmingly for the continuance of the NFFF as a separate entity. The collapse of the ABF in July 1925 seemed to bear out the wisdom of this decision, although Loftas was later to argue that its demise was largely due to the NFFF's failure to join. This seems an unlikely contention, a piece of retrospective self-justification, for the other fish trades were powerful enough to have carried the new organization without the ill-organized friers, who had in any case subscribed to the ABF without actually merging into it. Meanwhile the NFFF struggled on, casting envious glances at bodies like the Retail Newsagents' National Federation with its 13,000 members and tight control of the trade.[30]

At almost the lowest point in its fortunes, the NFFF took the risky, ambitious step of introducing a monthly periodical, which began in April 1925 as the

National Fish Caterers' Review, with a print-run of 3,000. It changed its name to the *Fish Friers' Review* two years later. On its first appearance the NFFF was down to 18 widely scattered branches: six in Lancashire, two in Yorkshire, four in South Wales and the others ranging from Northumberland and Durham to Bristol and Portsmouth by way of Leicester, Nottingham and Coventry. But the *Review*'s appearance coincided with a modest revival of the Federation's fortunes, although it was to be several years before it regained anything like the level of influence and apparent representativeness that it held at the end of the war.[31]

It was not until 1934 that the NFFF returned to vitality and growth in response to new threats to fish friers' livelihoods from government intervention in the fish and potato markets. During the intervening years the organization campaigned against restrictions on the spread of fish and chip shops into new residential areas, represented the trade before government commissions of inquiry into the fishing industry and tried to prevent new friers from setting up shop in old working-class areas where competition was already intense. Behind the scenes, it also lobbied against the trawler owners' efforts to secure legal restrictions on imports and prohibitive tariffs on foreign-landed fish. All this took place against a backcloth of deepening trade depression and declining demand among many of the trade's traditional customers. In 1933 the NFFF's twentieth annual report expressed despondency. This was the worst year in the Federation's history:

> so far as trading is concerned. Not only has the spending power of the public been reduced to a very low ebb, but almost every other commodity in so far as eatables are concerned, have been greatly reduced in price to the public, consequently, in view of the less spending power of the public and the other cheap commodities offered, fried fish and chips have become almost in price a luxury.[32]

The NFFF had been unable to counteract these trends and its membership and range of influence had stagnated. But hard on the heels of this report came two new developments that galvanized the NFFF into action and brought it a swelling flow of new branches and recruits. These were the 'Embargo' on fish caught in certain areas during the summer months and the activities of the Potato Marketing Board.

The NFFF had been resisting the British Trawlers' Federation's pressure on government for import restrictions and tariffs on foreign-landed fish since 1925; they saw the 'Embargo' as an alternative means to the same end, raising prices and profits for the producers at the expense of the friers and their customers. The 'Embargo' was officially labelled 'The Sea Fishing Industry (Restriction of Fishing in Northern Waters) Order, 1933'. It prohibited fishing in the recently developed Bear Island fishing grounds, in the far north, during August in 1933 and thereafter during June, July, August and September, and limited landings of foreign-caught fish to 90 per cent of the average of the last three years. There were other provisions but these were the ones which incurred the NFFF's wrath. Spokesmen immediately expressed the fear that the results would be as damaging as the trawler owners' previous proposal for a one-third tariff on foreign-caught fish; friers were particularly angry at the prospect of increased prices during their best and busiest months, when supplies were normally unproblematic. 'Reviewer' in the *Fish Friers' Review* issued a call to arms against the new regulations:

Ignored by the Government, undefended by the merchants, the Frier must fight alone.[33]

A sustained struggle ensued. The NFFF soon complained that the 'Embargo' had indeed artificially inflated summer costs; the trade's self-taught statistician, T. Harrison of Portsmouth, bombarded the civil servants and all who would listen with elaborate graphs purporting to demonstrate this point. Harrison blamed profiteering by fish merchants and railway companies as well as the machinations of the trawler owners. He was particularly incensed that the newspapers were regularly reporting examples of fish being sold to manure works at rock-bottom prices in time of glut, leaving the friers' customers to assume that these were the normal prices and to blame the friers for profiteering in their turn. He also attacked government policy, arguing that Whitehall should have taken over 'absolute control' of the fishing industry at the end of the war and blaming the current 'disastrous' tendency to favour producers against consumers, giving most to those who shouted loudest and were best organized.[34]

This view of the situation was, not surprisingly, not shared in ministerial and civil service circles. A meeting between civil servants of the Ministry of Agriculture and Fisheries and an NFFF delegation in May 1934 brought official denials of a relationship between the 'Embargo' and rising fish prices. The friers were reminded that their invoices now included the additional cost of heading, sorting and packing, or of filleting and packing, in most cases; and the long-term rise in prices (which pre-dated the 'Embargo') therefore reflected changes in the nature of the commodity. Moreover, Harrison's figures were based on cod, which was, incidentally, the main fish caught around Bear Island, and the civil servants wanted to look at a wider variety of species. In January 1935, after Harrison had bamboozled the Sea-Fish Commission with an incomprehensible disquisition on his graphs, the ministry's F.G. Barnard did a demolition job:

The Fish Friers may have a case but it wont [*sic*] be set out by their present statistician who is 'cod-minded' and assumes that all the cod landed is used by fish friers and that none has to be sold by merchants at offal prices . . . Moreover, cod is not the only fish that they fry.

There was also some scepticism about the representativeness of Harrison's own invoices, on which several of his graphs turned out to depend.[35] In 1939 the chair of the White Fish Commission provided an overview of the situation over the past few years, lamenting the friers' inability or unwillingness to come to terms with his analysis. He argued that the Bear Island fishing grounds were prolific but difficult, because even in the new long-distance trawlers the fish that was caught first had deteriorated by the time it was landed. The Bear Island fish were also overwhelmingly drawn from the cheapest varieties, which distorted the whole market. So the trawler owners limited the fish that could be brought back in each boat, limited the number of trawlers used and fixed a minimum sale price at the ports. The supply of fish as food was little reduced, with less wastage, and fish consumption had actually risen, despite an admitted increase in prices. This framework of analysis paid more heed to developments in the later 1930s than to the 'Embargo' itself, which was dismissed briefly as a groundless source for friers' complaints:

> it is good for the fishing grounds, prevents fish travelling long distances in hot weather, and was enforced, I think, to help the near water producers

who were suffering severely from the competition of the distant-water fleets. Alexander Gray endorsed these comments and complained that the NFFF continued to offer no new analysis and provided 'horridly confused' figures which they were now refusing to submit for scrutiny. The commissioners thought that the friers might be suffering from increasing competition from the fishmongers for what used to be friers' fish, but they were highly sceptical about the friers' complaints of rising prices and insufficient supplies.[36]

The NFFF's enduring obsession with the 'Embargo' thus found little sympathy in official circles and their limited resources inevitably meant that their statistics would be home-made, amateurish and vulnerable. The friers complained about the trawler owners' new devices for price-fixing and limiting supply, but the 'Embargo' became a kind of totem around which they conducted an angry but ineffectual dance, needing it as an explanation for their perceived woes even as they denounced it. Their sense of injustice was real enough, even though it was founded on a mistaken view of the current circumstances of the fishing industry.

The policies of the Potato Marketing Board added a further dimension to the NFFF's discontent with government policy. The Board was one of the first fruits of the policies of Walter Elliot, who had become Minister of Agriculture in 1932. He viewed society as a congeries of producer groups, which needed to be guided by government into the harmonious self-regulation of their own affairs through corporate organizations based on particular areas of economic interest. This was an influential strand of thought within Conservatism in the 1930s; but the NFFF found its practical expression, on their own territory, to be decidedly threatening. Elliot's views involved an acknowledgement that producers' interests should be put before those of consumers; in the case of the Potato Marketing Board the friers were relegated to quasi-consumer status.[37] The Board itself consisted of people elected by the registered producers, supplemented by two co-opted nominees of the Board's elected members, and two government nominees who turned out to be the stockbroker brother of the Earl of Moray and an agricultural adviser to ICI (though he did not wish to be so labelled). The chairman, Captain John Mollett, was a member of the council of the National Farmers' Union and chair of its potatoes committee.[38] The NFFF was eventually allocated, after protests, a single place not on the main committee but on the retail committee.[39] The Board appeared well-equipped to advance Stanley Baldwin's declared aim, enunciated before the Produce Markets Supply Committee in 1933: 'to rectify, if possible, the situation which under Free Trade had sacrificed the interests of the country to the interests of the town'.[40]

The NFFF's view of the Potato Marketing Board was soon being crisply enunciated. Harrison, again, provided an angry denunciation that set the tone for his colleagues. The Board was devoted to enriching farmers by raising prices and merchants by eliminating competition, all at the frier's expense. It had reduced the potato acreage and boosted prices spectacularly in its first year of operation and its luxurious offices and high administrative expenses merely added insult to injury. One result of all this would be ruin for large numbers of friers, but:

> I have ceased to take interest in the P.M.B. because I recognise how helpless Fish Friers are against the powerful stronghold the agriculturists are building up.[41]

Threatened increases in the price of friers' flour and frying media, again as a direct result of government policy, added further fuel to the indictment.

Harrison did not spare his own organization. He argued that the fish friers were treated in a cavalier fashion by government departments and policy-makers because they:

> know perfectly well that the NFFF are not, as a body, financially strong enough to represent a body of mosquitos.

His anger was stoked further by the knowledge that some friers were objecting to the existing affiliation fees, at a time when resources needed to be built up for the conflicts that lay ahead.[42]

By September 1934, when Harrison's denunciation appeared, the NFFF was already beginning to attract new members and affiliate new branches. Nine new branches were being planned in May and in the early summer the Potteries, Barry Dock, Rotherham and Chesterfield joined the NFFF empire. By January 1935 an NFFF delegation could tell the Sea-Fish Commission that the Federation had about 5,000 members who represented between eight and ten thousand fried fish shops. The first figure seems more likely than the second, but there are clear indications here of recent growth in response to the new threats to fish and potato supplies and prices. A year later the delegation was able to report an increase in membership to 7,000 and in branches from 34 to 57, with new initiatives still going forward. Indeed, the first half of 1936 saw 15 additional branches formed, in places as far apart as Bath and Accrington.[43]

At this point, in the early summer of 1936, the NFFF felt strong enough to threaten strike action for redress of the friers' grievances. The case was set out in bold type in the *Fish Friers' Review*. The trade's condition was said to be 'critical':

> Every piece of legislation referring to our trade that has had the Government's approval has, up to now, been at the expense of our particular section of the Fishing Industry. We have had as it were to give blood transfusions which we could ill-afford, to the Trawler Owners, through the Fishing Embargo, to the potato growers, through the PMB, and even to the wheat growers, through the quota on flour. For a time we paid dearly for cooking material because the price of raw fats rose because our Government was impotent to stay the exporting of raw fats to Germany.[44]

The strike threat was withdrawn when the government announced that the

Bear Island 'Embargo' was to be lifted during September. The NFFF's claim that this was a major victory was somewhat tendentious, as all the other grievances remained; 'Utility' in the *Fishing News* argued that the strike call was merely 'banging the big drum'. He claimed that the decision to lift the 'Embargo' in September had already been taken before the strike threat was made and that the strike would have been a fiasco: it would have done well to close one shop in four. The real problem of the fried fish trade, for other outside observers as well as 'Utility', was the surplus of small businesses that did not generate enough turnover to soak up their standing charges; the cure was to reduce competition and concentrate the trade into fewer, larger shops.[45]

This dispute over the real impact of the strike threat, with all its ramifications, led to something of a feud between the NFFF executive and the editor of the *Fishing News*; but whatever the facts of the case, the episode gave increased confidence to the NFFF's leadership while persuading them that a strong organization could wring concessions from government. Over the next few years the Federation continued to build up its strength and engage in the rhetoric of confrontation, while negotiating with more hope of an acceptable outcome than hitherto. This change of posture and expectations was clearly made easier by Elliot's departure from the Ministry of Agriculture and Fisheries in the autumn of 1936. The *Fish Friers' Review* welcomed his successor in lively style:

> We can hardly imagine that Mr Morrison can do more harm to the Fish Friers of England than has his predecessor, and from that point of view, the feeling engendered by this change of office was one of relief.[46]

Elliot's departure no doubt helped to take the heat out of the debate over the proposals for reorganizing the fishing industry that emerged from the Ministry in 1937. Some alarm was expressed in March at the scheme for regulating production and marketing under a Central Council or Joint Board under the agricultural marketing legislation that had produced the Potato Marketing Board. The NFFF originally feared that the trawler owners would be allowed to dominate such a body, just as the growers dominated the PMB. But their fears were allayed as they received increasing consideration and respect from government – and the scheme proved to be so administratively complicated that its establishment was eventually overtaken by the outbreak of the Second World War. Meanwhile, the NFFF continued to campaign against the 'Embargo' and in 1938 sustained pressure was rewarded when it was lifted during August, the key holiday month, as well as September. But this did not still the clamour from the branches and the rank and file about high fish prices and the trawler owners' quotas; other attempts to ration supplies also generated angry commentary. In April 1937 several branch meetings discussed a renewed strike threat; and in January 1939 the St Helens branch submitted a resolution to the Executive Committee, urging it:

> to immediately consider [*sic*] . . . asking all members to operate a general boycott of fish until a guarantee be given that supplies shall be at an economical price.

This was not taken up by the NFFF hierarchy, but it struck a chord with many of the friers whose complaints had been reverberating through the columns of the trade press for several years. Pleased as they were at the increasing influence they exerted on policy-making, the NFFF's leaders knew their limitations, and from time to time this made them unpopular with their local activists.[47]

These tensions became more obvious and sustained in the NFFF's dealings with the Potato Marketing Board, whose chair, Captain Mollett, had outraged the friers in a well-publicized speech in 1935:

> They had had potatoes below cost price for the past three years and they had looked upon them as a subsidy for their fish . . . It was not reasonable that the fish fryer should expect the potato grower to supply him with his potatoes at a loss.

This version of events was challenged by the NFFF at every turn. The Board's policy was said to aim:

> to restrict supplies and create a demand (by means of advertising) with the sole aim of forcing up the price of potatoes beyond the reach of their best customers.[48]

By the end of 1936 expressions of hatred for the Board and all its works were the staple fare of NFFF branch meetings. For the NFFF executive, however, results could only be achieved by negotiation; their understanding of this uncomfortable reality was demonstrated by the President's comment in late 1935 that:

> We are (now) in fact, at least we like to think so, on very good terms with the PMB, and they now recognise the value of the frier to the grower.[49]

This apparent cosiness was actually intermittent and conditional: the *Fish Friers' Review* produced a very circumstantial attack in late 1936 on the Board's advice to growers to hold supplies back in anticipation of price increases. But in March 1937 delegations from the two bodies met to draw up an agreement for future co-operation, 'including the possibility of establishing running contracts at a uniform price, irrespective of the rise and fall in the market price of potatoes'. This was a seductive goal and in pursuing it the NFFF executive asked for the suspension of public controversy among friers about the PMB's policies. But the critics were not to be silenced and two months later the Liverpool branch circulated a leaflet attacking the 'Potato Ramp', which the trade press had declined to publish. This led to a long dispute over NFFF policy, in which Liverpool found support from St Helens and temporarily disaffiliated from the Federation. What is most interesting, however, is the limited amount of official support from other branches for Liverpool's militant posture. The revelation that the PMB was to allow a much higher level of potato imports in the summer of 1938 was a welcome indicator of flexibility, especially when a supply gap between the old potatoes and the new created the temporary spectre of a potato famine at this time.[50]

The NFFF's policies might seem unduly conciliatory to a minority of organized friers, but they did not prevent it from continuing to grow and therefore to gain in credibility in its dealings with government departments. By the end of 1937 the number of branches had reached 130 and overtures were being made to the Scottish friers, who were responding to the pressures of the time and making a renewed attempt to build a federation of their own. By August 1938 seven Scottish branches had affiliated, and a year later the NFFF's membership had passed 10,000. The circulation of the *Fish Friers' Review* increased from 3,500 in September 1937 to 6,000 in September 1938; during this time the Federation acquired new offices, appointing a full-time secretary and a professionally trained editor for the *Review*. In the spring of 1939 the number of branches reached 160.[51] The NFFF was still reaching only one-third or so of Britain's fish friers as the war broke out, but it had come a long way in the previous five years. It had grown enough in stature and respectability to ensure that the friers were looked after much more carefully by the government during the Second World War than had been the case during, and especially after, the First.[52]

The central issues of fish and potato prices probably did most to boost recruitment, but they were not the NFFF's only concerns. The limited scope for influencing the Ministry's policies led friers into other ways of improving trading conditions. Attempts were made to restrict competition but here, too, government policies made life difficult in some respects. The most effective barriers to proliferation had involved local authority operation of Offensive Trades Orders. By the mid-1930s most towns seem to have scheduled fish frying as an offensive trade, but controls were becoming more difficult to enforce. In 1931 the West Riding Quarter Sessions had overturned a local authority's refusal to grant a licence for a new fish and chip shop, so the legal powers were seen to be less than watertight. Three years later the Ministry of Health sent out a remarkable circular to local authorities, asking them to 'think very seriously' before declaring fish and chips an offensive trade. The Ministry argued that the fried fish trade should be encouraged to expand to help the fishing industry, which was 'of primary importance, and is going through a very hard time'. New by-laws would also impose additional burdens on ratepayers and taxpayers at a time of austerity.

With advice like this going out from central government, it is not surprising that the Public Health Act of 1936 removed fish frying from the official schedule of offensive trades.[53] Meanwhile, the NFFF had high hopes of the proposed reorganization of the fishing industry which was being discussed during 1937–8. For a time it appeared possible that all fried fish shops wishing to register might have to be approved by the NFFF. But when this regulatory power turned out to be illusory, the Federation's spokesmen lost interest and by March 1938 the value of the registration scheme to the friers was expected to be 'very small'.[54]

Another way of restraining the proliferation of outlets lay through an agreement with the range manufacturers, in which they undertook not to supply ranges to new friers whose location and behaviour were not acceptable to the local association. By 1937 28 firms had subscribed to this agreement. But it worked less than perfectly in practice, and this is not surprising if the confidential memorandum which the National Federation of Fish Restaurant Engineers sent to the Sea-Fish Commission in 1935 is considered. They urged that all restrictions on the opening of new fried fish shops should be removed, apart from basic requirements about hygiene and fume disposal, which should be imposed and administered by central rather than local government according to national criteria. Barrington Hooper, the restaurant engineers' honorary secretary, added that the scope for expanding the consumption of cooked fish was 'almost unlimited', but:

> As it is, the Offensive Trades Order is being used as a kind of Trade Protection Act to protect the inefficient shop-keeper from the competition of an efficient one: where this operates it means that the possible demand for cooked fish is limited, and the middle and upper middle classes are deprived of fish cooked in a manner that would entice them to purchase and consume it.[55]

The NFFF would not have been pleased by this testimony, which accorded so well with official thinking; but Hooper's argument underlines their own dilemma. They wanted to raise standards but they also wanted to protect their members from 'unfair' competition, and these were not always mutually compatible goals.

At the local level, NFFF branches made increasingly determined efforts to reduce the stresses of the free market by introducing price-fixing arrangements. These went back to the earliest days of friers' organizations, but in the mid-1930s a combination of deepening economic problems and increasing local strength led to a rash of attempts to impose minimum prices and even standard lists. The late spring and early summer of 1937 saw initiatives of this kind from Bath to Harrogate, including attempts to define a standard weight for a penny portion of chips and a standard size of chip bag. Nelson set a list of minimum prices, which included fish scones as well as fish and chips. Preston and Chorley followed suit, in an area where the concept of a 'list' was familiar from the staple industry. But these arrangements did not always run smoothly. Preston's NFFF branch was plagued by dissidents and non-members who wanted to keep penny portions of chips, arguing that their customers could not afford twopennyworths. T. Reeder conducted a survey of portion sizes and found that almost all were over the agreed five ounces of chips for twopence. The Preston branch tried to persuade the suppliers' organizations to boycott the dissidents, but too many firms were outside the charmed circle and the arrangement proved impossible to police. Eventually the dissidents mounted a campaign of rumour and insult, accusing the local executive of 'making money out of the association' and 'waving the red flag', and calling them 'Bolsheviks'. By October the Preston association had abolished its price list by a very small majority, as the dissidents overcame the waverers. The list's fate seems to have been clinched by a widespread desire to continue selling pennyworths of chips to children, but an angry Reeder told his colleagues that 'you are letting twenty friers drive you to the workhouse'.[56] The Preston friers submitted unusually long, full and heartfelt monthly reports to the *Fish Friers' Review*, and similar sagas may well have taken place, unreported, elsewhere. It was almost impossible for a local association to impose a price list and make it work in the face of determined intransigence, and very few local associations could claim 100 per cent membership. But at least, by the late 1930s, the organized friers were often able to agree minimum prices over wide areas and among shops of a certain size and standard; this in itself must have helped to stabilize the trade.

The NFFF and its branches had less demanding and controversial advantages to offer. They provided insurance at cheap rates, and some were also supply companies that bought friers' requisites at wholesale prices for their members. Friers could wear celluloid membership badges and display the national sign of the NFFF, whose emblem was a lighthouse. Above all, perhaps, the associations offered friendly company and sociability to men – and, increasingly, women – who would otherwise have remained, in the words of a Dewsbury frier, 'lonely competitors'. Whist drives, outings, annual dinners and dances brought friers together and accounts of these occasions are full of shared humour and reminiscence. And extra free time was obtained by the arrival of Sunday closing and the spread of the half-day holiday movement, both of which were strongly advocated by the NFFF. The branches were also venues for formal and informal education about the trade, as friers heard talks and swapped experiences. Increasingly, too, the branches provided scope for women to display administrative as well as social talents, although the Cowdenbeath branch, whose officers were all female in 1941, was a wartime exception to the male-dominated rule.[57]

How, then, should we categorize the fish friers' organizations, and especially the NFFF? The NFFF delegation to the Sea-Fish Commission in 1935 accepted that 'you are essentially a Protection Society', although they went on to emphasize the social side and to stress the importance of comparing notes about merchants' prices and services and combining to provide affordable legal advice and to negotiate over gas and water supplies and prices, as well as offering cheap insurance.[58] But when we go further and ask what sort of ideals fish friers' organizations espoused or where they stood in relation to contemporary politics, we immediately run into cross-currents and complications.

The organized friers had at times a radical, collectivist face which belies easy generalizations about the individualism of the small trader. From an early stage the vocabulary of trade unionism was sometimes used, as when Bradford friers responded to a potato shortage in 1907 by forming a Fish and Chipped Potato Friers' Union.[59] The NCF's Yorkshire-dominated membership provided more substantial trade-unionist rhetoric through the pages of *The Frier*, whose resident poet stressed the importance of newcomers to the trade joining 'the union'. He offered the tale of 'The Newcomes', who had saved a little and wanted to purchase a comfortable retirement by 'A few short years of push and rush, of grabbing all the trade'. The NCF secretary tells them: 'They ought to join the union for on unionists that they lived'; but they resolved: 'To heed not others, sisters, brothers, but while within the trade/ To play for pelf, to seek for self, and others' custom – raid.' But this was a story with a moral and the Newcomes' reward was ultimate consignment to the workhouse. The chair of a meeting at Barnsley to set up an NCF branch was reported thus:

> Barnsley was in every way one of the best organised towns in England, and there was no reason to suppose that Fish Friers, who, in many cases were old unionists, would not renew their old time faiths in organisation and join up.[60]

The Frier also offered consistent support for the Co-operative movement, urging members to support collective purchasing schemes and to emulate the success of the Co-operative Wholesale Society: a posture that perhaps came easier to fish friers because they did not encounter the Co-op as a direct competitor.[61] Beyond this, a distinct strain of democratic socialism runs through the paper. An editorial on profiteering in 1919 began by citing Marx on the toll taken on a labourer's wage by landlords and shopkeepers, identifying friers with their customers as victims of the exploitation of trawler-owners and middlemen – although the indictment also embraced taxation. Less ambiguously, non-members were described as worse *even* than capitalists and a Stockton frier who sat on the NCF executive was described as 'a worker, a unionist, a student of economics'. He and others engaged in solidaristic, consumerist rhetoric, encapsulated by R. Vellam in 1919:

> Now that the fish is coming we can meet the increasing demand, and we can all give increasing value to our customers for their money. Let us all earn our fair wage by standing shoulder to shoulder with the worker in our shops by handing him his and her share of the increased production of the seas. Thus will the Fish Frier and his quiet, untiring, unselfish leaders, realise that they are doing their bit to build the new world, the promised land for all the sons and daughters of men.[62]

It is startling to find small shopkeepers talking in this vein. We must not make too much of it, however. We have no way of knowing how representative this kind of thinking was, although it accords well with some friers' attitudes to pricing and value for money in the depressed areas of the 1930s. *The Frier* was, however, a decidedly maverick production, and W. H. Wilcock of Leeds annoyed the editors in 1919 by telling them that its content was over the heads of the NCF membership in Leeds. Within its pages we also find anti-semitism and a sustained distrust of government regulation of the trade. But there was no perceived inconsistency in these juxtapositions of ideas and at very least *The Frier* gives us an unexpected window into attitudes that existed and found expression within the post-war petty bourgeoisie.[63]

Even within the ranks of the organized friers, however, the NFFF was much less radical than these NCF spokesmen. In 1923 the NCF denounced Loftas, who was still on the NFFF executive at this time, for his opposition to the offensive trades legislation. This was presented as support for untrammelled private enterprise, which would lead to ruinous competition.[64] This attack owed something to an enduring feud with Loftas, who once described *The Frier* as 'The Friers' Comic Cuts', and Loftas himself always emphasized that he had carried his trade-union principles into fish frying. He had adopted the widespread skilled worker's perception of the strike as a weapon of last resort and he favoured conciliation and arbitration, but his philosophy was in tune with the mainstream of the inter-war labour movement.[65]

Meanwhile, the NFFF's journal announced itself to be 'of course, strictly non-political' in 1925. This did not prevent the editors in July from running a fierce attack on Russian communism, from J. Hill of Blackpool; a riposte from C. Halstead of Halifax, who defended the Bolsheviks, pointed out that Hill's piece *was* political but it received short shrift. The editorial response was jingoistic:

> Communism cannot be recognised as practical British politics under our splendid Constitution, and may the day never come when we cannot sing 'God save the King' in our glorious England.[66]

Again, it is impossible to establish the representativeness of either set of views. But this exchange is a reminder that the NFFF had to avoid defining a political standpoint of its own if it was to build up its own strength and unity; henceforth the editor kept a lower profile. As the policies of the National Government generated increasing wrath among fish friers during the 1930s, however, the splendours of the British constitution began to pall and the NFFF visibly lurched towards the left.

As anger mounted against the 'Embargo' and the Potato Marketing Board, T. Harrison of Portsmouth revived notions of fish frying as an essentially proletarian activity which had been current in the NCF and had never disappeared at branch level. In November 1935 he proposed that the NFFF 'should seek entry to the trade union movement'. This idea was scouted by 'Reviewer' in the *Fish Friers' Review* for the obvious reasons:

> How . . . can an association of masters join in a body of workers? The object of a Trade Union is to gain better *working* conditions, etc., for its members, not BETTER TRADING CONDITIONS for a body of private enterprisers.

Interestingly, not everyone agreed with 'Reviewer' that the idea was, in a pejorative sense, 'fantastic'. It was taken seriously in Sheffield, for example, and it reappeared the following year when the proposed fish friers' strike was directly borrowed from the armoury of the labour movement. In July 1936, as plans were made for the strike, the executive committee of the NFFF decided 'to form a sub-committee to enquire into the possibilities of affiliation with the Trades Union Council'. At the same time, steps were taken to inform interested parties, including the Labour Party and the National Liberal Association but not the Conservatives. Nothing came of this initiative but, again, it is interesting that it happened at all.[67]

This episode was, admittedly, out of character as far as the NFFF leadership was concerned, although in 1928 one of its most respected administrators had married Edith Baxter, who was described as 'a prominent Trade Union leader and organizer in the clothing trade'. The *Fish Friers' Review* was capable of enlisting the aid of the *Daily Worker* against the Potato Marketing Board; but in the same issue the NFFF President, Henry Youngman, Edith Baxter's husband, sounded off against a proposed excess profit tax on the grounds that 'all taxation is bad for the community' because it discouraged capitalists' initiative and undermined all the values that had made Britain great. A few years earlier the NFFF's popular honorary secretary, Jackson Tomlinson, had praised Mr Holgate of the Leeds and District Estate Agents' and Rent Collectors' Association as the 'greatest opponent' of Leeds Corporation's 'socialist' slum clearance schemes, although the Leeds branch of the NFFF, after hearing Holgate, had voted to invite the chair of the Leeds housing committee to their next meeting.[68] Tomlinson's perspective on this issue was undoubtedly influenced by the difficulties then being experienced by Leeds friers as a result of slum clearance and the uncertain status of fish frying on the new council estates. The executive could convey a very different-looking political outlook when established friers were disappointed by the rejection in parliament of a proposal to impose a 'proper distribution' of fish and chip shops as part of the wider regulation of the fish trades. This issue provoked a particularly interesting editorial in the *Fish Friers' Review*:

> The principle of private enterprise, unrestricted in any way, is one which is very firmly established in this country. With certain people, it has become a religion. But what is the sense of demanding that private enterprise should go absolutely unchecked when it has become out of hand and is being misused by certain utterly selfish and unscrupulous members of the community.[69]

Taken in the round, the 'official' pronouncements of the NFFF cannot be used to enlist its leaders for any overarching political ideology. The perceived interests of the trade were paramount and the 'common sense' of the leadership often cut across political orthodoxies. This should not surprise us; but it is important that the fish friers were neither rampant individualists nor die-hard opponents of state intervention under all circumstances. They were ambivalent about government and their attitudes to it varied according to the perceived impact of its policies. At this level the politics of fish frying were essentially pragmatic.[70]

Despite the occasional 'free enterprise' rhetoric of some of the leadership, the centre of gravity of the organized frying trade was probably closer to Labour than to the Liberals or Conservatives. The Conservative MP for Camberwell North, A. L. Bateman, was a staunch defender of the friers in parliament until he lost his seat in 1935. But overwhelmingly, from their beginnings, the friers' organizations chose to work through Labour MPs, especially those whose proletarian origins made them seem approachable and likely to be sympathetic. Links with Labour were rarely formal – though in 1936 at least three of the branches chose to meet on labour movement premises, although they were far outweighed by the eleven pubs, eight restaurants and two temperance halls. Above all, the occasional rhetoric of branch meetings suggests a solidaristic outlook. North Staffordshire, a branch that came to contain at least two Labour local councillors, was urged to bring 'every frier in the area into one large brotherhood' and Wisbech advocated a Co-operative vision of the NFFF, with its own trawlers and potato distribution centres, a 'great Family of Friers'.[71]

In spite of all this, however, a year after its flirtation with the TUC the NFFF affiliated to the Federation of British Industries, 'undoubtedly the premier Trade Organisation of the country'. This belated formal admission that fish friers were businessmen rather than wage-earners was, however, capable of coexisting with a persisting perception of the fish frier's income as a wage, paid not by a capitalist employer but by neighbours of similar status who bought the frier's product. Within this framework of attitudes, what concerned friers above all was a form of respectability: an acceptance from the rest of society that they were performing a useful, responsible, skilled role that was vital to the national economy. To protect and nurture this recognition, the trade had to be policed, from within or without, in order to discourage or eliminate the irresponsible, unhygienic, old-fashioned, price-cutting friers at the bottom end of the market: just as the skilled trade unions from which so many friers came sought to maintain standards in order to protect their position in the labour market. Thus the NFFF looked kindly on proposals to regulate the frying trade, especially if, as at one time seemed possible, the Federation itself was to be put in charge of the regulation. The goal was to ensure for the respectable fish frier an adequate return on his or her investment of capital and labour.[72]

At times, and especially in the early 1920s when parliamentary bills were being envisaged to impose minimum standards and codes of conduct on the trade, the NFFF almost embraced the professionalization of fish frying. Friers supplied expertise as well as food and they could be presented as being equal in importance to doctors in preserving and promoting working-class health. They should be trained, trusted and respected in their communities. As with the rest of this chapter, we are dealing with the aspirations of an organized and relatively articulate minority among friers, and we need to bear in mind that many back-street friers must have pursued survival by hook or by crook as viciously competitive individualists. But the values I have been describing were undoubtedly widespread and influential within the trade. Fish frying may well have been unusual among the small businesses, because it combined craft production and retailing in a way that was becoming increasingly uncommon, but it would be interesting to look comparatively at other retail occupations and organizations to test the extent of the NFFF's distinctiveness.

Despite the widespread aspiration to craft or even quasi-professional status among fish friers, their persisting identification with neighbours and customers needs to be stressed. The overwhelming majority of friers continued to identify with the working-class society from which they were drawn, as the frequent proletarian and communal rhetoric of friers' organizations testifies. This, again, sets the friers apart from the more affluent and aspiring of their fellow retailers. It brings them squarely into Hosgood's 'domestic shopkeepers' category, specialists though they were, and in spite of a small top-dressing of substantial restaurateurs. The relationship between friers, customers and communities needs further investigation; this will be pursued in the next chapter, which also looks at the consumers and consumption of fish and chips and at its impact on working-class living standards.[73]

7 Consumers and Communities

One of the main obstacles to the fish friers' quest for respectability was the identification of their product with slums and slum-dwellers, with unpleasant smells and dubious hygiene and with the encouragement of 'secondary poverty' through injudicious domestic budgeting by unskilled housewives. These perceptions of the trade were widely shared among middle-class observers, journalists and social commentators – and the prejudices with which they became associated have proved to be enduring. Matters were not helped by the public consumption of fish and chips in the streets, out of newspaper, using unwashed fingers instead of cutlery: these aspects of the trade violated powerful taboos in respectable circles, involving such sacred issues as cleanliness, privacy and domesticity. And when, in the inter-war years especially, fish and chips became the butt of 'low' music-hall comedians and cartoonists, its disreputable proletarian image was doubly reinforced. If we examine the evidence, however, it appears that many of the stereotypes about fish friers and their customers date from the earliest years of the trade. The truth about fish and chip consumption during the first four decades of the twentieth century is complex, involving changes over time and geographical variations; but it adds up to something much more respectable than the myth about dissolute, improvident slum-dwellers living on fish and chips and little else. Fish and chips became part of mainstream, respectable working-class culture in the early twentieth century and moved further up-market in some places during the 1930s. There is also convincing evidence that it made a positive contribution to working-class diet and to the sustaining of neighbourhood life and local solidarities. In developing these arguments, I begin with the questions of who ate fish and chips, how often and under what circumstances, before moving on to questions of dietary value and the place of the fish and chip shop in working-class culture.

Anyone who tried to base a study of working-class diet on the numerous dietary surveys conducted house-to-house by social investigators between the 1880s and the 1930s might be forgiven for giving fish and chips a very low profile indeed. It is hardly mentioned and as a result fish consumption figures are presented as being lower than they really were. When Ian Gazeley attempted to recalculate A. L. Bowley's cost of living index for the years between 1881 and 1912, using sources of this kind to refine and expand the basis for changing food price indices, he found that where fish was separately recorded in surveys during these years, it accounted for between 1.94 and 8.21

per cent of expenditure on food in working-class households; but the high figure, from Liverpool, was aberrant and came from a small sample. In any case, hardly any of the recorded expenditure was on fried fish. When Gazeley made a tentative attempt at incorporating fish prices into his index, he had to use tinned salmon in the absence of any other remotely plausible price series. Gazeley does, rightly, note the problems posed by food consumed outside the home, which was less likely to be recorded. He acknowledges that: 'It is likely that the expenditure on convenience foods increased during this period.' There was also the problem of 'specific non-disclosure' among the survey population of expenditure of which the investigators might be thought to disapprove. Gazeley cites drink and tobacco; but in the light of the widespread prejudice in social investigating circles against fish and chips, which will emerge later in this chapter, there is a strong case for assuming that the same problem applies here. Moreover, households that were sensitive about aspects of their expenditure were particularly likely to refuse to participate in the surveys, which were biased in their composition towards the literate, numerate and respectable.[1]

These speculations are given added weight when we look at the Ministry of Agriculture and Fisheries' report on 'The consumption of fish at different income levels in Great Britain', prepared in 1935. This used the original records from about 2,500 family budgets from several surveys conducted in the early 1930s and its authors came to very clear conclusions. On the evidence of the surveys:

> expenditure on fried fish is very variable and, apart from the Co-operative groups, there is little indication of any definite trend of expenditure with increasing income. Moreover, the average expenditure per head in the northern industrial towns seems to be too low in view of the importance of the fish frying trade in the north of England. It is probably that the cost of fried fish was not included when the fish was eaten away from home or was not purchased out of the housekeeping allowance. It is felt, therefore, that the existing budget data relating to fried fish are probably misleading . . . It is probable that consumption of fish away from home is consider-able since it forms the basis of a large proportion of midday meals.

Exactly the same was said about chips later in the report.[2]

This evidence was put together and evaluated by people with a particular professional interest in levels of fish consumption, people who knew enough about popular eating habits from their own experience to adjust for the obvious deficiencies in the survey data. Other commentators occasionally showed a similar awareness. Thus the Manchester University Settlement's survey of Ancoats in 1937-8, noting that only 23 per cent of the families surveyed responded positively to a specific question about fish and chip consumption, commented:

> It is possible that (fish and chips was mentioned) only when (it) formed part of the regular weekly expenditure and (was) eaten for the principal meal. Before the days of 'black-out', the fried fish shops appeared to do their best trade in the late hours of the evening, and it is probable that these bed-time snacks were not considered of sufficient importance to be included in the weekly food budget.[3]

The sources differ about the circumstances under which fish and chips might have been hidden from the investigators, but their overall drift is entirely convincing. The dietary surveys, on which most historians of working-class food consumption have leaned heavily, simply cannot be trusted as indicators of fish and chip consumption. For that, we must go to other sources, and the picture we obtain of the importance of fish and chips in working-class diet will be dramatically different.

Fish and chips clearly originated in the back streets and slum districts of London and the industrial towns, becoming associated with the poor and with the disreputable pleasures of late-night revellers. In Birmingham in about 1880 'many of the shops bore a bad character, and were the resorts of persons of questionable morals'. They and the streets in which they were situated were centres of 'scrimmages' and 'sloggings', 'at all hours of the night'.[4] At about the same time J. B. Burnley gave a lurid description of a Bradford fish and chip shop, which was much resorted to by the patrons of dram shops and dubious saloons after closing time. Burnley was taken around Bradford's Saturday night underworld by a cabbie, who promised to show him some 'rum 'uns' and led him into 'a shop that seemed neither properly open nor properly closed', where 'the smell of fried fish assailed our olfactories as we entered, and made us feel greasy and uncomfortable':

> It was hot in more ways than one. In the rooms to which we were now introduced there was . . . a scene of a very strange character. Round several large tables sat a number of men and women, eating and drinking in the indifferent style which shows plainly enough that eating and drinking is not the chief object for which they are assembled. The language they selected for the expression of their sentiments was . . . several degrees stronger than the language of the Coal Hole [a low drinking den from which Burnley had just emerged] . . . There was a boy of fifty there, who had missed his train to Shipley, and had come to rest himself before seeking lodgings. The only thing that troubled him was the thought that his mother would be sitting up for him. There was another gentle youth of about forty-five, who told the sad tale that he had 'dropped sixteen quid' at some billiard-rooms the night before, and had come to enjoy the consolation of the fried-fish shop. He treated his female companions to any amount of fish and horehound beer, and made himself familiar with everybody. There was an antique German there also, who leered in a way that would almost justify a commission of inquiry into his sanity. One girl actually fell asleep over her plate of fish and potatoes, it being clear that she had been feasting on something stronger than horehound beer earlier in the evening. Girls to whom the dram-shop now refused admittance, could come here and obtain refuge, and refreshment, and companions; girls whose every feature betokened deplorable depravity could here prolong their excesses, and put themselves beyond the reach of the law.[5]

There were, apparently, three or four 'midnight fried fish shops' of this kind in Bradford, and the overtones of prostitution and excess are clear enough in this self-censored prose. The association between fish and chips and a subculture of crime, depravity and misapplied resources originated in a widespread dim awareness of the existence of such places, and proved almost impossible to disperse.

Some shops actively perpetuated the early identification with poverty, squalor and unseemly revelry. Fish and chip shops continued to follow the geographical rules that were observed in Southampton at the turn of the century, where 'the shops were situated in the low valleys; they must be where the population was thick'. They continued to meet 'a public want for poor people', as in Andover in 1905.[6] And they continued to be frequented by men on their way home from the pubs after closing time, and sometimes by prostitutes, as in the Barnsley shop where police found 'five men and three prostitutes' on the premises at 11.40 p.m., or in the Manchester case where a frier was fined in 1935 for harbouring 'undesirable women'.[7] A less disreputable association with pleasure and courting persisted. In Derby in 1906 and in many other places, a music-hall (and later a cinema) was deemed a desirable neighbour for a fish and chip shop, and in Barrow there would be a rush for fish and chips at 11.00 p.m. as men came home from the clubs (the Working Men's, the Gasworkers', the Irish Nationalists') and another rush on Saturday at midday as men dropped in on the way to the afternoon's soccer or rugby league games.[8] But by the early twentieth century these identifications with poverty and pleasure – and therefore with secondary poverty and perhaps the unbalanced allocation of resources between family members (with men getting more than their fair share) – were becoming only part of the story. Fish and chips was becoming part of the mainstream family economy of the industrial working class; and it was already making tentative steps up-market and taking root, sometimes controversially, in or on the fringes of more respectable areas.

The *Fish Trades Gazette* surveys of 'The Trade in the Provinces' in the Edwardian years convey a notion of the ubiquity of the fish and chip trade in northern industrial towns that is backed up by the proliferation of recorded outlets in the trade directories. Manchester's friers were said to 'serve a most useful purpose in supplying good wholesome and nourishing food to the poorer and lower middle-class population'.[9] Exactly what this meant is unclear, but at the very least it endorses what was said about Bolton and Warrington, Lancashire towns with markedly contrasting economies. In Bolton special emphasis was laid on the regular patronage of 'cotton operatives and others of the artisan class', in a setting where 'there is a shop in every street, and in some thoroughfares there are half a dozen'. In Warrington 'fried fish is a great institution . . . a favourite article of food with thousands of the inhabitants . . .'[10] Much the same could have been said of most Lancashire towns and although fish and chips was less overwhelmingly popular in the Edwardian Midlands, it was still far more than just a staple of the poor and a late snack for roisterers. The same applied to London, where a survey conducted for Southwark's Medical Officer of Health in 1904 claimed that 42 per cent of the population within a quarter-mile radius of one fish and chip shop had recently eaten fried fish from it; a further 16 per cent had had fried fish from else-where.[11] Beyond these impressions and isolated instances, the case for fish and chips as a staple item of diet among the Edwardian working class in general is made by the evidence on the proliferation of shops which was offered in Chapter 2.

Already, too, there is evidence that fish and chips was beginning to inch its way up-market. Customers who put on airs were not always welcome, admit-tedly, as a popular story reproduced in the *Fish Trades Gazette* illustrates:

> A man strolled into a busy fried fish shop in a big London suburb the other evening and, with much affectation, asked for 'a penny-piece of fish and a penny-worth of

potatoes, please'. 'Spuds up', bawled the proprietor, which caused great amusement among the other buyers, but the customer in question seemed quite annoyed at their merriment.[12]

The farmers of the Northallerton area probably did not have this problem. They were well catered for by the local friers in their supper-rooms on market day, when farm labourers from the Bedale area and 'country cousins' from the villages around Macclesfield also made the acquaintance of fish and chips.[13] But in the Nottingham of 1906 we find a less rustic extension of the market. Mr Wilson of Lenton was said to include 'among his patrons many of the well-to-do residents of the neighbourhood', and Mr Sanderson did well out of people who went boating on the Trent or promenading on its banks on summer evenings.[14] More generally, in 1910 Chatchip took it as read that the trade's improving status was due to the custom of 'our better-class working man and the low middle classes', although he later admitted that this did not extend to City clerks or to 'those middle classes which wield such immense power in this country'. He urged the development of a 'family order trade' for the weekends, to break down the prejudice of those who still did not want to be seen in a fish and chip shop.[15] But Sir Shirley Murphy, the London County Council's Medical Officer of Health, was clearly right in observing that fish and chips had 'grown to its present considerable dimensions, encroaching more and more upon respectable neighbourhoods, and appealing to a clientele possessed of more and more critical tastes'.[16]

During the inter-war years the trade began to attract middle-class custom more confidently and consistently – and not just in new up-market restaurants which made a special effort in this direction. It was not just propaganda when Dr E. S. Russell of the Fisheries Laboratory at Lowestoft announced that:

> Many fish consumers recognised that the product of the up-to-date fried fish shop in respect of finish and flavour compared favourably with the fried fish in the middle-class home.[17]

Chatchip provides a supporting reminiscence of supplying fish and chips three times a week to a lady with five servants whose cook was most annoyed at not being able to match his quality; and in 1925 we find a frier in a respectable district of Brixton delivering fish and chips to order at specified times, serving middle-class housewives who did not want to cook in hot weather or on the maid's evening out.[18] By 1930 'Macte Animo' of the Fish Friers' Review was identifying high mortgages, hire-purchase furniture and expensive leisure pursuits as economic trends that threatened the trade's well-being alongside more predictable themes such as unemployment and short-time working.[19] Two years later a general stock-taking article in the Fishing News made the point that: 'It has been a delight to see in recent years the progress made by fried fish shops in more residential areas.'[20] The Sea-Fish Commission was emphatic about the trend in middle-class districts of the North-East, where a motor-car trade had developed after entertainments finished, and there was a good-class residential trade where 'people who liked a fish supper two or three times a week' were 'finding it more convenient to have the fish cooked by a professional frier than to incur the trouble and smell of cooking it at home'.[21] John Stephen summed up the developing trend of the 1930s:

Fish and chips are growing in popularity among the better-class people. Business men, women shoppers, cinema fans, and now motorists, are being catered for.[22]

It was not all plain sailing, of course. Many – perhaps most – middle-class people regarded fish and chips with suspicion and disdain; similar sentiments were in evidence among some sectors of the respectable working class. In almost all industrial districts, however, and in many other settings besides, fish and chips became an accepted and inevitable adjunct to everyday life. It added variety to limited diets and enriched the sociability of the weekly routine, as well as adding to the enjoyment of special occasions. But we need to go further than this and ask how often it seems to have been consumed, by which members of the family and under what circumstances.

The *Fish Trades Gazette* survey identifies fish and chips especially with particular days of the week: and other kinds of evidence bear this out. Everywhere, Saturday was a particularly busy day and in most places Friday rivalled it, although parts of the Midlands were exceptional in this respect, including Stafford, Burslem and Walsall. In some places Monday was also mentioned as a continuation of the weekend peak. The towns where this was so had a strong tradition of the observance of 'St Monday', especially among their mining populations: they included Bolton, Wigan, Burslem and Wolver-hampton. This weekend peak of fish and chip consumption was associated with a post-payday spree in the eyes of the *Fish Trades Gazette* correspondent. Thus in Bolton:

> On Friday the cotton operatives and others of the artisan class receive their wages, and many of them spend the greater part of their pocket money before Tuesday arrives.

Similarly, the weekends in Wigan saw the 'horny-handed sons of toil' having 'a good blow-out'.[23] Fish and chips on Friday was clearly associated with payday. A Preston woman, whose husband was, exceptionally, paid on Thursdays, remembered:

> It was always a gala night. We used to go to the confectioner's and get these pancakes, and then next door to that was the fish and chip shop. That was the highlight of the week, I think.[24]

But the frier's trade was also augmented by those who abstained from meat on Fridays, who might eat 'butter pies' (potato and onion with a lot of butter melted on the top) as well as fish and chips.[25]

Fish and chips on Saturday was obviously associated with the weekend's relaxation, entertainment and relative affluence: for most working-class people there was a weekly poverty-cycle as well as those which had a longer timescale. But there might also be more conventionally reputable reasons for recourse to fish and chips at the weekend. An engaging equation between fish and chip consumption and domestic cleanliness was offered for Fleetwood in 1906:

> Fridays and Saturdays are the busiest days. The reason is that the men engaged at the docks or the works . . . draw their wages on Friday or Saturday, and their good wives

are busy cleaning on Friday, and do not, therefore, care to do any cooking on that day; and on Saturday they are even less disposed to engage in cooking when their houses are so clean and bright as the women in this locality delight in having them. Moreover, they like to take their ease on Saturday or enjoy their half-holiday to the full.[26]

For whatever mixture of reasons, the Friday and Saturday peak was enduring. A rare piece of quantitative evidence, from the late 1930s, surfaces in the Mass-Observation material on Bolton. Among an assortment of scruffy bits of card and paper containing assorted gnomic calculations is a day-by-day return of fish and steak pudding sales for a week in late March at 'Harry's' fish and chip shop. In orders of magnitude it was probably representative of most of the trade in industrial towns throughout the period, although there is an apparent echo of the 'St Monday' tradition that may be unusual:[27]

Table 7.1 Day-by-day sales of fried fish and steak puddings at Harry's fish and chip shop, Bolton, for a week in late March, 1938

	Dinner-time Steak Pudding	Fish	Night Steak Pudding	Fish
Monday	Closed		10	41
Tuesday	7	15	5	33
Wednesday	9	24	6	19
Thursday	7	20	7	31
Friday	21	71	11	70
Saturday	12	40	8	61*
Total for week	56	170	47	255

* Ran out of fish on Saturday night; could have sold between 75 and 90.

This is not an impressive volume of trade and one problem with the figures is that they ignore sales of chips without accompaniment, which must (as we shall see) have been considerable. Nevertheless, the weekly rhythm of sales that emerges here is entirely convincing in outline.

Clearly, fish and chip consumption was far from being confined to the weekend: there was a steady trade through the week and a large number of people bought fish and chips two, three or four times a week. This estimate by 'Macte Animo' in 1930 accords well with the oral evidence.[28] It also fits in with the remarkable calculation from Bradford in 1917 that the city's friers supplied enough meals to feed every man, woman and child in the city two and a half times per week, even if due allowance is made for exaggeration.[29] A Tyneside frier, writing in the thick of the supply crisis of the same year, explained how some families might come to depend more heavily on the fish and chip shop, as he described a family among his customers:

The father is a labourer, the mother a charwoman, and the two daughters are employed close at hand. All have only an hour for dinner, and as all go to work at 6 in the morning it is almost impossible for food to be cooked in advance, or even left simmering unattended. This family, when they came home for dinner, came four days out of six to my place for fish and chips, of which they made a cheap and good meal. Now they cannot get a warm dinner, they have to make shift with a cold meal, such as a pork pie and a cup of tea, a diet that doctors condemn as most indigestible. Their case is but one of hundreds.[30]

Obviously there is an element of propaganda and special pleading about this version of events, at a time of crisis in the trade, but it would be difficult to argue with the central theme. For much of working-class Britain, Chatchip's provocative claim in 1919 had some genuine substance behind it:

to-day fried fish and chips are in almost as universal demand as milk. They are a fundamental part of the people's food supplies.[31]

This is not to suggest that fish and chips became the staple diet of the industrial working class: it is to argue that it was a regular, important and sustaining part of mainstream working-class diet between the Edwardian years and the Second World War. As the Tyneside frier remarked in 1917, it was particularly popular as a time-saving hot meal for a factory dinner-break, especially for those who worked at a distance from their homes. Thus in Nottingham in 1906: 'A large number of warehouse girls and others make their midday meal frequently off fried fish to save the time and trouble involved in going home to dinner.'[32] Fetching fish and chips from the nearest shop was one of the tasks of the apprentice, as a Bolton upholsterer remembered:

Workers' canteens were unknown, so at a quarter before the mid-day break, I went to the local shop for their requirements, which usually consisted of the following items. A portion of chips 3 pence. Fish also 3 pence. Meat or meat and potato pies were the same price.[33]

For those who did not have apprentices at their beck and call, other arrangements might be made. Another Bolton witness remembers:

Then nearly all the girls that worked in the mills, there was a fish and chip shop at the bottom of Halliwell Road . . . they use to take a basin when they were going to work in the morning, probably six o'clock in the morning and this place was open then and they'd put a paper in this basin what they wanted . . . they'd leave these basins . . . and then at dinnertime when they were coming home for dinner all these were ready for em and that would be their dinner you see.[34]

This would help the fish frier to anticipate the level of demand on any particular day. Another widespread practice, which helped to keep the young Harry Ramsden going, was the bespoke delivery of fish and chips in bulk to a large workplace. Mrs Ada Vincent, who worked on the fish dock at Grimsby, had fish and chips twice a week at her workplace, delivered five minutes before the dinner break in an enormous wicker laundry-basket before being handed out to those who had ordered it.[35] Teenage factory workers who still 'tipped up' their pay packets at home would be given money for meals out, which would usually be spent at the fish and chip shop, although, as a Chorley frier complained in 1937, not all the money found its way to the intended target:

> Many of them had youthful customers from nearby factories and workshops who asked for pennyworths [of chips]. He was certain that parents supplied more than 1d for [the] midday meal of a 15 or 16-year-old. But if they could get chips for 1d they would have something left to buy cigarettes or, in the case of girls, lipstick.[36]

All in all, fish and chips as a midday meal was an institution in industrial Britain; and as Mass-Observation discovered in the Bolton of 1938, opening hours were geared-up to factory demand. The meal break ended at 1.15 p.m.:

> Obs[erver] went in 3 Chip & Fish Shops on Tuesday 12/4/38 at 1-20 p.m. and could not obtain any Chips as cooking stopped at 1 p.m. Proprietors say no trade at all after that time.[37]

Fish and chips might also be important as an easily available, instant hot meal at the end of the working day. A Bolton weaver used to have chips waiting for her at home when she came back off her late shift, which finished at 10.00 p.m., but at times in her late teens conflict with her father meant that she had to display some dexterity in order to enjoy them, as he resented the lateness of her return home:

> so when it come I was ready for getting married I did turn round and have a real argument with him, me mother used to get me some chips at night, one peneth worth and she used to leave them wrapped up in the paper on top of the old hob and he used to get them and throw them at me, well if I weren't aware the first few times they'd go on the floor and I had had nothing proper from going to work at dinnertime. So I kind of got used to this and I used to catch them and it really annoyed him then you see.[38]

Note the assumption here that chips were 'proper' food. It was shared by the South Wales miners and tinplate workers who worked the late shift from 3 p.m. to 11 p.m. and bought their suppers from the fish and chip shop on the way home to avoid disturbing 'their womenfolk', who were in bed because they had to be up at five to prepare breakfast for others in the household who were on the early shift. This was apparently a common situation among families with teenage (or older) sons.[39]

Mining families were heavy consumers of fish and chips anyway. Women were incorporated into the economy of the pit through the endless round of washing and heating water which the life imposed, before the introduction of pit-head baths; they might have as little time to cook as the factory workers who lived the 'double shift' of employment and housework, and were also prominent among the friers' best customers. Laundry workers were also proverbially avid consumers of fish and chips: a shop in North Acton was advertised in 1908 as in a 'splendid position, surrounded by laundries'.[40]

Whether or not they were employed outside the home, many working-class women increasingly used the fish and chip shop to take some of the pressure off the routine drudgery of housework, or simply as the provider of an occasional treat. Thus a Lancaster family would have fish and chips on Wednesdays 'which enabled mother to get on with whatever she was doing' and the wife of a Bolton man who worked for a potato wholesaler bought fish and chips regularly when she was too busy to cook: 'It would ease her situation, she just get chips and she'd have no worry about getting a meal prepared'.[41] In Manchester in 1935 many housewives were said to buy in chips and peas to save the trouble of cooking two vegetables for a main meal.[42] And a Bolton man remembered that his mother preferred sitting in at night to joining his father in the pub ('use to like sitting in the house, warm chair') but she insisted on being brought a pint of beer in a jug and a piece of fish from a nearby 'chip shop in George Street down a cellar'.[43]

Among the many contexts in which fish and chips might be eaten, there were plenty that included children. As a Preston woman (born in 1913) remembered: 'It was really a family meal in those days [her childhood]. It was a main meal.'[44] Children might have smaller portions, or do without fish, but they often participated in the meal: indeed, they were often sent to buy it. The same Preston woman remembered that in her family the parents would have a fish each, and a half for each child: 'In those days it was a thick fish, not a lot of batter as you get them today. So that a half-fish for the children was sufficient to fill them.' A Barrow man (born 1897) explained how children could be catered for more cheaply:

> You see you've got a big fish, well it wouldn't be exactly the head, you'd cut the head off the fish and then you'd get into the next portion. Now if it was a big fish they'd cut that off and that is what they used to call 'tops', it was fish but it was quite bony. So when we were kids we'd go for ha'porth of chips and ha'porth of tops. Five tops, and ha'porth of chips: a child's meal – a Saturday night supper – something special. Or if you were poorer again you might have $1/2$d of chips with batter scraps – if you were well in.[45]

Mrs Vincent of Grimsby remembered that only her parents would get fish – perhaps not surprisingly, with a family of eleven – but the children would have chips and batter bits and any fragments of fish that might happen to fall from mother's fork, for which there was excited competition. She also remembered buying 'skate knobs', a tasty gristly attachment to the jaws, at four for a penny.[46] By the late 1930s chips, at least, had become almost a routine children's treat in industrial areas, as Henry Youngman of Leeds pointed out when explaining why it was so difficult to raise the minimum price of chips from a penny to twopence:

> It was particularly noticeable that during the first hour of the evening's trade in most fish friers' shops, the demand was almost entirely for chips alone, mostly from factory hands in factories nearby and from parents for children about to go to bed. The parents would send for 1d worth each for perhaps three or four children but could not afford to spend 2d for each child. Each portion had to be sold separately. This alone satisfied the children. Division undertaken by the parents led to discontent.[47]

Children also bought fish and chips on their own account, from whatever pocket money they could muster. Thirty years earlier Olive Malvery had noticed this in London's East End:

Many of the customers were little children who came straight from school. Their purchases generally consisted of a halfpennyworth of fish and a halfpennyworth of potatoes. Sometimes, one more hungry-looking and more raggedly dressed than the others would come in and ask for 'a 'aporth of cracklings'. Mrs M. would give these poor children two large handfuls of tiny pieces of fish, broken potatoes, and the chips of fried batter which remained in the wire baskets after the cooked fish had been removed from them.[48]

As a Lancaster man remarked: 'As lads you'd do anything for a copper, and then it was the fish shop first stop . . . You'd run a message, do quite a lot of things.'[49]

Fish and chips also became a ubiquitous accompaniment to all kinds of leisure activities. The film buff Leslie Halliwell took in chips on the way home after most of the films he shared with his mother – and in this he was not alone. 'Macte Animo' of the *Fish Friers' Review* took it as read that the cinema, like the theatre, was an ally of the trade, although the whist-drives and dances that provided cheap refreshment in the 1920s were its enemies.[50] Fish and chips was inseparable from working-class courting rituals. Ralph Glasser of Glasgow's Gorbals, like so many others, remembered buying 'a tuppenny bag of chips to eat together as we walked', only to find 'that we had forgotten to eat them, and that the greasy chips were stone cold'. Glasser also recounts the story of a friend's affectionately remembered sexual initiation with a Glasgow prostitute driven by cold and hunger and purchased with a bag of fish and chips.[51] But the fish and chip shop was also the centre of a masculine republic of adolescents. Pat O'Mara, in the middle of the worst of Liverpool slumdom during the First World War, still took his nightly visit to John the Greek's fish and chip shop in St James Street as a natural phase of a night on the street corner with his friends; and on the other side of the country Jack Common's fictionalized memories of Tyneside tell much the same story.[52] The association between fish and chips and seaside holidays is just as strong. It applies especially to Blackpool, where Mass-Observation found that: 'Everywhere . . . the holidaymaker is offered opportunities to eat' and that: 'Chips and fish . . . easily lead the holiday-maker's eating, especially for those 30 per cent who take all their meals out.'[53] Blackpool was unique only in its scale: at Port Talbot fish friers were competing on the beach in 1929 and in 1931 Canvey Island Urban District Council came under fire for allowing fish and chips to be sold from a kiosk on the foreshore, although the Chairman fought back by pointing out that 'the fish was fried in High Street, and was sold on plates, not paper'.[54] Special fish and chip tents were provided for a Territorial Army Camp in 1931, staffed by Army personnel, and in 1925 cold fried fish 'went like hot cakes' when offered to Ascot racegoers on the course.[55]

It is not surprising that fish and chips became an institution, celebrated in song as well as music-hall joke and comic postcard. Fred Austin's 'Chips and Fish', sung by Ernie Mayne and published in 1920, made the inevitable allusions to Blackpool and Wigan and culminated in a celebratory chorus:

Chips and Fish ! Chips and Fish !
Eh! by gum it's a Champion Dish.
Oh! what a smell when they fry 'em,
Just get a penn'orth and try 'em.

Put some Salt and Vinegar on, as much as ever you wish,
You can do, do, do without supper when you've
Had a bob's worth o' Chips and Fish![56]

By the 1920s, too, the fish and chip habit was penetrating the remotest
country districts. In 1922 W. H. Boomer of Leeds fitted out a one-ton Ford van
in red and gold with a white clerestory roof as a mobile fish and chip shop to
trade with outlying villages. It was said that this spectacular vehicle drew
'amazing' crowds wherever it went, but this was merely an unusually vivid
example of an increasingly common phenomenon, which brought fish and chips
to the rural fastnesses of Hertfordshire and Northamptonshire as well as
Yorkshire.[57] Perceived levels of demand and opportunity were such that few
potential outlets were neglected for long: thus in 1936 Keighley friers were told
that one of their number was 'carrying out Fish and Chips in his motor-cycle
and side-car to a new Estate at Woodhouse'.[58]

The legends that proliferated about fish and chips being part of the urban
pathology of the slum should be placed in this context. Plenty of isolated
examples could be used to illustrate such a thesis, such as the petition of the
inmates of Mitcham workhouse in 1910 for the inclusion of fish and chips in
their diet at least once a fortnight, or the *Daily News'* investigation of allegations
that babies were dying through being fed on fish and chip pieces instead of a
proper infant diet.[59] Such stories no doubt helped to form the agenda for
assumptions about the dietary preferences and deficiencies of the urban working class which regularly surface in the literature. They fuel the widespread
assumption that evacuees from the slums at the start of the Second World War
were unable to adjust to wholesome country living. As one art teacher commented: 'Many were so used to chips that it took a long time to persuade them
to eat fresh vegetables': a statement that reveals 'commonsense' but contestable
assumptions about rural diet as well as about what chips are made from.[60] This
frame of mind responds to and perpetuates a view of fish and chips as
unhealthy, wasteful, expensive and productive of secondary poverty through
misapplied resources – a view that has been assiduously propagated by 'official'
commentators and elements within the media since the turn of the century and
still affects the attitudes of some historians and politicians. But the impact of
fish and chips on working-class diet and living standards is a complex matter
and deserves extended discussion.[61]

Attacks on fish and chips from Medical Officers of Health,the popular press
and assorted civic dignitaries and representatives of officialdom began in
earnest at the turn of the century and persisted throughout the period and
beyond it. Before the First World War the accent was on fish and chips as an
instigator of disease. In London, Drs Hamer and Murphy of the London
County Council made sustained efforts in the early twentieth century to
connect fish and chips with enteric or typhoid fever. In 1904 Dr Murphy
reported that: 'The phenomena commonly met with in food outbreaks were
found by Dr Hamer . . . to be always associated with two conditions – poverty
and fried fish eating. It was, indeed, almost impossible to discover an area of
London in which the one set of circumstances existed apart from the other'.[62]
The defective logic in this reasoning was exposed in a *Fish Trades Gazette*

editorial. Although Hamer added substance to his argument by pointing out that many of the smallfish sold for a halfpenny were not properly cleaned or gutted and that frying for a short time might not sterilize the contents of the intestines, the *Gazette* remained unconvinced.[63] But the campaign continued, in association with the attacks on defective ventilation in the Edwardian years, and buoyed up, no doubt, by occasional inquest findings that blamed bad fried fish and described gruesome circumstances. Thus at a Lambeth inquest in 1909: 'One witness who had been shown the fish said that it was green in colour and smelt of chloride of lime'.[64] Some of the evidence was unimpressive: in 1907 only 14 out of 513 cases of enteric fever were 'possibly' ascribable to fried fish. But in 1911 Dr Hamer returned to the attack on the same lines as hitherto, provoking a fierce, effective retort from Chatchip, who pointed out that during 40 years of attacks on the fish and chip trade from Medical Officers and the press, it had enjoyed an enormous expansion and the people's health had improved markedly:

> Now I cannot prove that fried fish and chips have done anything towards that desirable state of affairs, but I have just as much right to co-ordinate the improved health of the people with the increased consumption of fried fish and chips as, say, Dr Hamer has to co-ordinate fried fish and typhoid fever. In his co-ordination he has no more proof than I have, and my only proof lies in the fact that both things are coincident. If coincidence may be taken as proof from Dr Hamer, then what hinders it from being taken from your humble servant?[65]

Some of the other attacks were even less effective, if considered dispassionately. The Medical Officer for the north-eastern district of Bedlingtonshire was castigated by Chatchip for blaming cases of ptomaine poisoning on fish and chips fried in beef dripping adulterated with grease and tallow, on the grounds that the alleged adulterants were more expensive than pure frying media; the allegation seems to have been unsupported by any hard evidence.[66] More entertaining was the claim of the Wednesfield (Staffs.) Medical Officer to have discovered a new syndrome, fish and chip poisoning, which was:

> due to the oil in which they are fried. The main symptoms . . . are vomiting, diarrhoea, prostration, urticaria, and a very itchy and unsightly rash.

He advocated the compulsory use of dripping or lard instead of cotton-seed oil and again incurred the wrath of Chatchip, who pointed out that refined cotton-seed oil was used in salad oil, margarine and artificial lard with no apparent ill-effects.[67] Meanwhile, attacks like that of the penny monthly magazine *Good Health* in 1904, which based themselves on nothing more than prejudiced assertion, were even less convincing.[68] We do not have to take the friers' apologists on trust to be clear that their enemies were quite unable to make their charges stick. Nevertheless, the sustained, well-publicized barrage had its effect on public opinion, especially among those who smelt the shops without using their products. The Mayor of Hemel Hempstead, Mr. E. A. Mitchell-Innes, KC, was representative of much élite opinion, garnered from the casual reading of newspapers, when he said in 1913: 'I think that probably the fish frying trade is the most terrible in existence.'[69]

After the war the hostility of local officialdom took a different line. Fish andchips was attacked as an irrational way of spending limited resources and a cause of malnutrition in children whose parents – and especially their mothers – were too lazy or too ignorant to provide a 'proper' diet. Thus in 1928 Blackpool's School Medical Officer complained that:

> A few of the poorer and less thrifty parents supply fish and chips, a food . . . which is indigestible and unwholesome, for their children's dinners. Food of this type used persistently and in the almost complete absence of milk and vegetables, tends to undermine a child's health and produce an ill-nourished condition.[70]

A few months later Blaenavon's Medical Officer blamed the town's unenviable infant mortality rate on lazy mothers who fed their children on tinned foods and fish and chips, relegating such issues as defective housing, sanitation and water supply to the status of contributory factors.[71] Such attacks on a whole imagined lifestyle – 'the fish and chips diet of the poor city children' – call to mind Charles Webster's argument that when dealing with working-class health and living standards Medical Officers of Health were all too likely to parade the prejudices of their class as if they were scientific medical judgements.[72] As 'The Idler' in the *Blackpool Gazette* commented, a great deal of the opposition to fish and chips had its roots in snobbery.[73]

Another manifestation of these attitudes was also reported in 1928, when the Stepney (London) Poor Law Guardians reaffirmed their policy of not allowing outdoor relief recipients to exchange relief tickets at fish and chip shops. The chair justified this policy on the grounds that fish and chips was not good value for money – 'one of the most expensive foods to buy' – and that the unemployed, who by definition were in no hurry, would find it cheaper to cook their own fish. The friers argued against these assumptions but without apparent success.[74] There were renewed complaints in 1932, when some northern friers alleged that families applying for public assistance were similarly being issued with selective food tickets that excluded fish and chips as a 'luxury' food. In May Chatchip claimed credit for securing the removal of this restriction but it is significant that it was imposed in the first place.[75] After this, official attitudes to fish and chips seem to have mellowed, from this perspective at least; but the frame of mind that induced a headmistress in Bishop Auckland to ban her pupils from eating fish and chips at lunch-time, on the grounds of smell and because 'the girls adopt the practice of eating the food with their fingers', remained pervasive.[76] Meanwhile, the hazards of salt and vinegar were seldom discussed, although in 1921, when the dangers of eating too much salt were being canvassed, Chatchip commented:

> Some people who get their salt for nothing from the fried-fish shops should . . . be in quite a bad way by this time . . . Lots of people spoil fried fish and chips by the amount of salt and vinegar they consume with them.[77]

The perils of vinegar were dramatically illustrated by the fate of a Wainfleet farm labourer, who died after snatching a two-pint bottle of concentrated vinegar in a fish and chip shop after the pubs shut and taking a long and determined drink from it.[78]

The tide of contemporary opinion was far from universally hostile to fish andchips and the friers found plenty of support outside the trade for their insistence on the value of their product as a provider of cheap, wholesome nourishment. The friers' greatest coup before the First World War came from the brain surgeon Dr Crichton Browne's presidential address to the Sanitary Inspectors' Association conference in 1910. Browne suggested that Sanitary Inspectors should encourage the poor to eat more fish as an escape from the 'monotonous round of bread, dripping and tea' and he recommended fried fish, from shops that supplied 'wholesome and acceptable meals', as the best way of achieving this. He even speculated that fried fish might be 'a useful auxiliary in the crusade against tuberculosis', praising those groups within the working class, such as weavers and 'laundry girls', who had 'discovered for themselves that fried fish was especially adapted to their wants'. All this was lavishly publicized in the national press. The *Fish Trades Gazette* was particularly pleased that the comments came from a well-known popular figure with a reputation for common-sense, a man who was emphatically not a food faddist:

> He was the champion of the mutton chop and of the beef steak against vegetarian votaries, and when he declares that fish is next in value to meat his opinion carries weight with the great majority of people who love to look upon the flesh when it is red.

Chatchip echoed this, expressing special pleasure at Dr Browne's rout of the 'scare-mongers' who in recent weeks had been frightening the housewife by attaching the spectre of ptomaine poisoning and appendicitis to 'every conceivable article of food'. No wonder Dr Browne's words were treasured and hoarded by the fish friers, to be brought out and displayed like an amulet or talisman at every hint of criticism for the next generation.[79]

A steady trickle of further endorsements came to the trade's attention during the inter-war years. In 1921 Chatchip seized enthusiastically upon Dr E. J. Spriggs' contention that every healthy adult should eat a pound of potatoes per day as the basis for an encomium of fish and chips, with 'some fresh greens', as 'a meal containing all the nourishment that the body needs'.[80] Two years later, *The Times*, in its Fishing Industries Supplement, praised fish and chips as an ideal diet and urged its wider diffusion among the 'poorer class', praising the fried fish shop as 'having already passed the shabby stage' and 'now being run in almost a fastidious way, and is capable of huge expansion in the interests of better nutrition . . . and of national economy in eating'.[81] Here the impact of the war on significant sections of élite opinion is made explicit. And there were further favourable medical opinions. The Leeds children's surgeon Dr Vining spoke in support of the food value of fish and chips at a meeting of Leeds Poor Children's Holiday Camp Association in 1928, although he subsequently became irritated at the publicity given to his praise by friers' organizations.[82] In 1931 the Leeds Medical Officer of Health, Dr Jervis, 'could state with confidence that Fish and Chips . . . contained all the vitamins necessary to build up the tissues of the human body', and two years later there was a similar endorsement from the Sanitary Inspector for Carlton, who saw it as 'a valuable pure and cheap food' which contained nothing injurious to health.[83] In 1934 'A Medical Man' was similarly supportive in the *Daily Dispatch*:

Although I do not recommend fish and chips as a daily diet, I certainly think that it can be eaten two or three times a week with advantage. It is a cheap, health-giving food, and is entitled to rank much higher in the social dietary than it does at present.[84]

And in 1937 Professor R. M. Picken of the Welsh National School of Medicine set the seal on all this testimony by denying that fish and chips were either dear or indigestible, suggesting that there was nothing necessarily to be regretted about 'the rise of articles of diet which saved labour, if they were nutritious and not extravagant'.[85]

So fish and chips had its defenders as well as its enemies among informed contemporary opinion and careful readers of the popular press who enjoyed their fish and chips need not have gone short of authoritative arguments to give backing to their own common-sense. It is important to emphasize that even if the defenders of fish and chips were wrong, the consumers at the time could have justified themselves by an appeal to selected but perfectly respectable authorities. In fact there is a strong case for accepting that fish and chips was not only popular and tasty, but also a rational choice for working-class families in terms of cheapness, convenience and nutritional value. This is not recognized by the few historians to have considered the matter, but it can be supported in various ways. The views of Dr Crichton Browne can be seen to carry more weight than those of the assembled Medical Officers of Health on the other side.

This argument goes against the prevailing orthodoxy among historians, such as it is, so it will have to be elaborated a little. Elizabeth Roberts damns fish and chips mainly indirectly, by associating it with a 'textile diet' which she sees as prevailing in Preston and by extension in other factory towns where women worked outside the home. She contrasts fish and chips with a healthier 'traditional north Lancashire diet' that allegedly prevailed in Barrow and Lancaster and in 'some non-textile families in Preston'. The 'textile diet' is supposed to have relied heavily on convenience foods (pies, tripe and 'various cold cooked meats' as well as fish and chips) and to have been less satisfactory than the nourishing stews and imaginative use of offals and vegetables identified with the 'traditional north Lancashire diet'.[86] Stephen Mennell's attack is more direct. He associates fish and chips with the 'deleterious' aspects of the influence of continuing urbanization during the second half of the nineteenth century. More food had to be bought in rather than grown and inadequate cooking facilities necessitated general recourse to 'convenient and quickly prepared food'. As part of this pattern: 'From the late nineteenth century, recourse to the fish and chip shop was also a feature of working-class life.' The implications of the next sentence drive the critical message home: 'According to Campbell, these trends undermined even the hitherto healthier diet found in Scotland.'[87] And in a fascinating piece of paradox, Hamish Fraser goes against the fishing industry orthodoxy that fish and chips was essential to the growth of demand by (speculatively) blaming the allegedly poor fresh fish supplies in parts of urban Lancashire at the turn of the century on taste having been 'artificially restricted by the well-known Lancashire enthusiasm for fried fish and chips'.[88] Beyond these findings of guilt, by association or otherwise, some historians of the urban working class ignore fish and chips altogether, like Carl Chinn, whose concern to celebrate the strength and resourcefulness of working-class matriarchs in Birmingham leads him to emphasize their skills at making a little food go a long way, while leaving the fried fish shop out of his account.[89]

Elizabeth Roberts' indictment of fish and chips as part of a 'textile diet' is misleading on several counts. In the first place, a re-examination of her oral interview material suggests that the contrast between the 'textile' and 'traditional north Lancashire' diets is overdrawn, as befits a situation in which Preston, for example, had at least as many fruiterers and greengrocers as fish and chip shops. In practice, fish and chips formed part of a varied dietary pattern in both kinds of setting. Here is an example from a rather superior working-class family in Lancaster, in response to the question: 'What did you have for your dinners?':

> It was pretty routine – a roast on Sunday, cold meat on Monday, cottage pie on Tuesday, perhaps fish and chips on Wednesday which enabled mother to get on with whatever she was doing, Thursday was usually hot pot or potato pie because that was bedroom day and rice pudding, Friday possibly stewed steak and chips from the chip shop which was just across the road.[90]

The consumption of fish and chips *alongside* home-made soup, vegetables, home baking and the gathering of nuts and blackberries recurs in other Lancaster families. On the other side of the country, Mrs Vincent, a brewery worker's daughter from Grimsby, ate fish and chips regularly along with sheep's-head broth, shin beef and the produce from her father's allotment, which included peas, beans, lettuce, celery and tomatoes. She was full of praise both for her mother's cooking and for the local fish and chips, in which she took an almost proprietorial pride.[91] But the families of cotton workers had similar memories. A Preston card-room worker had fish and chips two or three times a week but also enjoyed tripe and cow heel, stewed with an appetizing mixture of vegetables. Another textile family consumed Sunday roasts with vegetables, as well as stews and hot-pots, while paying regular visits to the fish and chip shop.[92] Bolton families who were interviewed as part of a different research project also consumed fish and chips alongside home-made bread, cakes, soups and stews, even in households where great pride was taken in the mother's domestic skills and the wholesomeness of her cooking.[93] These were families in which the mother did not work outside the home, and the pressures on women working the 'double shift' were such that the 'textile diet' cannot have been entirely mythical. But it seems to have been more a matter of emphasis rather than of stark contrast, and it was probably associated more with shop-bought pies and cakes and perhaps with tinned foods, than with a distinctive identification with fish and chips. The Bolton interviews reveal strong prejudices against cheap frozen meat (women who went to the Argenta shop were the butts of gossip), brown sugar ('it was like for poor people because it [was] a lot cheaper') and tinned foods ('people who had tinned stuff weren't very good housekeepers it was opening tins of food how awful') – but there were no such comments about fish and chips.[94] All this tends to confirm the other evidence that fish and chips was part of the ordinary diet of the respectable working class.

It is also possible that reference to fish and chips in Roberts' own interviews (and perhaps in those of other researchers, too) has been distorted by the context and manner in which questions about it were put. Interviewees were asked about fish and chips in the context of discussions about tinned foods and convenience foods, and leading questions were sometimes asked which invited respondents to say that fish and chips was expensive.[95] It is also significant that (as with the contemporary household dietary surveys) information about fish and chips was not necessarily forthcoming unless specifically requested. Thus two Bolton interviewees, asked about fish, responded without mentioning fish and chips; but a specific question elicited that in both cases it had been a regular part of the diet.[96] At times, questions about fish and chips have undoubtedly been posed in an atmosphere of implicit or explicit disapproval which may well have affected the outcome of the interview; but at other times they have not been asked at all.

The indictment of fish and chips is based on the assumption that it formed part of a dietary pattern that was 'not necessarily unnutritious, but . . . monotonous, conspicuously lacked vegetables, and was expensive'.[97] This is Roberts' comment on the 'textile diet' more generally, but fish and chips is very much a part of this picture. It is also viewed as an index of bad housekeeping on the part of working-class housewives, whether as a result of laziness, exhaustion or domestic incompetence. These allegations require investigation.

In the first place, fish and chips was clearly not expensive. We have seen that prices were held down by competition, custom and consumer resistance. And although there were some critical comments from friers' customers, most of them seem to have perceived fish and chips to be cheap, except perhaps during the most difficult years of the war. A Barrow interviewee said straightforwardly: 'Yes, we used to buy a lot of fish and chips, they were cheap.' In similar vein, a Preston woman said: 'At one time you could get a penny-worth of chips and with a few pieces of bread and butter you were filled up.'[98] Bolton respondents also remembered the cheapness of the dish and Mrs Vincent of Grimsby emphasized how cheap it was ('absolutely cheap').[99] A migrant from York to Preston who had strong opinions on the deficiencies of Lancashire cooking, but adored fish and chips, put a different point of view: 'It is not a cheap meal but it is a good meal'; and the only real dissidents were people whose childhood memories had been shaped by the First World War, with its uniquely difficult trading conditions for fish friers.[100] Chatchip was an interested party, but nevertheless his comments in 1913 sum the situation up very well:

> The one thing I think we overlook, even when we keep the extremely poor in mind, is this important fact – that there is no other diet, either cooked or uncooked, which is nearly so cheap as the diet to be obtained from the fried-fish shop . . . On Friday and Saturday dinner-times I often have working men, who are working somewhere in the neighbourhood, call in at my place for their dinners. 'A penn'orth of chips, a penn'orth of peas, and two pieces of fish,' generally is the order. In normal times the cost of that dinner is fourpence, in abnormal times fivepence. Where can a working man go and get anything like it either in nutrition or quantity for anything like the price?[101]

He reiterated the same claim in 1937 and it still carried weight.[102]

The proposition that fish and chips was associated with dietary monotony is even less tenable. We have seen that for families in the Lancashire oral interview samples, this was simply not the case. For those less fortunate families who subsisted on bread, dripping, jam and tea, it was an *escape* from monotony, an attainable treat – for we have also seen that it was seldom, if ever, a staple diet in itself. Moreover, the chips, with the frequent addition of peas and beans, provided a vegetable component in diets that would otherwise have been dominated by bread, pies and the ubiquitous fry-up of bacon or chops.[103] It seems that fish and chips was damned more for the company it kept in the dietaries of the poor than for any deficiencies of its own as a foodstuff. The way in which this could happen is beautifully demonstrated by the way in which the title of Charles Segal's *Penn'orth of Chips* emerged. The book's sub-title was 'Backward children in the making' and it was based on a study of 'the mental, educational, physical and environmental conditions of a class of twenty-six backward boys' in a North Kensington school. As part of an investigation into home environments, a boy was quizzed about his diet, which consisted of bread, margarine and tea: and 'we never have any supper, except on Saturday night, when we get a penn'orth o' chips'. Out of the whole study of the roots of 'backwardness' the chips were chosen as the most telling symbol, even though they had been the only *alleviation* of the monotony and inadequacy of the child's diet. This way of presenting a book published in 1939 tells us a great deal about perceptions of fish and chips and how they were perpetuated, but it reveals nothing useful about the real contribution of fish and chips to working-class living standards.[104]

In Segal's book, as elsewhere, fish and chips symbolize the domestic failings of working-class wives and the misplaced spending that plunged families into secondary poverty. This was part of an important political agenda of the 1930s. As Madeleine Mayhew points out, the growing understanding of nutrition that was spreading in parts of the scientific community by the 1930s posed problems for the National Government: it could be used to demonstrate that the children of the unemployed, especially, were chronically and measurably malnourished due to insufficient purchasing power rather than misallocation of resources within what might have been adequate family budgets. This had to be rejected, and Mayhew states that:

> Throughout the 1930s, the ministry steadfastly denied that malnutrition was purely a matter of food intake, or that it could be clinically tested. Officials maintained that there was no connection between low income and malnutrition; if sections of the population were malnourished, then the fault lay with individual idiosyncrasies or ignorant housewives.[105]

From this perspective fish and chips as part of 'slum culture' was a convenient scapegoat, calling to mind allegations about the domestic incompetence of working-class wives that were at least as old as the factory system and the emergence of the social investigator.

There were, however, plenty of good reasons for working-class families to have recourse to fish and chips two or three times a week. Most obviously, it saved time, an invaluable commodity for working-class women whether or not they also had paid employment. It substituted a short period of sociable queuing, which could easily be delegated to a child (who in turn might look after the needs of several neighbouring households), for a substantial allocation of time for preparation and cooking.[106] Fish and chips itself simply could not have been prepared in many working-class homes, with their primitive domestic technology, so it was especially welcome in households where the only domestic cooking possible was toasting, grilling or frying over an open hearth. It allowed some respite from the cooking fumes that were inescapable in badly-ventilated houses and its use provided an opportunity for houses to be kept relatively clean and fresh for longer at weekends.[107] Fish and chips also economized on fuel, and there was much to be said for the friers' claim that their economies of scale as (relatively) mass-caterers enabled them to provide better-quality fare at a cheaper price than the housewife could supply.[108] And the assertion that fish and chips was relatively expensive leaned heavily on the assumption that working-class women's domestic labour had, by definition, no monetary value. The popularity of fish and chips in the warm summer months owed much to the fact that families did not need to heat their houses at this time, and resented lighting fires and consuming fuel purely for cooking purposes. Fish and chips was also easy to assimilate for that overwhelming majority of the working class who had bad teeth, no teeth, or ill-fitting false teeth. This applied especially to chips, peas and beans but also to fish – especially after filleting became general.[109] And beyond all this, people liked the taste; and a lot of the shops' customers liked the smell. These are points that were especially easy for the compilers of social surveys to overlook or discount, but they were very important indeed to the consumer. On this issue Mrs Vincent of Grimsby deserves the last word:

And I'll tell you what used to be my favourite. Skate knobs. Now they used to buy skate knobs, and they was beautiful . . . Well, you get a skate . . . well, the knob is in the jaws . . . And when you eat 'em – y'know – there was a bone of gristle. And if we was that hungry, we'd have one of those as well – 'cos it couldn't stick in your throat, it was all gristle. But it was good, and nourishment.

And it was tasty?

Tasty, yes. And nourishment was in it. We couldn't bear to chuck that lovely skate knob bone away.

[And what did they fry the fish in?]

Oh, it was always pure dripping . . . Buckets, white buckets, full of beautiful beef dripping . . . That's why the fish shop used to smell so nice. Made your mouth water. 'Cos it was dripping they was frying them in. Beautiful.[110]

So fish and chips had important practical advantages within working-class culture, as well as being enjoyable in itself. Why, then, did it come to be so widely equated with bad housekeeping? In the first place, it should be emphasized that this association was generally made by people from outside the working class: we have seen that fish and chips did not attract the stigma among working-class people that frozen meat and tinned foods might do. It arose from, and was sustained by, powerful ideological forces that associated being a good woman with going a good housewife, which in turn entailed providing a wholesome diet based on careful buying and labour-intensive cookery. This was a potent symbol of family unity and social stability among whose who worshipped at the shrine of the angel of the fireside. Home cooking was emblematic of maternal affection and security. It is easy to see how fish and chips and other convenience foods appeared to threaten this still-pervasive ideal. Jan Harold Brunvand's story of the 'urban legend' of the 'Kentucky Fried Rat', which has its British counterparts, is apposite here. Its central theme is a fear that food cooked outside the home is all too likely to contain disgusting ingredients disguised as wholesome and tasty fare. One researcher, noting that 'the victim [in the stories] is always a woman', suggests that this is because:

> by neglecting her traditional role as food preparer [she] helps to destroy the family by permitting the transfer of control from the home to amoral profit-making corporations . . . the rat is appropriate symbolic punishment.[111]

It is hard to recognize the fish and chip shop of the 1920s or 1930s as a 'corporation', but the rest of the analysis rings true. And the whole argument is supported by the work of Nickie Charles and Marion Kerr, who document the deep roots and enduring importance of values associating 'proper' foods and 'proper' homes and treating with distrust all food that has been worked on outside the home.[112]

Fish and chips may well have owed part of its popularity to the lack of tasty alternatives in a British diet that lacked the flair, interest and capacity to generate enthusiasm (among cooks and consumers alike), which Stephen Mennell finds in evidence in France.[113] For a lot of contemporaries, however, plainness was equated with virtue, as manuals such as Lever Brothers' *Good Plain Cookery* indicated. Fried fish was not excluded from this (or other) recipe books but it was never mentioned in its shop-bought guise, although Chatchip and other votaries of fish frying as a profession would have warmed to the way in which the section on 'Frying fish' was introduced: 'Perhaps there is nothing in the whole range of cookery which will so test the powers of a cook as a plainly fried sole or whiting.'[114] The voluntary social workers and calorie-obsessed nutritionists of the turn of the century were staunch advocates of the boring and virtuous, as their sustained efforts to persuade 'the poor' to go over to porridge and lentils bore witness. Paton's work on Edinburgh put the perceived conflict between preferences and resources in working-class diet in a nutshell. The 'lazy diet' of tea, bread and butter (or margarine) was faulty; it could be amended either by expensive animal foods, or by 'the free use of oatmeal with milk, or of peas or beans, without extra cost'; and 'to correct the faults of a tea and bread diet, either money spent on animal food or labour spent in the cooking of vegetable food is necessary; if they have not . . . the money, they must use . . . the labour of properly cooking more nutritive foods'.[115] What was overlooked, or discounted, is that fish and chips went some way towards squaring this intractable circle.

The text-book orthodoxies of the inter-war years played down the value of fish and chips in other ways that must (along with the agenda and content of domestic science lessons) have reinforced the other negative images. What contemporaries called 'the newer knowledge of nutrition', involving an

improved understanding of dietary components and deficiencies through vitamins, minerals and amino acids, brought forth studies of the comparative value
of foods for different purposes which, as expressed in the mainstream literature, kept white fish firmly on the sidelines.[116] Professor Mottram, in the sixth
edition of a popular primer, pronounced in 1938:

> *The Poverty of Fish.* – On the whole, fish are very expensive as a means of purchasing
> calories, the only real exception being the herring. The fact is, fish are a poor source
> of almost everything except protein and iodine, and might well be banished from the
> poor man's table.[117]

In a more substantial standard text, Mottram lent his name to a more positive
view of fried fish, pointing out (with supporting statistics) that: 'Fish can . . . be
made to take up a considerable amount of fat in the process of cooking, and so
have its nutritive value greatly increased.' In the process, he also reiterated
earlier attacks on popular beliefs that fish was 'brain food' and had 'aphrodisiac
qualities', ideas that must have boosted the popularity of fish and chips at a
working-class level. Mottram provided nothing of substance to counteract the
prejudices against fish and chips in respectable society, although the discovery
of Vitamin C and the importance of the potato as a protective against scurvy
were positive developments. The problem was to make a connection with fish
and chips, and this was something the friers themselves began to address, as
part of their wider attack on the negative connotations of their product.[118]

The friers' efforts to justify the rationality of buying fish and chips as a
genuinely cheap, nourishing meal began in earnest with an article in the *Fish
Trades Gazette* in March 1917, a few months before potato shortages played
their part in precipitating outbreaks of scurvy in Manchester, Newcastle and
Glasgow.[119] This article, 'The value of the fried fish shops', was almost
certainly written by the ubiquitous Chatchip. It sought to emphasize the
'energy-value in calories' of fish and chips, drawing attention to protein and fat
content and stressing the value and importance of the fat content, 'because fat
has more than twice the energy-value of protein'. The writer calculated that an
average pre-war twopenny portion of fish and chips would be equivalent in
calories to half a pound of steak or a pound of chicken and asked: 'Can any
cheaper or more nourishing food be got anywhere else?' Admittedly 'The fried
fish diet is excessive in fat' but this made it an ideal diet for miners and manual
labourers, who had 'a largely increased need for fuel without any corresponding
increase in the need for protein or for other specific nutrients'. The same
argument might have been applied to working-class housewives. For a balanced
diet, fish and chips needed to be combined with peas, beans, bread, green
vegetables and a little fruit; but the nutritional ideas of the time could be used to
make a powerful-looking case for the defenders of this controversial dish.

Vitamins were later incorporated into this argument. In 1935 the Sheffield
friers were proclaiming, in a poster campaign, that fish and chips, 'as we cook
them', contained Vitamins A, B and C, and it is surprising that this theme was
not pursued in H. T. Reeves' substantial trade manual two years earlier.[120] But
Chatchip was aware of all the developments in nutritional thinking when he
returned to the fray in 1937, asserting that chips, in particular, were 'still by far

the best food value for money to be obtained almost anywhere in the world' and that:

> If a human being could get nothing else to eat except fried chipped potatoes freshly cooked, for many days on end, he or she would suffer no material harm thereby.[121]

The friers and their growing band of medical supporters failed to overcome the prejudices of respectable society during the inter-war years, despite the support that could be obtained from the 'newer knowledge of nutrition'. But a recent survey of the fast-food trades in Britain confirms that fish and chips has its virtues, although it makes the Sheffield friers look unduly optimistic. Fish and chips is said to be a 'good source' of protein, calcium and Vitamins B6 and B12. It supplies 'useful amounts' of Vitamins B1 and C, iron, dietary fibre and zinc. It is unduly high in fats, though not saturated fats, although a separate analysis of fish and chips in Leeds told a different story, and the contrast between animal fats and vegetable oils as frying media is clearly crucial here. It is short on Vitamins A, B2, D and E, and on folic acid, although the peas or beans that often accompanied fish and chips would make up for this latter deficiency. All this demonstrates that fish and chips three or four times a week could be, and probably was, either part of a balanced diet or an enhancement of a generally deficient one. It would be especially useful for those in heavy manual occupations who would need the protein and burn up the fat – and we should include housework under this heading. Fish and chips stands out from this survey as much better in terms of food value than other kinds of 'fast food' and this may have applied in earlier years as well, although we lack similar analyses of such alternatives as tripe, meat pies or jellied eels from the pre-Second World War years. But it is clear that contemporaries who damned fish and chips as lacking in nutritional value, as poor value for money, or as part of a pathology of working-class laziness and incompetent housekeeping, were very wide of the mark.[122] Dr Crichton Browne and the author of the *Fish Trades Gazette* article in 1917 may have been right for the wrong reasons, but the general tenor of their conclusions has been vindicated. On balance, and especially in the context of the time, fish and chips clearly made a decidedly positive contribution to working-class diet and living standards.

But there was more to fish and chips than dietary value. It also became an important focus of working-class sociability, and the shops came to perform a variety of functions over and above the supply of meals. They were centres of gossip and neighbourly competition, and the public nature of the purchase and (often) consumption of fish and chips no doubt helped to damn it in the eyes of those who valued privacy and domesticity and shunned the communal conviviality of the street. The fish and chip saloons of Warrington in 1906, which look like an extension of or alternative to the predominantly masculine world of the pub, are interesting but far from representative:

> Not a few of the proprietors of the 'saloons' sell mineral waters, tobacco and cigars, so that if the patrons happen to be 'flush', they can spend a very pleasant hour or two . . . especially if, as is sometimes the case, there happens to be a pianoforte in the room.[123]

This harks back to the early days in Bradford or Birmingham, and the trend in the twentieth century was towards a very different kind of customer behaviour, as set out by the 'Reviewer' in the *Fish Friers' Review* in 1933, with considerable emphasis on the importance of friendly – but not *too* friendly – conversation with regular customers who needed to be made to feel at home:

> fully 75 per cent of my customers are women and children. Care in serving children is always well rewarded. With obviously single ladies, apart from being as pleasant as possible, one must talk with care . . . it's so easy to get out of your depth. Married ladies – they're different. They've got two great interests, home and children.

So that is what the friers should talk about, while treating male customers as experts on their sport and their work but leaving politics firmly on the sidelines – 'they're dynamite'.[124] These perceptions of customers and their concerns may tell us at least as much about 'Reviewer' and his assumptions as about anything else; but the evidence of Mass-Observation a few years later bears out the notion that fish and chip shop conversation was expected to be cosy, neighbourly and uncontroversial. Harry, the Mass-Observers' tame fish frier, recorded the exchanges between his Bolton customers in a semi-literate pencilled scrawl, telling the curious that he was writing a novel: the subject matter was dominated by safe topics of guaranteed mutual interest, especially health, the weather, enjoyments and the football pools.[125] Not that everything was always perfectly respectable: one Preston fish frier failed partly because he was unable to exchange civilities with his customers on their own terms. His son remembered:

> We had moved into a rough sort of district and my people could not get down to their ways. One needed to be table to talk football, horse-racing and pass on bets, plus saucy tales to the right people at the right time.[126]

For those who fitted into the established patterns of neighbourhood life, the fish and chip shop might be viewed much more positively, as in the case of the Preston card-room worker who remembered going for the family meal with her basin and commented on the friendly competition for 'who could get the nicest basin', with floral decorations and careful coverings. At different times of the day, in different ways, the fish and chip shop became an important focus for neighbourhood life in industrial towns.[127] It was more inclusive than pub or chapel, opening its doors to men, women and children without distinction of belief. It was associated with warmth, comfort and pleasure and its opening hours were restricted and well-defined, expressing a local consensus about meal-times. It became a centre for the exchange of gossip and sociability, but often it was also more than that.

Some of the additional roles played by fish and chip shops were mildly disreputable. As the Preston man with the distaste for 'saucy tales' hinted, fish and chip shops were obvious conduits for illegal off-course betting and every so often evidence of this came to the surface, as when a Sale frier was fined £10 in 1914 for an offence of this sort.[128] Gambling of other kinds might become part of a frier's attractions, especially if he had a lot of youths and young men among his customers. Thus the manager of a Bo'ness fish restaurant was fined £5 in 1931 for keeping a 'gaming house' and six of his young customers were fined £1 each. This kind of activity could become divisive locally. In 1934 a Nottingham frier who had hired a fruit machine was fined £2 after parents had complained of their children losing change and spare coppers by playing it.[129] More in tune with the values of his customers was Alfred Yeomans of Hull, who tried to boost trade by offering lottery tickets. Each purchaser at his shop was given a numbered ticket, a draw was made on Fridays and the winner received a bag of coal for twopence. The police prosecuted, as they pointed out, partly in fear that other friers in the locality would have to follow suit.[130] The fish and chip eating contest reported from the Potteries in 1925, involving several men sitting on kerbstones eating fish and chips against the clock for a five-shilling prize, was an altogether more remarkable event.[131] A good store of jokes and a sense of humour were prized assets for fish friers, however, and these might often coexist with a willingness to extend the range of services provided. We do not know how many took up Keith Prowse and Co.'s offer to supply penny-in-the-slot 'electric pianos' in 1928, nor do we know how many illicitly sold beer to their customers, as was reported from Preston in 1937.[132] In most places, these would perhaps also have been divisive initiatives, losing more customers than they gained. Fish friers also gave credit to trusted customers, as did most small shopkeepers, and some friers would lend flour and even cash in the locality.[133] And the friers' need for newspapers often drew them into a local informal economy of barter, especially involving children who would collect papers in exchange for cinema tickets or free chips.[134]

The fish and chip shop, then, became a working-class institution. Children treated themselves, and were treated, there, and took pleasure in being well enough known to receive extra chips or free batter bits. Adolescent boys met their friends there and adolescent gangs identified them as territorial markers. Courting couples ate fish and chips together as one of the rituals of 'going out'. Fish and chips punctuated the working day and the working week, for men and women alike, and it even responded to the rhythms of the seasons. It was both holiday and workaday fare. It was so universal that it has been ignored by social surveys, condescended to by social commentators and investigators and relegated to the bottom of the historian's agenda. Where it has not been taken for granted, it has been attacked. In this chapter I have suggested that those attacks have no foundation and that fish and chips was beneficial to working-class health and living standards during the difficult years covered in this book. In the next and final chapter, I draw the threads of the argument together at greater length.

8 Fish and Chips in Context

Fish and chips became ubiquitous, mundane, inescapable and taken for granted in Britain in the first half of the twentieth century. It was at the heart of a multitude of daily and weekly routines and social rituals. But it could also – inevitably, in the light of its universality – be at the centre of dramatic, exciting events. Fiction acknowledges this, though very rarely: Gerald Priestland offers us a love story, a ghost story and a murder story, all set in and around fish and chip shops.[1] In real life, too, fish and chips could become a matter of life and death. Arthur Harding's memories of his heyday as a 'terror' in London's East End includes a gruesome portrait of a man called Scabby, who:

> would pick his victims from people who showed fear, and make them give him money for protection. One night in a doss-house in Dorset Street Scabby came in with a parcel of fish and chips. He offered the chips round, which was the custom then and still is. But one drunken fool took his piece of fish instead of just the chips and started eating it. Scabby had a knife in his hand, because he was about to cut a loaf of bread. When he realised what had happened he stabbed the man fatally. He was put on trial for murder, pleaded provocation and was acquitted.[2]

Some aspects of this story need to be taken with a pinch of salt, no doubt; it is also the kind of tale that reinforces the image of fish and chips as enduringly tied to low life and the culture of the slums. But we have seen that, as it developed, there was much more to the trade than that. It mattered to individuals; and if they were poor and short of resources, fish and chips might be worth fighting over. By the First World War, however, it was capable of playing an important part in a much greater fight.

The role of fish and chips in feeding the people and sustaining morale in the latter days of the First World War has been missed by previous historians. But contemporaries were aware of it, and it fits in well with recent interpretations of the war that emphasize the importance of the combatants' relative abilities to provide and distribute sufficient food to their soldiers and citizens.[3] Within this framework of argument, the persisting emphasis on agriculture and trade rather than fisheries merely perpetuates a lasting imbalance in government priorities which has been passed on to affect the agenda of historians. The sea fisheries, whether in near or distant waters, have always lacked the glamour and political clout associated with stately homes and landed estates. And potatoes have never shared the charisma of the waving wheatfields. The war record of the fish and chip trade may have fallen short of actual heroism, despite the friers' own rhetoric, but it undoubtedly made a difference. And the events of 1917-18 drove home the trade's ubiquity and importance in working-class areas as never before. Whether fish and chips was really a prophylactic against revolution, as one friers' organization claimed, is another matter – but not a laughing matter.

A more conventionally heroic, though indirect, association with fish and chips can be found in its crucially important contribution to the rise of the fishing industry, especially in the cold, winter darkness and ever-present danger of the distant-water fishing grounds within the Arctic Circle. As Jeremy Tunstall has expressed it, deep-sea fishing is an 'extreme' occupation, and its most 'extreme' characteristics were most in evidence in the long Arctic voyages of the Hull trawlers of the inter-war years, under the most bleak and spartan of living conditions.[4] The industrial fisheries of the 'big five' ports added up to a major element in the British economy between the turn of the century and the Second World War, with a multitude of spin-offs in other sectors, from shipbuilding, railways and coal-mining to ice manufacture, fertilizer and glue. The systematic exploitation of the fishing grounds had its own incalculable consequences for marine ecology; but it generated sufficient employment for one commentator to present the fishing industry as Britain's sixth largest.[5] This was a matter of definition and potential controversy; but more generally, the importance of the industry is undeniable. And it was widely accepted that the trawlermen's role extended beyond their often-romanticized battle with the elements to feed an expanding industrial population. They were also called upon to give assistance of the most direct kind to the Royal Navy in wartime. Trawlers were called up for minesweeping service and their crewmen were obvious recruits for the bigger warships and Merchant Navy vessels. Even on an ordinary fishing voyage, a medical academic was moved to comment that the fishermen's fatigue 'reminded me of what I saw among soldiers during the retreat to Dunkirk in 1940'; he was also able to confirm that 'trawler fishing had a higher occupational death rate than coal mining', with no effective safety legislation.[6] The risks in wartime were much greater and the fishermen's contribution was much praised by naval officers and military historians. This is relevant to our theme because it was, above all, the rise of the fish and chip trade that generated the demand which enabled the industry to grow in a sustained, spectacular way between the 1880s and the 1930s; and it was the everyday heroism of the crews in distant waters that brought back the cheap cod which increasingly sustained the frying trade in the depressed areas of the inter-war years. On the more conventionally heroic military stage, H. T. Reeves made the connection between the fish friers and the navy quite explicitly in 1936 and his logic is difficult to challenge, unexpected though its conclusions might seem:

> the more successful the fishing is made possible by the success of the fish frying trade, so much the better for the Navy's first line of reserve.[7]

This builds on John Stephen's acknowledgement of the necessity of the fried fish trade to the growth of the fishing industry, two years earlier, and takes it to its logical conclusion.[8]

The fish and chip trade may have generated the demand that made the rise of a concentrated, highly-capitalized fishing industry, as such, possible; but in

its turn its supplies and profits depended on the exploited labour and outra-
geous working conditions of the trawlermen. From time to time the friers
remembered this. As we saw in Chapter 3, there were many other linkages of a
less emotive kind between fish and chips and other aspects of the British and
international economies, from primary producers to the manufacturers of
sophisticated technical equipment (by the inter-war years) and the purveyors of
assorted business and personal services. There is no need to reiterate those
points here. Nor should it be necessary to go over the ground covered in
Chapter 7, emphasizing the value of fish and chips in dietary terms, in the
context of the times, and its positive contribution to working-class living
standards.

What is most remarkable, in some ways, is the persisting prejudice against
fish and chips in 'respectable' and official circles, which still affects many
people's perceptions even today. Fish and potatoes can be praised as the basis
of a healthy diet for Scottish crofters in the nineteenth century, while fish and
chips as a staple foodstuff of the urban working class is damned without a
hearing.[9] As I suggested in Chapter 7, the roots of these attitudes can be found
in the powerfully promoted Victorian ideal of female domesticity: the identification of the woman's sphere with hearth and home, cooking, cleaning and
needlework. One aspect of this was the stigmatization of women's work outside
the home; another was the condemnation of family budgets that included 'lazy'
and 'expensive' foods. At the very time in the late nineteenth century when fish
and chips was starting to become popular, these values were being assiduously
propagated through the schools as the 'domestic subjects' lobby successfully
pushed for extra time and status for cookery and housecraft lessons for
working-class girls.[10] Girls were to be trained to be wives, mothers and
domestic servants, on an approved plan and in spite of the protests of many
parents who saw it all as a waste of time. The obsession with eugenics and the
future of the race, which reached its height at the turn of the century, gave an
added dimension of urgency to the agenda of intending reformers of working-
class household management. From this point of view the emergence of fish
and chips as an item of mass consumption came at a very inconvenient
moment.[11]

The enduring power of the ideology of feminine domesticity and full-time
motherhood and its identification with the preservation of order and authority is
exemplified in this extract from *This England* in 1986:

> Nowadays, children mostly arrive home from school to an empty house . . . The
> television is provided to keep [the child] quiet until [mother] arrives home from work
> in an office or shop. Poor mum is too tired then to listen to childish chatter. She has
> no time to bake a cake or prepare a nourishing meal of stew and dumplings, so she
> feeds her family on deep-frozen, micro-waved convenience foods . . . Soaring crime
> and a breakdown of morals are the ultimate effects of evil. But the cause lies in the
> home . . . Whatever damages the family unit will eventually destroy the nation.[12]

From this perspective, fish and chips looks like the start of a very slippery slope
indeed, even though on a different occasion the same magazine might regard it,
in passing, as a nostalgic emblem of Englishness. The notion that fish and chips
is part of a way of life which is downright immoral, subverting the basic values

of home and family, still finds expression in ministerial pronouncements as well as in the editorial 'common sense' of right-wing magazines. Most of all, perhaps, it has affected the outlook of the 'respectable' middle classes, rather than those social inferiors at whom the propaganda of domesticity was more overtly aimed. But there is more to the enduring prejudice against fish and chips even than this.

Fish and chips has been widely seen and presented as 'common': something of low status with which respectable people should not become involved, except perhaps on holiday or special occasions when neighbours and acquaintances are unlikely to find out about a frivolous flirtation with it. Eating with the fingers and in public was, and for some people remains, an important taboo here. In this respect the status of fish friers has had as much influence as that of the commodity they sell. The association with smell and grease is very much part of this story, and we have seen that it made it hard for fish friers who sought a measure of social acceptability beyond their customers and neighbourhood. But the working-class origins of most fish friers and the low status of most of their customers also told against them.

The organized friers were forever trying to escape from these images and connotations, with increasing but always limited success. The trade retained its proletarian associations, and part of Harry Ramsden's success came from the way in which he defied the down-market expectations of his customers. Paradoxically, however, one of the most important aspects of the fish and chip trade was the way in which it offered a route out of wage-labour – and sometimes unemployment – for the alienated skilled worker who sought an independent living and (sometimes) a more comfortable lifestyle. Like other kinds of relatively small-scale retailing, but perhaps more so than most, fish and chips took aspiring, assertive people out of the workplace and the trade union movement, distancing them from the day-to-day workplace concerns of their former comrades. Fish and chips was a demanding trade, mentally, physically and in terms of working hours. It absorbed the energy and attention in ways that help to explain the problems experienced by the National Federation of Fish Friers in gaining and keeping recruits and organizers. The trade also offered satisfactions of its own, allowing skilled workers to devote their inventive capacities to testing, refining and improving their equipment.[13] And if the business failed,the disaster was more likely to be ascribed to the individual's own failure or ill fortune than to the workings of the overall economic system, although friers' adversarial attitudes towards the Ministry of Agriculture and Fisheries and the Potato Marketing Board complicate this picture somewhat.[14]

This diversion of creative energy and commitment into cottage industry and into what might be called enterprise culture was part of wider patterns of fragmentation and division within the inter-war working class. They were already appearing in late Victorian times in some respects, as Gareth Stedman Jones has pointed out. The decline of a workplace-centred popular culture and the development of more family-centred values and a preference for domestic pursuits was increasingly widespread in the inter-war years, epitomized by the growth of gardening as a popular recreation.[15] This may have been accompanied by a growing trend for working people to set themselves up in small businesses: greengrocery and confectionery, for example, as well as fish and chips. The shared routines of the factory and the workshop, the collective solidarities of industrial labour, were being supplemented by or exchanged for privacy and domesticity. This demanded a remaking of working-class politics, which is well analysed in Mike Savage's study of inter-war Preston.[16] In the short run, however, it distanced people from the organized working class and the trade union movement. In this respect, aspects of the rise of the fish and chip trade intersected with and reinforced more general social and political trends that helped to defuse class conflict. And the distinctive recruitment pattern of the fish and chip trade probably robbed large-scale industry, ossified as it often was, of much creative potential that went instead into the improvement of ranges and the calculation of thermal efficiencies. As we saw in Chapter 6, the fish friers' own political attitudes cut across conventional divisions; but the implications of the trade's development, in context, were undoubtedly politically stabilizing. If we take into consideration the friers' role in feeding the unemployed and helping to make life in the distressed areas bearable, that conclusion is more firmly reinforced.

Issues of this sort are difficult to pin down, but they should not therefore be neglected. Nor should we ignore the most difficult question of all, hard though it is to answer. Why did fish and chips, in particular, become so outstandingly popular, so universal an item of working-class diet, in these years? It did so, after all, in the face of a sustained barrage of official disapproval and snobbish scorn, which only began to lift a little at the end of the First World War and again in the 1930s. And the rise of fish and chips was achieved by a host of small back-street entrepreneurs whose publicity system worked by word of mouth, in sharp contrast to the centralized publicity resources and sophisticated image-building that has fuelled the rise of more recent franchised fast-food developments. Fish and chips had no sustained help in this respect from the fishing industry, the agricultural lobby or central government until the 1930s: and even then it was rarely at the centre of the stage. The growth of the fish and chip trade was a quiet, unassuming, populist, almost subterranean process.[17]

Fish and chips met an unfulfilled need for a cheap, convenient, tasty, all-the-year-round foodstuff for working-class families. It had no real rival in this niche at the turn of the century and for many years afterwards. Its rise coincided with the decline of oysters and other shellfish in popular esteem, partly as a result of well-publicized typhoid fever scares; but these were never full meals in the way that fish and chips came to be.[18] It had rivals of various kinds: tripe and meat pies in the Lancashire cotton district, eels and pie and mash in London's East End; but they never achieved general parity of esteem and never matched the fish friers' sheer density of outlets, even in the places where they were most popular.[19] The emergence of fish and chips as a national institution would have been unthinkable without the railway system, the steam trawler and the industrial fishing port. It is difficult to imagine it developing far without the combination of cheap fuel, cramped living conditions, inadequate cooking facilities and close-packed terraced housing that characterized so much of urban and industrial Britain in the late nineteenth century. But it is also significant that its rise coincided with the sustained rise in working-class purchasing power that took place almost everywhere in Britain in the late nineteenth century and was most pronounced in the areas in which the trade took earliest and deepest root: industrial south Lancashire, the West Riding of Yorkshire and London. This was a period when the balance of working-class spending was being tilted away from men and drink towards families, food and consumer durables, despite the emergence of professional football as a new male leisure pursuit. As fish and chips developed into a family meal rather than, or as well as, an accompaniment to a night out, so it fitted into a developing (though incomplete) pattern of working-class domestication. The availability of fish and chips, after all, itself contributed towards making the home a more comfortable place and easing the lot of those who did the housework. What all this adds up to is the overwhelming importance of working-class demand to the rise of the fish and chip trade. The other influences were the handmaidens of this great first cause. Without the overwhelming consumer enthusiasm that is so generally apparent, the developments on the supply side would have come to nothing.[20]

Whatever we may think about the reasons for the rise of the fish and chip trade, its importance and influence cannot be denied. They have been missed hitherto, despite central government endorsement, because historians assumed that fish and chips was too trivial to have a history that merited serious, sustained investigation. It was a matter for journalists and the popular media. This frame of mind can itself be explained in terms of the history of ideas, values, assumptions and prejudices. One of the messages of this book must be that historians should look carefully at their ideas about what constitutes the proper stuff of history. The inherited agenda has been challenged in the past and will need to be challenged in the future, if the new social history of the 1970s and 1980s is to consolidate its gains. Meanwhile, the importance of the fish and chip trade and its ramifications to an understanding of the social history of industrial Britain should now be clear. Unanswered questions – perhaps unanswerable ones – remain, and there is plenty of scope for further work. But the impact of the fish and chip trade on popular culture and social change in the first industrial nation can no longer be underestimated or ignored.

Notes

1 The Importance of the Fish and Chip Trade

1 *This England*, 1 (4), 1968, editorial.
2 Walter Wood (ed.), *The fish retailer and his trade* (London, 1933), II, p. 399.
3 Bill Naughton, *Saintly Billy: a Catholic boyhood* (Oxford, pbk. edn., 1989), p. 116.
4 Margery Allingham, *Flowers for the judge* (London, 1936; Penguin edn., 1988), pp. 92–3. Jenny Smith kindly found this reference.
5 A. H. Halsey, *Change in British society* (third edn., Oxford, 1986), p. 1.
6 John K. Walton, 'Fish and chips and the British working class, 1870–1930', *Journal of Social History* 23 (1989–90), p. 243; *Private Eye*, 16 Feb. 1990.
7 *FFR*, Jan. 1950; *FN*, 14 May 1932; *FFR*, Aug. 1933.
8 *FFR*, Mar. 1935.
9 D. J. Oddy, 'Food, drink and nutrition', in F. M. L. Thompson (ed.), *The Cambridge Social History of Britain*, II (1990), pp. 251–78.
10 G. Priestland, *Frying tonight* (London, 1972). See also the reminiscent history of the trade published by 'Chatchip' (William Loftas) in *FFR* 1951, and the history of the NFFF in *FFR*, April 1938.
11 W. H. Chaloner, 'Trends in fish consumption', in T. C. Barker et al. (eds), *Our changing fare* (London, 1966), pp. 109–10.
12 W. H. Fraser, *The coming of the mass market* (London, 1981), pp. 108–9; E. Roberts, *A woman's place* (Oxford, 1985), pp. 151–61.
13 R. Salaman, *The history and social influence of the potato* (Cambridge, 1949). The revised edition of 1985 contains a new introduction by J. G. Hawkes, which incorporates critical comments by historians, but still ignores fish and chips. The reference to potato crisps is on p. 566 in both editions.
14 The only complete run of *FFR* issues, as far as I know, is at the NFFF headquarters at Dewsbury Road, Leeds.
15 *Daily Mail*, 15 Aug. 1990. Jayne Southern kindly provided this reference.
16 *FTG*, 28 Sept. 1907; *FFR*, Nov. 1949.
17 *FTG*, 29 Oct. 1910; *cf.* Fraser (1981), p. 162.
18 The clearest evidence of this comes from Jean Turnbull's comparison of trade-directory listings with Medical Officer of Health reports in Carlisle: see below, Chapter 2.
19 *FFR*, July 1927.
20 PRO MAF 29/12 SFC 157.
21 *FFR*, Jan. 1939; and see below, Chapter 2.
22 *FFR*, Jan. 1931; *FN*, 16 Jan. 1932, for Chatchip's estimate that 90,000 people were

employed in the shops themselves,with no account being taken of indirect employment.

23 P. Ford, 'Excessive competition in the retail trades. Changes in the number of shops, 1901–1931', *Economic Journal* 45 (1935), p. 507.

24 For a good summary, Fraser (1981), pp. 159–63.

25 *FFR*, June 1934. See also Chatchip in *FTG*, 19 July 1913, for a list of ancillary fishing trades with an interest in fish and chips.

26 *FTG*, 16 July 1910; 31 Mar. 1917; 20 Oct. 1917; Fraser (1981), p. 162.

27 *FTG*, 4 July 1914.

28 PRO MAF 29/12 SFC 157.

29 *FFR*, Nov. 1935; Mar. 1939; PRO MAF 23/4/2 WFC 574.

30 *FTG*, 16 July 1910, 20 Oct. 1917; Sir W. H. Beveridge, *British Food Control* (New Haven and London, 1928), p. 154.

31 Ministry of Agriculture and Fisheries, *Report on the marketing of potatoes in England and Wales* (London: HMSO, 1926), p. 59.

32 *Bolton Journal*, 26 Sept. 1924. Peter Taylor kindly supplied this reference.

33 PRO MAF 86/365; G. Walworth, *Feeding the nation in peace and war* (London, 1940), pp. 412, 427–8.

34 *FFR*, Nov. 1935; but Harrison's figures were almost certainly based on his local experience in Portsmouth, which may have been misleading. See also *FN*, 5 Mar. 1932, for an estimate of 30 per cent.

35 The changing ratio between fish and potatoes suggested by these figures must reflect a change in the balance between fish and chip consumption, with fish becoming more important both relatively and in absolute terms. For further discussion see below, Chapters 5, 7.

36 *FTG*, 16 July 1910, 24 May 1919.

37 *FFR*, Nov. 1935. A lower estimate of 125,000 tons was actually cited, again without any supporting evidence, in *FFR*, Sept. 1940.

38 *FTG*, 2 Mar. 1907; H. T. Reeves, *The modern fish frier* (London, 1933), I, pp. 201–8.

39 *FFR*, Feb. 1950.

40 *FTG*, 22 Oct. 1910.

41 *FTG*, 16 July 1904, 28 July 1921.

42 *FTG*, 5 Oct. 1907; and advertisements in the trade press, *passim*.

43 *FFR*, Mar. 1951; *FTG*, 9 July 1910, 7 June 1919, 8 May 1920; MO, Worktown Box 12C, *Bolton Fish Friers' Journal*, 1938.

44 *FFR*, Sept. 1933; *FTG*, 15 Aug. 1908, 19 Sept. 1908, 24 April 1909, 26 Feb. 1910.

45 *FTG*, 22 Aug. 1908, 14 Oct. 1911.

46 *FTG*, 21 May 1921; *FFR*, June/July 1926.

47 *FFR*, July 1927.

48 *FTG*, 13 Oct. 1906.

49 *FTG*, 6 Feb. 1909.

50 *FFR*, Jan. 1950.

51 *FFR*, April 1927; *FN*, 13 Feb. 1932, 21 May 1932. We can be impressed by the orders of magnitude indicated by Loftas' calculation even if we remain sceptical about his extrapolation from the case of Great Yarmouth. For the first electric range, *FFR*, Jan. 1951.

52 *FTG*, 19 June 1909; *FFR*, Dec. 1949.

53 Priestland (1972), p. 67.

54 *FFR*, Oct. 1927.

55 *FTG*, 4 June 1910, 14 Oct. 1911.

56 PRO MAF 29/18 SFC 198; *FFR*, April 1928, for Nelson and Co.; *FFR*, Jan. 1951,

Mar. 1951, for developments in the 1920s and 1930s.

57 *FTG*, 1 Jan. 1910, 29 Jan. 1910; Reeves (1933), I, pp. 99–104.

58 Reeves (1933), I, pp. 70–8; *FFR*, April 1933.

59 Reeves (1933), I, Chapter 5.

60 For this and what follows, see the surveys of 'The trade in the provinces' in *FTG* 1905, and Chapter 2, below.

61 *FTG*, 9 July 1904.

62 *FTG*, 17 Mar. 1917, 22 Dec. 1917. And for all this see below, Chapters 7–8.

63 Priestland (1972), pp. 71–7; and see below, Chapter 6.

64 *FTG*, 2 July 1904, 6 Sept. 1913; and quotation from *FN*, 5 Mar. 1932.

65 See below, Chapter 8; and for Crichton Browne, *FTG*, 3 Sept. 1910; *FFR*, Mar. 1950.

66 Dorothy L. Sayers, *The unpleasantness at the Bellona Club* (London, 1974 edn.), p. 91. This reference is another product of Jenny Smith's addiction to detective stories.

67 *FN*, 12 Mar. 1932.

68 Information from Audrey Cox and Joan Wilkinson; and see below, Chapter 7.

69 Jack Common, *Kiddar's Luck* (third edn., Newcastle upon Tyne, 1990); Jack Common, *The Ampersand* (London, 1954); Ralph Glasser, *Growing up in the Gorbals* (London, 1986); Richard Hoggart, *A local habitation* (London, 1989).

70 For more on these themes, see below, Chapter 9.

71 M. J. Winstanley, *The shopkeeper's world* (Manchester, 1983); John Benson, *The penny capitalists* (Dublin, 1983); G. Crossick (ed.), *The lower middle class in Britain* (London, 1977); G. Crossick and H.-G. Haupt (eds), *Shopkeepers and master artisans in nineteenth-century Europe* (London, 1984); C. P. Hosgood, 'The "pigmies of commerce" and the working-class community: small shopkeepers in England, 1870–1914', *Journal of Social History* 22 (1988–9), pp. 439–59; G. Shaw and M. T. Wild, 'Retail patterns in the Victorian city', *Transactions of the Institute of British Geographers*, N. S., 4 (1979), pp. 278–91; G. Shaw, 'Retail patterns', in J. Langton and R. J. Morris (eds), *Atlas of industrializing Britain, 1780–1914* (London, 1986), pp. 180–4; and see also J. K. Walton, *The Blackpool landlady: a social history* (Manchester, 1978), and for pawnbrokers M. Tebbutt, *Making ends meet* (Leicester, 1983).

72 Fraser (1981), offers a way in to most of this literature. See also M. Purvis, 'The development of Co-operative retailing in England and Wales, 1851–1901', *Journal of Historical Geography* 16 (1990), pp. 314–31.

73 B. Harrison, *Drink and the Victorians* (London, 1971); L. L. Shiman, *The crusade against drink in Victorian England* (London, 1988); M. Girouard, *Victorian pubs* (New Haven and London, 1984); A. Crawford et al., *Birmingham pubs 1880–1939* (Gloucester, 1986); P. Bailey (ed.), *Music-hall: the business of pleasure* (Milton Keynes, 1986).

74 The Scottish campaign, which was also directed against ice-cream parlours, can be followed in *FTG* during 1913, or in (especially) the Glasgow press. We return to it in Chapter 5.

75 See below, Chapters 4–6.

76 See below, Chapter 5.

77 *FFR*, Nov. 1935.

78 *FFR*, Oct. 1935.

79 See below, Chapter 6.

80 See above, note 71.

81 *The Frier*, 1 Mar. 1919.

82 *FTG*, 8 Sept. 1917; and see also 28 April 1917, 25 Aug. 1917.

83 *FTG*, 1 Dec. 1917.
84 *FTG*, 8 Dec. 1917; *FFR*, April 1938.
85 Beveridge (1928); J. M. Winter, *The Great War and the British people* (London, 1985), pp. 215–17; PRO MAF 60/56, especially Austen Chamberlain to Secretary of War Cabinet, 5 Dec. 1917.
86 Winter (1985), pp. 213–29, 244–5.
87 PRO MAF 60/326.
88 *FTG*, 19 Jan. 1918; the Government purchased the entire Egyptian cotton-seed crop.
89 *FTG*, 2 Mar. 1918; and see below, Chapter 6. Fish price ceilings were fixed in January 1918: *FTG*, 26 Jan. 1918.
90 *FTG*, 3 May 1919; *FFR*, June 1950. Price ceilings were fixed but fish and potatoes remained unrationed.
91 *FTG*, 25 Aug. 1917, 27 Oct. 1917; *The Frier*, 1 Mar. 1919.
92 Winter (1985), p. 245.
93 PRO MAF 29/12 SFC 157.
94 *FFR*, Jan. 1941.
95 PRO MAF 72/253 is the file in question.
96 PRO MAF 23/2/1 WFC 117; *FFR*, Jan. 1940.
97 PRO MAF 75/46; see also MAF 86/365 for the potato subsidy, MAF 86/24 for white fish price regulations and MAF 85/18 for the working of the oils and fats regulations.
98 George Orwell, *The road to Wigan Pier* (London, 1965 edn.), p. 91. *Cf.* also the Leo Baxendale cartoon, 'I *love* you Baby Basil!', in the *Guardian*, 4 Aug. 1990, for a shrewd analysis of fish and chips as part of 'the politics of distraction', although it is not for me to say how seriously it is intended.
99 *Observer Colour Supplement*, 'The forging of the north', 1966 but anon. and not otherwise dated. Elaine Knox kindly supplied this material.
100 PRO MAF 29/12 SFC 157, Verbatim Evidence of Northern Area of Fish Friers' Federation to the Sea-Fish Commission, 13 Aug. 1935.
101 PRO MAF 29/12 SFC 191, Retail Fish Survey (SFC 80), pp. 40–3.
102 PRO MAF 34/335 sheds interesting light on the mode of nomination to the Potato Marketing Board and its domination by the farming interest. For further discussion of the issues in this paragraph see below, Chapter 6.
103 PRO MAF 23/4/2 WFC 574.
104 PRO MAF 29/17 SFC 196; MAF 86/365.
105 PRO MAF 29/12 SFC 157.

2 Origins, Growth and Spread

1 *FFR*, Aug. 1949.
2 Priestland (1972), p. 61.
3 F. Volent and J. R. Warren, *Memoirs of Alexis Soyer; with unpublished receipts and odds and ends of gastronomy* (London, 1859), p. 74. Mary Delorme kindly provided me with this reference.
4 London County Council report, 'The fish frier and his trade', reproduced in *FTG*, 23 Feb. 1907.
5 *FTG*, 14 Oct. 1911, 29 July 1922.
6 Priestland (1972), pp. 63–5; *FTG*, 12 Jan. 1907, 29 Aug. 1908.
7 Priestland (1972), p. 63; *FTG*, 23 Feb. 1907.
8 *Modern Housewife* (1848–9), p. 329; *Soyer's Shilling Cookery* (*c.* 1854), p. 114. Mary

Delorme supplied photocopies of these references.
9 *FTG*, 3 July 1920.
10 *FTG*, 28 Oct. 1911.
11 Priestland (1972), pp. 66–7.
12 R. Poole, 'Oldham Wakes', in J. K. Walton and J. Walvin (eds), *Leisure in Britain 1780–1939* (Manchester, 1983), p. 83.
13 Barrett's *Directory of Blackburn and District* (1894).
14 PRO MAF 23/1/7, WFC 68, minute sheet.
15 Priestland (1972), pp. 68–9.
16 *FTG*, 13 Mar. 1906, 15 Sept. 1906, 6 Oct. 1906, 7 Aug. 1909, 3 Mar. 1906.
17 *FFR*, Nov. 1933, Feb. 1950.
18 *FTG*, 23 Feb. 1907.
19 *FTG*, 13 Jan. 1906, 7 Aug. 1909.
20 *FTG*, 18 Mar. 1905, 30 Sept. 1905, 28 July 1906.
21 *FTG*, 20 Jan. 1906, 10 Mar. 1906.
22 The Newcastle figure comes from a local trade directory, by courtesy of Dr Lynn Pearson.
23 *FTG*, 9 Dec. 1905, 16 Dec. 1905, 6 Jan. 1906, 28 July 1906, 6 Oct. 1906.
24 *FTG*, 14 Oct. 1911. This article was not formally attributed to Chatchip, but the style is his and it deals with his part of the country.
25 *FTG*, 21 April 1906; see also 28 April 1906, 5 May 1906.
26 See below, Chapters 7–8.
27 *FTG*, 7 Jan. 1911.
28 G. Shaw and A. Tipper, *British directories: a bibliography and guide to directories published in England and Wales (1850–1950) and Scotland (1773–1950)* (Leicester, 1988).
29 For problems of this sort see, for example, M. J. Winstanley, *The shopkeeper's world* (Manchester, 1983), pp. 13–14; J. K. Walton and P. R. McGloin, 'The tourist trade in Victorian Lakeland', *Northern History* 17 (1981), pp. 167–70.
30 *FTG*, 12 July 1913; and thanks to Jenny Smith for counting the friers in the Burnley trade directory.
31 These figures are by courtesy of Jean Turnbull.
32 M. Savage, *The dynamics of working-class politics: the labour movement in Preston 1880–1940* (Cambridge, 1987), Chapter 4.
33 *FTG*, 2 June 1906.
34 See below, Chapter 6.
35 *FTG*, 3 Feb. 1917.
36 *FTG*, 7 July 1917, quoting letter dated 29 Dec. 1916.
37 *FTG*, 21 July 1917.
38 *FTG*, 2 Mar. 1918, 13 Feb. 1909, 23 Feb. 1918.
39 Based on information from Jean Turnbull.
40 *FFR*, Sept. 1930.
41 *The Frier*, 5 April 1919.
42 *FTG*, 8 Feb. 1919, 22 Feb. 1919, 3 Jan. 1920, 10 Jan. 1920; *The Frier*, 7 June 1919.
43 *FFR*, Aug. 1928.
44 *FN*, 9 Sept. 1925.
45 *FFR*, Oct. 1927, Jan. 1928.
46 *FTG*, 5 June 1920.
47 *FFR*, Jan. 1926, Feb. 1926, Dec. 1926, May 1927, Sept. 1928.
48 *FFR*, Jan. 1926, Sept. 1929.
49 R. A. Taylor, *The economics of white fish distribution in Great Britain* (London, 1960), pp. 145–7.

50 *FN*, 2 Jan. 1932, 18 June 1932.
51 PRO MAF 29/12 SFC 157, Verbatim evidence of Northern Area of Fish Friers' Federation, North Shields, 13 Aug. 1935; *Observer Colour Supplement* (1966), for interesting reminiscences of Jarrow.
52 *FFR*, Nov. 1949.
53 *FFR*, Feb. 1950; *FTG*, 19 May 1906.
54 *FFR*, Jan. 1951, Nov. 1950.
55 *FTG*, 11 Aug. 1923; *FN*, 8 Aug. 1925.
56 *FFR*, Feb. 1951; Don Mosey and Harry Ramsden, Junior, *Harry Ramsden: the uncrowned king of fish and chips* (Clapham *via* Lancaster, 1989), pp. 23–4, 34.
57 *FFR*, April 1934, May 1934, Loftas told the Sea-Fish Commission in October 1935 that '. . . last year I had a very bad misfortune', as a result of which he had had to work extra hard for his living over the previous 12 months: PRO MAF 29/12 SFC 157, evidence of Manchester friers, 14 Oct. 1935.
58 *FN*, 16 Jan. 1932.
59 *FN*, 9 Jan. 1932.
60 *The Caterer and Hotel-Keeper's Gazette*, 19 Mar. 1932. Julian Demetriadi kindly suggested that this source might be useful.
61 *MO*, Box 3, File B, Brown's of Chester. Thanks to Bill Lancaster for passing on this reference.
62 *FFR*, April 1939.
63 *MO*, Box 55D.
64 *FFR*, Nov. 1934. For more general worries about this trend, *FFR*, Dec. 1936 (Wakefield).
65 Tower Hamlets Local History Library, Mile End Old Town Vestry Harford Street Widening Scheme papers, 1887–9, Deeds Nos. 5093 and 5100. Geoff Crossick very kindly provided transcripts of this material.
66 *FTG*, 9 Dec. 1905, 16 July 1921.
67 R. Samuel (ed.), *Village life and labour* (London, 1975), Plate 14.
68 *FTG*, 28 Dec. 1907; Barrett's *Directory* for Preston, 1892, by courtesy of Jenny Smith.
69 *FTG*, 16 July 1921.
70 *FFR*, July 1925.
71 PRO MAF 29/12 SFC 157, evidence of Manchester friers to Sea-Fish Commission.
72 PRO MAF 23/1/7.
73 *Fish Trades Annual*, 1939.
74 *FN*, 4 June 1925.
75 M. Rogers, 'Italiani in Scozzia', in Billy Kay (ed.), *Odyssey: voices from Scotland's recent past* (Edinburgh, 1982), pp. 13–15; *Evening Times* (Glasgow), 4 Sept. 1980, pp. 18–19; L. Sponza, *Italian immigrants in nineteenth-century Britain: realities and images* (Leicester, 1988), Chapters 2–3; and information from Eric Leaver.
76 *FTG*, 2 June 1906.
77 *FTG*, 8 Mar. 1913.
78 Sponza (1988), pp. 110–11.
79 *FTG*, 6 June 1914.
80 *FTG*, 29 April 1905, 14 June 1913; Sponza (1988), p. 111; John Stephen, in Wood (1933), II, p. 384.
81 *FTG*, 10 April 1909.
82 Information on Italian migration patterns to Dublin was kindly provided by Brian Reynolds of the Department of Geography, Trinity College, Dublin. For Cork, *FTG*, 9 Mar. 1912.

83 Reeves (1933), I, p. 15.
84 Reeves (1933), I, pp. 15–16.
85 *FTG*, 27 Sept. 1919, 18 Oct. 1919; Priestland (1972), p. 114.
86 *FTG*, 11 June 1921. But Priestland (1972), p. 113, is more sanguine about British Columbia and Nova Scotia.
87 *FFR*, Oct. 1936.
88 *FN*, 19 Sept. 1925; Priestland (1972), p. 113.
89 *FFR*, Jan. 1951; *FTG*, 8 Nov. 1919; *FFR*, Oct. 1928; Reeves (1933), I, p. 15.
90 *FN*, 15 Aug. 1925.
91 Reeves (1933), I, pp. 16–17.
92 Reeves (1933), I, p. 16; and information from my colleague Paolo Rossi on Barga.
93 Priestland (1972), Chapter 10.

3 Fish Friers and Other Industries

1 *FTG*, 19 July 1913.
2 *FTG*, 28 Sept. 1907.
3 *FFR*, Jan. 1930.
4 R. Robinson, *A history of the Yorkshire coast fishing industry 1780–1914* (Hull, 1987), Chapter 5.
5 Paul Thomson et al., *Living the fishing* (London, 1983), p. 17.
6 Fraser (1981), pp. 160–1; Jeremy Tunstall, *The Fishermen* (third edn., London, 1972), pp. 19–22.
7 E. Gillett, *A history of Grimsby* (Hull, 1972), Chapters 17–18.
8 Robinson (1987), pp. 72–3; Fraser (1981), p. 162.
9 *PP* 1900 vii, Special Report and Report from the Select Committee on the Sea Fisheries Bill, p. 530.
10 Fraser (1981), pp. 162–3.
11 *PP* 1900 vii, p. 530; Thompson et al. (1983), p. 90.
12 Figures derived from the annual reports on sea fisheries in *PP*, by courtesy of Gill Parsons.
13 *PP* 1900 vii, Q. 690–1, 2627.
14 Ibid., Q. 2583.
15 *FTG*, 3 April 1909, and information from Dr Gordon Jackson.
16 See above, note 12; and *PP* 1935–6 x, Sea-Fish Commission of the United Kingdom, second report: the White Fish Industry, p. 323.
17 *FTG*, 27 Feb. 1909.
18 *FTG*, 21 Sept. 1907.
19 *FTG*, 17 Feb. 1906; Thompson et al. (1983), Chapter 5 and 6.
20 *FTG*, 20 Aug. 1904; 3 July 1909; 24 July 1909.
21 *FTG*, 8 Oct. 1910, 3 July 1920, 2 Oct. 1909.
22 *PP* 1935–6 x, pp. 320–34.
23 *PP* 1935–6 x, p. 326.
24 *PP* 1935–6 x, pp. 328, 349.
25 *The Frier*, 1 Mar. 1923.
26 *FFR*, Sept. 1934.
27 *PP* 1929–30 viii, Committee of Civil Research, First Interim Report of the sub-committee on the Fishing Industry, p. 538.
28 Tunstall (1972), p. 36.
29 *PP* 1929–30 viii, p. 539.
30 *PP* 1935–6 x, pp. 341, 351–2, 357.

31 *FFR*, Sept. 1929.
32 *PP* 1935–6 x, p. 340.
33 G. Dow, *Great Central*, II (London, 1965), pp. 263–4, 322–3; W. A. Tuplin, *Great Central Steam* (London, 1967), p. 59.
34 Ray Batcheler, 'Fish, filth and the food brothel', seminar paper, MA programme, Victoria and Albert Museum, London, 1989, p. 11; *FFR*, Sept. 1949.
35 *FFR*, Sept. 1949.
36 *FTG*, 5 Nov. 1904.
37 *The Caterer and Hotel-keepers' Gazette*, 15 Feb. 1913.
38 *FTG*, 25 Mar. 1905. 21 April 1906, 12 May 1906, 6 Oct. 1906.
39 *FTG*, 11 Mar. 1905, 25 Mar. 1905, 24 Mar. 1906.
40 *FTG*, 24 Feb. 1906, 17 Mar. 1906.
41 *FTG*, 12 July 1913; see also the claim made by Faulkners of Hollinwood, *FTG*, 15 Feb. 1908, 4 April 1908, 19 June 1909.
42 Batcheler (1989).
43 *FFR*, Oct. 1927, July 1933.
44 *FFR*, May 1937.
45 *FN*, 11 June 1932.
46 *FFR*, May 1931; *FN*, 21 May 1932.
47 Batcheler (1989); *FFR*, Dec. 1936, May 1937.
48 *FFR*, Feb. 1930; *FN*, 30 Jan.– 13 Feb. 1932; *FFR*, May 1935, Oct. 1936.
49 *FFR*, July 1928, Dec. 1930; *FN*, 12 Mar. 1932.
50 Batcheler (1989); *FN*, 12 Mar. 1932.
51 Batcheler (1989), p. 24.
52 *FFR*, Feb. 1938.
53 Harold W. Brace, *The History of Seed Crushing in Great Britain* (London, 1960).

4 The Friers and their Fortunes

1 *FFR*, Nov. 1949; and see also *FN*, 11 July 1925, 5 Sept. 1925.
2 *FTG*, 30 Sept. 1905.
3 *FTG*, 7 Aug. 1909.
4 *FTG*, 3 Nov. 1906, 21 Oct. 1911, 1 Feb. 1913.
5 *FTG*, 14 Oct. 1911.
6 Information from my colleague Paolo Rossi.
7 *FTG*, 7 July 1921; and for Lipton see P. Mathias, *Retailing revolution* (London, 1967).
8 *FTG*, 19 Feb. 1910.
9 *FTG*, 29 Nov. 1919.
10 *FFR*, May 1927, May 1933.
11 *FN*, 26 Mar. 1932.
12 *FFR*, April 1939.
13 Taylor (1960), p. 142.
14 *FTG*, 29 Nov. 1919.
15 *FN*, 26 Mar. 1932.
16 The Northamptonshire entries were found by Jenny Smith in the Co-operative movement directory for 1940 in the C. W. S. Library in Manchester; and for Ipswich, *FFR*, April 1939.
17 Taylor (1960), p. 142.
18 *FFR*, June 1931.
19 *FFR*, Oct. 1949.

20 N. Griffiths, *Shops Book: Brighton 1900–1930* (Brighton, n.d.), pp. 8–9.
21 Benson (1983), Chapter 10.
22 Winstanley (1983), Chapter 3.
23 A. Howkins and T. Vigne, 'The small shopkeeper in industrial and market towns', in Crossick (1977), pp. 184–209.
24 Benson (1983), p. 127.
25 Hosgood (1989), pp. 450–3; G. Crossick, 'The petite bourgeoisie in nineteenth-century Britain: the urban and liberal case', in Crossick and Haupt (1984), pp. 78–9, 86–7.
26 *FTG*, 5 Nov. 1910.
27 Benson (1983), pp. 4–5.
28 *FFR*, June 1928.
29 *FTG*, 17 Feb. 1912.
30 *FTG*, 31 May 1913.
31 Griffiths (n.d.), p. 36.
32 *FTG*, 15 Feb. 1913.
33 *FTG*, 11 Dec. 1909.
34 Gracie Fields, *Sing as we go* (London, 1960), pp. 11–12.
35 *FTG*, 18 Feb. 1905.
36 *FTG*, 3 Aug. 1907.
37 *FTG*, 17 Oct. 1908.
38 *FTG*, 15 March 1913.
39 *FTG*, 12 Oct. 1907.
40 Joe Robinson, *The life and times of Francie Nichol of South Shields* (London, 1975), pp. 94–6. I owe this reference to Bill Lancaster and Elaine Knox.
41 *FFR*, Nov. 1949.
42 *FTG*, 5 Oct. 1907.
43 *FTG*, 10 Oct. 1908, 17 Oct. 1908, 5 June 1909.
44 Mosey and Ramsden (1989), pp. 11–12.
45 *FTG*, 3 Sept. 1904.
46 *FTG*, 11 June 1910, 30 July 1910.
47 *FTG*, 2 July 1910.
48 *FFR*, Oct. 1929.
49 *FTG*, 7 Jan. 1905; and see also *FTG*, 4 Aug. 1906, 3 Aug. 1907.
50 *FTG*, 15 Aug. 1908.
51 Stephens, in Wood (1933), II, p. 284.
52 *FTG*, 10 May 1919.
53 *FTG*, 13 Sept. 1919, 10 Jan. 1920.
54 *FFR*, May 1929, July 1931.
55 *FFR*, Nov. 1935.
56 *FFR*, Dec. 1931.
57 *FTG*, 3 Jan. 1920, 1 May 1920, 15 May 1920.
58 *FFR*, Aug. 1931.
59 *FN*, 27 Feb. 1932.
60 PRO MAF 29/12 SFC 157, evidence of Messrs. Scott, Cooper and Barret of the Northern Area of the NFFF, 30 July 1935.
61 *FTG*, 15 May 1920, 12 June 1920.
62 *FTG*, 27 May 1922.
63 *FFR*, Oct. 1929.
64 *FN*, 2 Jan. 1932.
65 *FFR*, Sept. 1930, Oct. 1929; *FN*, 11 July 1925.
66 Robinson (1975), pp. 91–3.

67 *FFR*, Nov. 1949.
68 *FTG*, 10 Oct. 1910, 2 Dec. 1911.
69 *FFR*, April 1931.
70 *FTG*, 22 Aug. 1914.
71 *FFR*, Jan. 1935.
72 *FFR*, Mar. 1930.
73 *FTG*, 17 June 1922; *FFR*, Aug. 1935.
74 *FFR*, April 1927.
75 *FTG*, 19 June 1920.
76 *FN*, 18 July 1925.
77 *FFR*, July 1929.
78 *FFR*, Oct. 1929, July 1929.
79 *FFR*, 4 April 1925.
80 *FFR*, Mar. 1936, April 1949.
81 *FFR*, May 1939.
82 *FTG*, 3 Mar. 1906.
83 Kay (1982), pp. 16–17; information from Paolo Rossi; *FTG*, 13 Feb. 1909, 27 Nov. 1909, 4 Mar. 1911.
84 Priestland (1972), p. 7.
85 See below, Chapter 5.
86 Robinson (1975). This book is Francie Nichol's autobiography as told to a relative and it is possible that this may have affected the tone and ordering of the memories in places; but the whole thing carries conviction.
87 *FFR*, 4 April 1925, 1 July 1925, Jan. 1931.
88 P. Barrett and Co., *Directories* for Preston and District, 1885–1913, and for Blackburn and District, 1894.
89 *FTG*, 13 Nov. 1909.
90 *FFR*, Feb. 1939.
91 *FTG*, 7 June 1919.
92 Robinson (1975), pp. 90–1.
93 Robinson (1975), pp. 91–8.
94 *FFR*, April 1927.
95 *FFR*, Nov. 1949.
96 See below, Chapter 6.
97 *FTG*, 2 July 1904.
98 *FTG*, 3 Aug. 1907.
99 *FTG*, 4 Aug. 1917.
100 *FTG*,12 April 1919. For similar misleading impressions, Walton (1978), Chapter 6.
101 *FN*, 23 April 1932.
102 *FFR*, Feb. 1934, Oct. 1937 (columns by H. T. Reeves and 'Gossipyum').
103 *FFR*, April 1937.
104 *FTG*, 2 March 1912.
105 Ibid.
106 *FTG*, 28 July 1906, 12 July 1913.
107 *FFR*, Sept. 1928.
108 *FFR*, Dec. 1927.
109 *FFR*, Sept. 1931.
110 *FN*, 9 Jan. 1932.
111 *FTG*, 22 Nov. 1913.
112 *FFR*, Jan. 1930.
113 *FFR*, Aug. 1935.
114 Preston trade directories, as in Table 2.1, above; J. K. Walton, 'The social

development of Blackpool, 1788–1914', Ph.D. thesis, Univ. of Lancaster, 1974, p. 152, Table 3.8; and information from Geoff Crossick.
115 *FTG*, 13 Jan. 1894, 20 Jan. 1894.
116 *FTG*, 24 May 1919, 8 Nov. 1919.
117 *FTG*, 2 Feb. 1906.
118 *FFR*, Feb. 1934.
119 *FFR*, Aug. 1937.
120 *FTG*, 16 Aug. 1919, 30 Aug. 1919.
121 *FFR*, July 1929.
122 *FFR*, Feb. 1938.

5 The Nature of the Business

1 PRO MAF 29/12 SFC 157, evidence of NFFF to Sea-Fish Commission, 18 Jan. 1935; *FFR*, Jan. 1930. Chatchip, in *FTG*, 13 Sept. 1919, reckoned that even then 'the average fried fish shop' would turn over between £35 and £40 per week, but this is out of line with other evidence, including his own to the Sea-Fish Commission: PRO MAF 29/12 SFC 157, evidence of Manchester friers.
2 Bolton Archives, Oral History Collection, Tape 28b.
3 See above, Chapter 4.
4 *FTG*, 5 Nov. 1910.
5 *FTG*, 6 Sept. 1919.
6 Oral evidence kindly collected in Somerset by Jenny Paull and Robbie Smith.
7 *FFR*, Jan. 1928.
8 *FFR*, July 1931.
9 *FFR*, April 1929.
10 *FN*, 19 Mar. 1932.
11 Kent University Oral History Collection, interview with Mrs Jennings of Ramsgate, transcript kindly provided by Mike Winstanley.
12 *FFR*, Feb. 1951.
13 *FTG*, 2 Sept. 1905.
14 *FFR*, Dec. 1949.
15 *ER*, Mr M7B.
16 *FFR*, Mar. 1927.
17 *FFR*, Mar. 1939.
18 L. Davidoff and C. Hall, *Family fortunes: men and women of the English middle class, 1780–1850* (London, 1987).
19 R. Roberts, *The classic slum* (Manchester, 1971).
20 Robinson (1975), pp. 102–3.
21 *FTG*, 19 Feb. 1919.
22 M. Prior (ed.), *Women in English society 1500–1800* (London, 1985), p. 95.
23 *FFR*, Aug. 1927.
24 *FFR*, May 1928.
25 *FFR*, Mar. 1929; and see also his comments in *FFR*, July 1933.
26 *FFR*, Nov. 1934.
27 *FFR*, Feb. 1937.
28 *FTG*, 27 Oct. 1917.
29 *ER*, Mr D2P.
30 *FTG*, 15 July 1922, 12 Aug. 1922.
31 *FFR*, Feb. 1930, Feb. 1931; *FN*, 26 Mar. 1932.
32 *FTG*, 1 Feb. 1913.

33 *FFR*, Nov. 1927; Robinson (1975), p. 102.
34 *FTG*, 25 Nov. 1911, 10 June 1922.
35 *FFR*, April 1933.
36 *ER*, Mr M7B.
37 *FFR*, Nov. 1936.
38 *FFR*, Feb. 1951.
39 *FFR*, June and July 1933.
40 See above, note 11.
41 *FTG*, 13 Dec. 1919.
42 *FN*, 23 Jan. 1932.
43 *ER*, Mr D2P.
44 *FFR*, May 1927.
45 *FFR*, Sept. 1934.
46 *FFR*, April 1936.
47 *FFR*, Jan. 1937.
48 *FTG*, 18 Dec. 1909.
49 *FTG*, 19 June 1909.
50 *FTG*, 2 Sept. 1905.
51 *FTG*, 29 May 1920; *FN*, 18 July 1925.
52 *FTG*, 10 June 1922; *FFR*, Nov. 1934.
53 *FFR*, May 1939.
54 *FFR*, May 1939.
55 *FFR*, May 1930.
56 *FN*, 13 Feb. 1932.
57 *FFR*, Mar. 1933.
58 PRO MAF 29/12 SFC 157, evidence of Manchester friers to the Sea-Fish Commission, 14 Oct. 1935.
59 *FTG*, 25 Oct. 1919; *FN*, 8 May 1925.
60 *FFR*, June 1931.
61 *FFR*, Aug. 1935.
62 *FFR*, Nov. 1937.
63 *FTG*, 22 Feb. 1919, 15 Feb. 1913.
64 *FTG*, 7 June 1913.
65 *FTG*, 8 Mar. 1913; *Glasgow Herald*, 24 Sept. 1909; *FTG*, 7 June 1913, 14 June 1913, 28 June 1913.
66 *FTG*, 18 Jan. 1919, 22 Feb. 1919, 1 Mar. 1919, 9 Aug. 1919, 16 Aug. 1919, 20 Sept. 1919.
67 *FTG*, 7 Oct. 1905, 5 Nov. 1910, 19 Nov. 1910.
68 *FTG*, 23 Oct. 1909.
69 *FFR*, Aug. 1930.
70 *FFR*, May 1937, June 1937, Jan. 1939.
71 *FTG*, 'Trade in the Provinces' feature, 1905–9.
72 PRO MAF 29/17 SFC 191, Retail Fish Survey, labelled SFC 80, pp. 28–9, and comment on 'The consumption of fish at different income levels', p. 5.
73 Annual returns of fish catch, 1889–1902, kindly supplied from Parliamentary Papers by Gill Parsons.
74 *FFR*, Nov. 1937; PRO MAF 23/4/2 WFC 574, Gray to R. G. R. Wall, 20 Aug. 1939.
75 *FTG*, 21 Oct. 1911.
76 See above, Chapter 2.
77 *FN*, 16 Jan. 1932, 23 Jan. 1932; *FFR*, April 1939.
78 PRO MAF 29/17 SFC 191, Retail Fish Survey, p. 30.

79 *PP* 1900 vii 371, Special Report and Report from the Select Committee on the Sea Fisheries Bill, Q. 690–1, 2656–61, 3419–23, 3464–7.
80 *FTG*, 4 Aug. 1906, 17 April 1909; *FFR*, July 1927.
81 *FTG*, 6 May 1905; PRO MAF 29/12 SFC 157, evidence of NFFF to the Sea-Fish Commission, 18 Jan. 1935.
82 *FTG*, 22 Aug. 1914, 6 Jan. 1917, 22 Dec. 1917.
83 PRO MAF 29/12 SFC 157, evidence of North-Eastern friers to the Sea-Fish Commission, 30 July 1935.
84 *FFR*, July 1927.
85 *FTG*, 18 Nov. 1905, 14 Nov. 1911.
86 *FTG*, 15 Feb. 1919; Reeves (1933), II, p. 273.
87 *FFR*, Aug. 1937.
88 *FFR*, Sept. 1928.
89 *FTG*, 6 Aug. 1904.
90 PRO MAF 29/17 SFC 191, Retail Fish Survey, pp. 51–4.
91 *FFR*, Oct. 1931; Reeves (1933), I, p. 163.
92 *FTG*, 15 Feb. 1908.
93 PRO MAF 29/17 SFC 191, D. Maitland to Lloyd, 15 Mar. 1935, and SFC 197 on Glasgow Corporation's fish market.
94 *FTG*, 16 July 1904.
95 Reeves (1933), I, p. 163.
96 *FTG*, 26 Sept. 1908, 21 May 1910, 16 Aug. 1913.
97 *FFR*, Sept. 1950.
98 *FTG*, 4 Feb. 1911.
99 Reeves (1933), I, p. 181; PRO MAF 86/365.
100 *FTG*, 4 Feb. 1911; PRO MAF 86/365, E. Norkett to D. Struthers, 12 Dec. 1942.
101 *FTG*, 1 Nov. 1913; PRO MAF 29/12 SFC 157, evidence of Manchester friers to the Sea-Fish Commission.
102 *MO*, Box 28D.
103 Ministry of Agriculture and Fisheries (1926), p. 60.
104 *FTG*, 4 Feb. 1911; Reeves (1933), I, Chapter X.
105 Reeves (1933), I, pp. 201–2.
106 *FTG*, 'Trade in the Provinces' survey, 1905–9.
107 *FTG*, 11 Feb. 1911.
108 *FTG*, 25 Nov. 1905; *FFR*, April 1933.
109 *FTG*, 9 May 1908.
110 *FTG*, 1 Jan. 1910, 29 Jan. 1910, 18 Oct. 1913.
111 *FTG*, 28 July 1923; *FFR*, Feb. 1933, Mar. 1933, Jan. 1937.
112 *FTG*, 8 Sept. 1917; *FFR*, Feb. 1933.
113 Reeves (1933), I, pp. 99–102.
114 *FFR*, Sept. 1949, which is also used extensively in the rest of the paragraph.
115 *FTG*, 2 July 1904, 15 April 1905, 30 Sept. 1905.
116 *FFR*, April 1927.
117 *FTG*, 26 April 1913, 27 June 1914, 18 July 1914; *FN*, 25 June 1932; *FTG*, 11 Feb. 1911.
118 *FFR*, Sept. 1930; *FN*, 6 Feb. 1932; *FFR*, Sept. 1931.
119 *FFR*, June 1931.
120 *FTG*, 27 Aug. 1904, 18 Mar. 1905; *FFR*, Feb. 1951; *FTG*, 11 Sept. 1909, 1 Feb. 1913; Mosey and Ramsden (1989), p. 20.
121 Mosey and Ramsden (1989), pp. 26–7.
122 *FTG*, 31 Oct. 1908, 11 Feb. 1911; *FN*, 2 Jan. 1932; *FFR*, June 1937, May 1938, Feb. 1939, April 1939.

123 *FFR*, June 1928, Aug. 1928, May 1931, May 1935, Jan. 1939; *FTG*, 3 April 1911, 12 April 1913, 22 Mar. 1913; Mosey and Ramsden (1989), p. 20; *FN*, 19 Mar. 1932.

124 *FTG*, 11 Mar. 1905

125 *FTG*, 4 Oct. 1913.

126 *FTG*, 9 Mar. 1907; Priestland (1972), p. 73; *FTG*, 4 April 1908, 6 Feb. 1909, 13 Feb. 1909, 19 June 1909, 11 Jan. 1913, 5 April 1919; *FFR*, July 1929; Reeves (1933), I, p. 54.

127 *FFR*, Mar. 1951.

128 *FTG*, 3 Sept. 1904, 17 Sept. 1904.

129 *FTG*, 8 Aug. 1908; *FFR*, 1 April 1926; and information from Mrs Bennett of Barnsley.

130 *FFR*, Feb. 1937; and see also *FFR*, July 1936, Sept. 1936, Mar. 1937.

131 Bolton Archives, Tape 28B.

132 This was one of the great discoveries of Mass-Observation in the Bolton and Blackpool of the late 1930s.

133 *FTG*, 25 Feb. 1911.

134 *FTG*, 12 April 1913, 25 Feb. 1911.

135 *FFR*, Dec. 1928, Aug. 1931.

136 *FFR*, Feb.–April 1937; PRO MAF 29/17 SFC 191, Retail Fish Survey, pp. 40–3 and 51–4.

137 PRO MAF 29/12 SFC 157, evidence of NFFF to Sea-Fish Commission 17 Jan. 1936.

138 *FTG*, 18 Jan. 1913, 7 Jan. 1911; and see above, Chapter 1.

139 *FTG*, 13 Sept. 1913.

140 *FTG*, 4 July 1914, 11 July 1914.

141 *FTG*, 3 Sept. 1904, 24 Sept. 1904; Mosey and Ramsden (1989), p. 23.

142 *FTG*, 18 June 1910, 15 Oct. 1910, 17 June 1922; *FN*, 19 Mar. 1932.

143 *FFR*, Aug. 1927, Nov. 1927.

144 *FFR*, Nov. 1927.

145 *FFR*, Nov. 1928, May 1929, July 1929, May 1931, Feb. 1933; S. Constantine, *Buy and build* (London, 1986), for Empire Marketing Board poster. Reeves (1933), Chapter 25, shows some of the B. T. F. posters.

146 Mrs Jennings interview; *FTG*, 2 Sept. 1905.

147 *FTG*, 18 June 1910, 31 May 1913.

148 *FFR*, Oct. 1950.

149 *FFR*, 1936–7, *passim*.

150 PRO MAF 29/17 SFC 196.

151 PRO MAF 29/17 SFC 191, Retail Fish Survey, pp. 64–5.

152 *FFR*, Sept. 1934.

153 *FTG*, 16 Mar. 1907.

154 *FTG*, 11 Jan. 1913, 8 Mar. 1913, 19 July 1913.

155 *FTG*, 31 May 1913.

156 *FTG*, 18 Nov. 1911, 1 Mar. 1913.

157 E. P. Thompson, 'The moral economy of the English crowd in the eighteenth century', *Past and Present* 50 (1971), pp. 76–136.

158 *FTG*, 19 Dec. 1914, 28 June 1919; *The Frier*, 2 Aug. 1919.

159 *FFR*, June 1929, June 1937, July 1937, and 1937–8, *passim*; and see above, Chapter 1.

160 *FFR*, July 1937.

161 PRO MAF 29/17 SFC 191.

162 *FTG*, 27 Aug. 1904, 30 Sept. 1905, 17 Feb. 1906.

163 *FTG*, 3 Feb. 1917.
164 *FFR*, July 1931, July 1937.
165 *FFR*, Mar. 1937; PRO MAF 29/17 SFC 191; *FTG*, 29 May 1920.
166 *FN*, 16 Jan. 1932.
167 *FTG*, 27 Sept. 1919.
168 *FTG*, 13 Oct. 1906.
169 *FFR*, June 1937. The figure of £1 'in the till' per stone of fish may refer to profits.
    Otherwise it is impossible to reconcile with the £6 per stone recommended in 1906.
170 *FTG*, 12 April 1913; *The Frier*, 6 Dec. 1919.
171 *FFR*, July 1927.
172 *FFR*, April 1934; PRO MAF 29/12 SFC 157.
173 *FTG*, 10 Sept. 1910.
174 *FTG*, 11 June 1921.
175 *FFR*, Nov. 1933; Dec. 1933, and *passim* during 1934; Jan. 1936.
176 *FFR*, Mar. 1933, June 1937.
177 *FFR*, April 1936, April 1949.
178 *FTG*, 23 July 1910.
179 *FTG*, 2 Oct. 1909.
180 *FTG*, 12 July 1913; *FFR*, June 1927, July 1927, June 1929; *FN*, 2 Jan. 1932; *The
    Frier*, 1 April 1923.
181 *FFR*, Nov. 1927, April 1933.
182 *FTG*, 21 Jan. 1905, 30 June 1906, 17 Oct. 1908, 4 Nov. 1911.
183 *FTG*, 9 Mar. 1912, 18 Jan. 1919, 11 Oct. 1919, 21 May 1921.
184 *FTG*, 15 Mar. 1919, 14 June 1919, 9 Aug. 1919, 19 June 1920.
185 *FFR*, June 1934, Sept. 1934, May 1935.
186 *FTG*, 9 Sept. 1905, for the first statement I can find on this perennial theme.
187 *FTG*, 29 July 1905, 10 July 1909, 27 June 1914.
188 *FTG*, 22 Jan. 1910.
189 PRO MAF 29/17 SFC 191, evidence of Victor Joseph to the Sea-Fish
    Commission, 29 Jan. 1935, pp. 2, 12–13.
190 *FFR*, April 1937, Dec. 1937.
191 See above, discussion of pricing policy and techniques, and below, Chapter 6.
192 *FTG*, 23 April 1910; *FFR*, April 1927, July 1935; *FTG*, 27 Aug. 1910.
193 *FTG*, 28 July 1906, 29 Nov. 1919, 22 Nov. 1919, 13 Aug. 1921; *FFR*, Nov. 1930,
    Jan. 1931, Oct. 1931.
194 *FTG*, 3 Aug. 1907, 7 Nov. 1908, 20 Oct. 1917; *FN*, 29 Aug. 1925; *FFR*, Sept.
    1935, Oct. 1935.
195 *FTG*, 20 Jan. 1906, 12 May 1906, 8 Dec. 1906, 16 April 1910, 1 Oct. 1910, 13
    Sept. 1913; information from Mrs Bennett of Barnsley; and *ER*, Mr D2P, p. 44.
196 *FTG*, 30 April 1910, 14 Dec. 1907.

6 Solidarity and Suspicion: Organization and its Limitations

1 M. J. Winstanley, *The shopkeeper's world* (Manchester, 1983), p. viii.
2 Ibid., especially Chapters 6 and 7.
3 G. Crossick and H.-G. Haupt (eds), *Shopkeepers and master artisans in nineteenth-
  century Europe* (London, 1984), pp. 78, 258.
4 C. P. Hosgood, 'The "pigmies of commerce" and the working–class community:
  small shopkeepers in England, 1870–1914', *Journal of Social History* 22 (1988–9),
  pp. 439–40, 450–4; Benson (1983), pp. 114–27, 133–40.
5 Crossick and Haupt (1984), Chapter 11; Winstanley (1983), Chapter 6.

6 J. K. Walton, *The Blackpool landlady* (Manchester, 1978), Chapter 8.

7 *FTG*, 9 Sept. 1905, 9 Dec. 1905.

8 *FTG*, 3 Sept. 1904.

9 *FTG*, 7 Oct. 1905, 3 Mar. 1906, 16 June 1906, 19 Nov. 1910.

10 *FTG*, 3 Aug. 1907.

11 *FTG*, 18 Jan. 1908; and for the rest of the paragraph, *FTG*, 2–16 Mar. 1907, 28 Sept. 1907, 5 Oct. 1907.

12 *FTG*, 7 Mar. 1908, 7 Aug. 1909, 13 Nov. 1909. According to Chatchip's reminiscences, in *FFR*, Feb. and Mar. 1950, the Lancashire Federation was in existence from June 1907.

13 H. A. Turner, *Trade union growth, structure and policy* (London, 1962); J. L. White, *The limits of trade union militancy* (Westport, Conn., 1978); A. Fowler and T. Wyke (eds), *The barefoot aristocrats* (Littleborough, Lancs., 1987).

14 *FTG*, 11 June 1910, 25 June 1910, 3 Sept. 1910, 22 Oct. 1910, 4 Jan. 1913; *FFR*, Mar. 1950.

15 *FFR*, Mar. 1950. For the Shops Act, Winstanley (1983), pp. 96–101.

16 *FFR*, Mar. 1950; *FTG*, 29 Oct. 1910, 5 Nov. 1910, 14 Oct. 1911, 21 Oct. 1911, 18 Nov. 1911, 4 Jan. 1911, 1 Feb. 1913, 8 Feb. 1913.

17 *FTG*, 12 April 1913, 10 May 1913, 28 June 1913, 5 July 1913.

18 *FTG*, 15 Nov. 1913. From its origins until the Bradford conference of 1917 the NFFF was officially known as the National Federation of Fish-friers' Associations: *FFR*, April 1938.

19 *FTG*, 15 Nov. 1913; *FFR*, Jan. 1933, April 1950.

20 *FTG*, 15 Nov. 1913; *FFR*, April 1938, April 1950.

21 *FFR*, May 1950, June 1950; *FTG*, 20 Jan. 1917, 3 Feb. 1917, 10 Feb. 1917, 24 Feb. 1917, 28 April 1917, 26 May 1917, 25 Aug. 1917; Beveridge (1928), p. 154.

22 *FTG*, 6 Oct. 1917, 22 Dec. 1917, 5 Jan. 1918, 12 Jan. 1918, 19 Jan. 1918; PRO MAF 60/326.

23 PRO MAF 60/326; *FTG*, 3 May 1919.

24 *FTG*, 3 May 1919.

25 *The Frier*, 6 Sept. 1919.

26 *FTG*, 15 Sept. 1917, 27 Oct. 1917, 10 Nov. 1917, 8 Dec. 1917, 12 Jan. 1918, 19 Jan. 1918, 2 Mar. 1918, 16 Mar. 1918; *FFR*, Feb. 1933, Mar. 1933, June 1950.

27 *The Frier*, 1 Mar. 1919, 3 May 1919, 1 April 1923; *FTG*, 10 July 1920; *FFR*, 1 Jan. 1926. According to *FTG*, 11 Oct. 1919, the NCF forbade the publication of any reports of its meetings outside the pages of *The Frier*, the exact nature of whose relationship with the NCF was never perfectly clear.

28 *FTG*, 3 May 1919, 24 May 1919, 12 July 1919, 25 Oct. 1919, 20 Dec. 1919, 10 Jan. 1920, 7 Feb. 1920, 1 May 1920, 27 Aug. 1921, 6 May 1922, 14 July 1923; *FFR*, 4 April 1925, 1 May 1925, 1 June 1925.

29 *FTG*, 21 June 1919, 5 July 1919, 13 Dec. 1919, 1 May 1920, 2 July 1921, 6 May 1922; *FFR*, April 1938, Sept. 1950.

30 *FFR*, April 1938, May 1938, Nov. 1950; *FTG*, 15 July 1922; *FFR*, 1 July 1925.

31 *FFR*, 4 April 1925, May 1930.

32 *FFR*, May 1933.

33 *FN*, 2 Jan. 1932, 19 Mar. 1932; *FFR*, Feb. 1933, June 1933, Sept.–Nov. 1933.

34 *FFR*, Sept. 1934; PRO MAF 29/12 SFC 157.

35 PRO MAF 29/12 SFC 157, A. M. Lowe to J. Tomlinson, 5 June 1934; evidence of NFFF to the Sea-Fish Commission, 18 Jan. 1935; memoranda of 23 Jan. 1935 (Barnard) and 2 May 1935; Economic Advisory Council, Report of the Committee on the Fishing Industry (Cmd. 4012, 1932), para. 27.

36 PRO MAF 23/4/2 WFC 574.

37 A. F. Cooper, *British agricultural policy 1912–1936* (Manchester, 1989), Chapter 9, especially pp. 165, 168.
38 PRO MAF 34/335, MAF 34/332.
39 *FFR*, Sept. 1934.
40 Cooper (1989), p. 2.
41 *FFR*, Sept. 1934; and see also *FFR*, June 1935, July 1935 (for a satire on the 'Periwinkle Marketing Board').
42 *FFR*, Sept. 1934.
43 PRO MAF 29/12 SFC 157, evidence of NFFF to Sea-Fish Commission, 18 Jan. 1935, 7 Jan. 1936; *FFR*, Sept. 1936.
44 *FFR*, July 1936.
45 *FFR*, Sept. 1936; PRO MAF 23/4/2 WFC 574.
46 *FFR*, Nov. 1936.
47 *FFR*, April, 1937, May 1937, Mar. 1938, June 1938, Jan. 1939.
48 *FFR*, Sept. 1935.
49 *FFR*, Nov. 1935.
50 *FFR*, Mar. 1937, May 1937, Aug. 1937, May 1938, Feb. 1939.
51 *FFR*, Oct. 1937, Dec. 1937, Aug. 1938, Jan. 1939, April 1939, Aug. 1939.
52 See above, Chapter 1.
53 PRO MAF 29/18 SFC 198, Appendix B; *FFR*, Mar. 1938.
54 *FFR*, Mar. 1938.
55 *FFR*, May 1937; PRO MAF 29/18 SFC 198.
56 *FFR*, May–Oct. 1937.
57 *FFR*, Jan. 1941; and see above, Chapter 5.
58 PRO MAF 29/12 SFC 157, evidence of NFFF to the Sea-Fish Commission, 18 Jan. 1935.
59 *FTG*, 27 July 1907.
60 *The Frier*, 3 May 1919, 1 May 1923.
61 *The Frier*, 1 Mar. 1919, 7 June 1919.
62 *The Frier*, 7 May 1919, 4 Oct. 1919, 1 Nov. 1919.
63 *The Frier*, 7 June 1919, 4 Oct. 1919, 1 Nov. 1919.
64 *The Frier*, 1 Aug. 1923.
65 *FTG*, 12 July 1919, 13 Sept. 1919, 18 June 1921.
66 *FFR*, 4 April 1925, 1 July 1925, 1 Sept. 1925.
67 *FFR*, Nov. 1935, Dec. 1935, July 1936.
68 *FFR*, Oct. 1928, June 1937, Nov. 1934.
69 *FFR*, Mar. 1938.
70 *Cf.* especially Winstanley (1983), pp. ix, 90–2.
71 *FFR*, Jan. 1936, April 1936, June 1935, Dec. 1935.
72 *FFR*, July 1937; and *cf.* Winstanley (1983), Crossick (1984).
73 Hosgood (1988–9).

7 Consumers and Communities

1 I. Gazeley, 'The standards of living of the working classes, 1881–1912: the cost of living and an analysis of family budgets', D. Phil. thesis, Oxford University, 1986, pp. 86, 117–22, 198.
2 PRO MAF 29/171 SFC 191, evidence to the Sea-Fish Commission on retailing.
3 Manchester University Settlement, *Ancoats: a study of a clearance area* (Manchester, 1940), p. 33. Thanks to Mike Rose and Jayne Southern for this reference. See also J. Boyd Orr, *Food health and income* (London, 1936), p. 68.

4 *FTG*, 28 July 1906.
5 J. B. Burnley, *Two sides of the Atlantic* (Bradford, 1880), pp. 315–16.
6 *FTG*, 25 Mar. 1905.
7 *FTG*, 21 Oct. 1905; *FFR*, Sept. 1935.
8 *FTG*, 20 Oct. 1906; ER, M7B.
9 *FTG*, 9 Dec. 1905.
10 *FTG*, 20 Jan. 1906, 6 Jan. 1906.
11 *FTG*, 9 July 1904.
12 *FTG*, 11 Feb. 1905.
13 *FTG*, 15 April 1905, 3 June 1905, 3 Mar. 1906.
14 *FTG*, 6 Oct. 1906.
15 *FTG*, 3 Sept. 1910, 5 July 1913, 9 Dec. 1911.
16 *FTG*, 2 July 1910.
17 *FTG*, 29 July 1922.
18 *FTG*, 25 June 1921; *FN*, 29 Aug. 1925.
19 *FFR*, April 1930.
20 *FN*, 2 Jan. 1932.
21 PRO MAF 29/17 SFC 191, Retail Fish Survey, pp. 62–3.
22 In Wood, *Fish retailer* (1933), II, p. 388.
23 *FTG*, 20 Jan. 1906, 27 Jan. 1906.
24 *ER*, Mrs B1P, p. 18.
25 *ER*, Mrs O1P, pp. 8, 36–7.
26 *FTG*, 19 May 1906.
27 *MO*, Worktown Box 28D.
28 *FFR*, Aug. 1930. So Sir William Crawford and H. Bradley in *The people's food* (London, 1938), were wrong to dismiss fish and chips as 'a luxury' (p. 201). In so doing they revealed their social distance from what they were writing about.
29 *FTG*, 17 Mar. 1917, 22 Dec. 1917; and see above, Chapter 1.
30 *FTG*, 3 Feb. 1917.
31 *FTG*, 3 May 1917.
32 *FTG*, 6 Oct. 1906.
33 Bolton Archives, Interview No. 57, dealing with the mid-1920s. This item is a Ms. autobiography and the spelling is as in the original.
34 Bolton Archives, Interview No. 47c.
35 Interview with Mrs Vincent.
36 *FFR*, July 1937.
37 *MO*, Worktown Box 28D.
38 Bolton Archives, Interview No. 28a.
39 *FTG*, 7 June 1913.
40 G. Preece, 'Pithead baths and the Miners' Welfare Fund', MA thesis, CNAA (Manchester Polytechnic), 1988, pp. 19–23; *FTG*, 10 Oct. 1908, 3 Sept. 1910.
41 *ER*, Mrs W2L, p. 8; Bolton Archives, Interview No. 79b.
42 PRO MAF 29/17 SFC 191, *Retail Fish Survey*, pp. 51–4.
43 Bolton Archives, Interview No. 43.
44 *ER*, Mrs M1P, p. 45.
45 *ER*, Mr B1B, pp. 105–6.
46 Interview with Mrs Vincent.
47 PRO MAF 86/365, meeting between NFFF and Ministry of Food, St. John's College, Oxford, 25 Sept. 1940.
48 *FTG*, 2 Sept. 1905.
49 *ER*, Mr A2L, interviewed with Mrs W2L, p. 138.
50 L. Halliwell, *Seats in all parts* (London, 1985), pp. 17, 27, 61, 87; *FFR*, April 1928;

and see John Holloway as quoted by Colin Ward, *The child in the city* (London, second edn., 1990), p. 69.

51 R. Glasser, *Growing up in the Gorbals* (London, 1987), pp. 81–2, 131–2.
52 Pat O'Mara, *The autobiography of a Liverpool Irish slummy* (London, 1934), pp. 139, 175; Jack Common, *The Ampersand* (London, 1954).
53 G. Cross (ed.), *Worktowners at Blackpool* (London, 1990), pp. 70–3.
54 *FFR*, May 1929, July 1931.
55 *FFR*, Sept. 1931; *FN*, 4 July 1925.
56 Published by Herman Darewski Publishing Co.; thanks to John Mackenzie and Jeffrey Richards for finding this.
57 *FTG*, 27 May 1922; *FN*, 2 Jan. 1932; *FFR*, July 1931.
58 *FFR*, Jan. 1936.
59 *FTG*, 24 Sept. 1910, 3 Aug. 1907.
60 Ben Wicks, *The day they took the children* (London, 1988), p. 11.
61 E. Roberts, *A woman's place* (London, 1985), pp. 151–61.
62 *FTG*, 2 July 1904.
63 *FTG*, 9 July 1904.
64 *FTG*, 4 Sept. 1909.
65 *FTG*, 13 Feb. 1909, 30 Dec. 1911, 6 Jan. 1912.
66 *FTG*, 28 May 1910.
67 *FTG*, 6 Sept. 1913.
68 *FTG*, 10 Sept. 1904.
69 *FTG*, 8 Feb. 1913; and see also *FTG*, 10 Sept. 1910.
70 *FFR*, May 1928.
71 *FFR*, Oct. 1928.
72 C. Webster, 'Healthy or hungry 'thirties?', *History Workshop Journal* 13 (1982).
73 *FFR*, May 1928.
74 *FFR*, Nov. 1928.
75 *FN*, 20 Feb. 1932, 7 May 1932.
76 *FFR*, April 1931.
77 *FTG*, 2 July 1921.
78 *FFR*, April 1936.
79 *FTG*, 3 Sept. 1910, 10 Sept, 1910.
80 *FTG*, 13 Aug. 1921.
81 *The Frier*, 1 May 1923.
82 *FFR*, April 1928, Dec. 1928.
83 *FFR*, June 1931, July 1933.
84 *FFR*, Sept. 1934.
85 *FFR*, Oct. 1937.
86 Roberts (1985), pp. 151–61.
87 Mennell (1985), pp. 226–7.
88 Fraser (1981), p. 162.
89 Carl Chinn, *They worked all their lives* (Manchester, 1988), pp. 56–66.
90 *ER*, Mrs W2L, p. 8.
91 Interview with Mrs Vincent.
92 *ER*, Mrs M1P, Mrs B1P.
93 Bolton Archives, Interviews Nos. 28, 39, 43, 47, 79, 89, 158.
94 Bolton Archives, Interviews Nos. 55b, 60b, 89a.
95 *ER*, Mrs W2L, p. 127; Mr B1B, pp. 105–6.
96 Bolton Archives, Interviews Nos. 79b, 89a.
97 Roberts (1985), p. 159.
98 *ER*, Mr B1B, p. 105; Mrs P1P, pp. 50–1.

99 Bolton Archives, Interviews Nos. 79b, 158a; interview with Mrs Vincent.
100 *ER*, Mrs M3P, p. 72; Mr G1P, p. 7; Mr D2P, p. 7.
101 *FTG*, 8 Mar. 1913.
102 *FFR*, Sept. 1937; and see above, Chapter 5.
103 R. Roberts, *The classic slum* (Manchester, 1971), pp. 82–3.
104 C. Segal, *Penn'orth of chips: backward children in the making* (London, 1939), pp. 18–19 and *passim*.
105 M. Mayhew, 'The 1930s nutrition controversy', *Journal of Contemporary History* 23 (1988), p. 452.
106 *ER*, Mrs P1P, pp. 50–1.
107 R. Roberts (1971); *FTG*, 19 May 1906.
108 *FTG*, 17 Jan. 1920.
109 I owe this important point to Richard Emmess.
110 Interview with Mrs Vincent. My own spontaneous leading question does not invalidate the argument here.
111 J. H. Brunvand, *The vanishing hitch-hiker: urban legends and their meanings* (London, 1983), p. 71. Thanks yet again to Jenny Smith.
112 N. Charles and M. Kerr, *Women, food and families* (Manchester, 1988), Chapters 2 and 6.
113 Mennell (1985), Chapter 9.
114 Lever Brothers, *Good plain cooking* (n.d., *c.* 1900), p. 55.
115 D. N. Paton et al., *A study of the diet of the labouring classes in Edinburgh* (Edinburgh, 1902).
116 Mayhew (1988), pp. 444–5.
117 V. H. Mottram, *Food and the family* (sixth edn., London, 1938; first published 1925), p. 117.
118 Hutchison's *Food and the principles of dietetics* (tenth edn., revised by V. H. Mottram and G. Graham, 1948), pp. 402–3.
119 *FTG*, 31 Mar. 1917; R. H. A. Plimmer and Violet G. Plimmer, *Food health vitamins* (sixth edn., London, 1933; first published 1925), pp. 95–6.
120 *FFR*, Aug. 1935; Reeves (1933).
121 *FFR*, Sept. 1937.
122 T. Lobstein, *Fast food facts* (London, 1988), especially pp. 43, 138. Lobstein's is a generally critical analysis of fast foods. See also J. M. Pascoe, J. Dockerty and J. Ryley, 'Fast foods', in R. Cottrell (ed.), *Nutrition in catering* (Carnforth, 1987), pp. 97–109.
123 *FTG*, 6 Jan. 1906.
124 *FFR*, July 1933.
125 *MO*, Worktown Box 28D.
126 *ER*, Mr D2P, pp. 43–4.
127 *ER*, Mrs M1P, p. 45.
128 *FTG*, 27 June 1914.
129 *FFR*, May 1931, Mar. 1934.
130 *FFR*, May 1929.
131 *FN*, 25 July 1925.
132 *FTG*, 20 Aug. 1921; *FFR*, Oct. 1928, April, 1937.
133 Bolton Archives, interview No. 28b; Chinn (1988), p. 59.
134 Interview with Mrs Vincent.

8 Fish and Chips in Context

1 Priestland (1972), pp. 144–8.
2 R. Samuel, *East End Underworld: the life of Arthur Harding* (London, 1981), pp. 106–7. This story was not traceable in the court records, despite John Mason's efforts to find it.
3 Avner Offer, *The First World War: an agrarian interpretation* (Oxford, 1989).
4 Jeremy Tunstall, *The Fishermen: the sociology of an extreme occupation* (London: third impression, 1972).
5 H. T. Reeves, quoted in *FFR*, July 1936.
6 Tunstall (1972), new introduction (unpaginated), quoting Professor R. S. F. Schilling.
7 *FFR*, July 1936.
8 *FFR*, June 1934; see above, Chapter 1.
9 See, for example, T. C. Smout, *A century of the Scottish people, 1830–1950* (pbk. edn., London, 1987), p. 11. Thanks to Mike Winstanley for advice on this topic.
10 Annmarie Turnbull, 'Learning her womanly work: the elementary school curriculum, 1870–1914', in Felicity Hunt (ed.), *Lessons for life* (Oxford, 1987), especially pp. 92–9; Carol Dyhouse, *Girls growing up in late Victorian and Edwardian England* (London, 1981), Chapter 3.
11 Dyhouse (1981), pp. 91–3.
12 *This England* 19 (1), Spring 1986. Thanks again to Jenny Smith for calling my attention to this passage.
13 *FFR*, May 1928.
14 See above, Chapter 6.
15 Gareth Stedman Jones, 'Working-class culture and working–class politics in London, 1870–1900: notes on the remaking of a working class', *Journal of Social History* 7 (1974), pp. 460–504; S. Constantine, 'Amateur gardening and popular recreation in the nineteenth and twentieth centuries', *Journal of Social History*, 14 (1981), pp. 387–406.
16 M. Savage, *The dynamics of working–class politics* (Cambridge, 1987), Chapter 7.
17 See above, Chapter 5, for fish friers and advertising.
18 Bill Luckin, *Pollution and control* (Bristol, 1986), p. 126. Gill Parsons is currently working for a Lancaster Ph.D. on the decline of the inshore fisheries in this period, with special reference to oysters.
19 For tripe in Lancashire see Marjory Houlihan, *A most excellent dish: tales of the Lancashire tripe trade* (Swinton, Manchester, 1988).
20 John K. Walton, *Lancashire: a social history, 1558–1939* (Manchester, 1987), Chapter 13, provides some context for this. See also J. Golby and W. Purdue, *The civilisation of the crowd* (London, 1984). I do not propose to pursue the question of any possible relationship between fish and chips and the 'civilising process' postulated by Norbert Elias' 'figurational sociology': see Mennell (1985), Chapters 1 and 2. To fit fish and chips into such a framework would require even more contortions of argument and distortions of evidence than the recent attempts by Eric Dunning and others to perform a similar feat with football hooliganism; I prefer not to change my agenda to accommodate a critical discussion of a theory to which I cannot subscribe at any but the most superficial level.

Index